STRATEGIC STAFFING

A Comprehensive System for Effective Workforce Planning

SECOND EDITION

Thomas P. Bechet

AMACOM

SHRM™
SOCIETY FOR HUMAN
RESOURCE MANAGEMENT

American Management Association
New York • Atlanta • Brussels • Chicago • Mexico City • San Francisco
Shanghai • Tokyo • Toronto • Washington, DC

Special discounts on bulk quantities of AMACOM books are available to corporations, professional associations, and other organizations. For details, contact Special Sales Department, AMACOM, a division of American Management Association, 1601 Broadway, New York, NY 10019.
Tel: 212-903-8316. Fax: 212-903-8083.
E-mail: specialsls@amanet.org
Website: www.amacombooks.org/go/specialsales
To view all AMACOM titles go to: www.amacombooks.org

This publication is designed to provide accurate and authoritative information in regard to the subject matter covered. It is sold with the understanding that the publisher is not engaged in rendering legal, accounting, or other professional service. If legal advice or other expert assistance is required, the services of a competent professional person should be sought.

Library of Congress Cataloging-in-Publication Data

Bechet, Thomas P.
    Strategic staffing : a comprehensive system for effective workforce planning / Thomas P. Bechet.—2nd ed.
        p.   cm.
    Rev. ed. of: Strategic staffing : a practical toolkit for workforce planning. c2002.
    Includes index.
    ISBN-13: 978–0-8144–0938–1
    ISBN-10: 0–8144–0938–5
    1. Manpower planning.   2. Strategic planning.   I. Title.

HF5549.5.M3B43   2008
658.3'01—dc22

                         2008002415

The Society for Human Resource Management (SHRM) is the world's largest professional association devoted to human resource management. Our mission is to serve the needs of HR professionals by providing the most current and comprehensive resources, and to advance the profession by promoting HR's essential, strategic role. Founded in 1948, SHRM represents more than 230,000 individual members in over 125 countries, and has a network of more than 575 affiliated chapters in the United States, as well as offices in China and India. Visit SHRM at www.shrm.org.

Printing number

10   9   8   7   6   5   4   3   2   1

To Ann and Leigh:
Thank you (once again!) for your love and support—
and for putting up with all those nights away from home.

Contents

Preface to the Second Edition   vii

Section 1: Setting the Stage   **1**

1. An Overview of This Book   2
2. What Is Strategic Staffing, Anyway?   6
3. How Should You Begin?   17

Section 2: Developing the Strategic Staffing/Workforce Planning Process   **21**

4. Placing Strategic Staffing/Workforce Planning in a New Context   22
5. Designing Your Strategic Staffing/Workforce Planning Process   41
6. Strategic Staffing/Workforce Planning at 30,000 Feet   77
7. Defining Required Staffing Levels   85
8. Defining Staffing Requirements Where Plans Are Uncertain   112
9. A Staffing Model Example   125
10. Effective Strategic Staffing/Workforce Planning: Case Studies and Examples   141

Section 3: Implementing and Supporting Your Strategic Staffing/ Workforce Planning Process   **165**

11. Implementing Your Process Effectively   166
12. Placing Strategic Staffing/Workforce Planning Within Your Business Context   177
13. Engaging and Involving Managers in Strategic Staffing   191
14. Developing a Strategic Staffing/Workforce Planning Web Site   205
15. Supporting Strategic Staffing/Workforce Planning: HR Structure and Required Skills   214
16. Getting Started: Conducting a One-Day "Kickoff" Session   227

Section 4: Beyond Staffing Plans: Analyzing and Applying the Results   **239**

17. Using Workforce Planning to Define the Impact of Retirements on Your Workforce   240
18. Using Workforce Planning to Support Management Succession and Development Planning   247
19. "Talent Planning": The Key to Effective Talent Management   261

20. Structuring Strategic Workforce Planning to Support Common
    Business Initiatives   270
21. Defining Staffing Reductions in a Strategic Context   283
22. Measuring Staffing Effectiveness and Efficiency   288
23. Calculating Staffing Costs and Evaluating Staffing Options   295

Appendices
A. Frequently Asked Questions   309
B. Using the Strategic Staffing Templates from the Web Site   317
C. Retrieving the Book's Computer Files   335
Index   **337**

Preface to the Second Edition

Most organizations understand the benefits that a longer-term approach to staff planning can bring. Many actually attempt to develop staffing strategies (or strategic workforce plans, as they are also known). Unfortunately, these companies often find that the traditional approaches to strategic staffing and workforce planning that they are trying to implement are ineffective, and that the expected benefits are not realized. To me, the solution to this problem lies not in trying to improve the effectiveness of the traditional approach, but in implementing a completely different kind of process for strategic staffing/workforce planning.

This book describes that process. It is a practical resource for both those who are just starting to implement strategic staffing and those who are searching for ways to make their current practices more effective. It can be followed step by step to initiate a strategic staffing process or used as a sourcebook that is referred to periodically to maintain or improve the effectiveness of a process that is already in place. It contains process descriptions, hints, tools, examples, and other practical advice. I've included only those approaches and techniques that have proved to be the most valued by clients and other practitioners.

Many of the ideas presented here were new when the first edition of this book was published in 2002. Five years later, those ideas are a bit better known to some, but most of them would still be new to many organizations. As I worked to update the text, I found that the basic direction and content of the process I suggest is as relevant now as it was then. However, my experience in the meantime has allowed me to develop a deeper understanding of strategic staffing/workforce planning and what the effective implementation of the process really entails. Consequently, I have significantly updated and edited every single chapter of the original manuscript. I have also included a wealth of new information, supplementing the existing material and providing eight entirely new chapters addressing issues and applications that were not covered at all in the first edition.

Some of my suggestions may still seem unorthodox at first, but based on my more than 25 years of consulting in this area, I know that they really work. Some of what I propose may challenge your understanding of what strategic staffing/workforce planning is and how it should be implemented. In some cases, I may seem to push the bounds of conventional thinking and challenge those more traditional approaches.

Needless to say, the workforce planning/strategic staffing processes described here are not the only ones that can be beneficial. Your organization may have been successful in implementing some of the very practices that I suggest should be avoided. In these cases, use my suggestions as a mirror in which you can reflect your practices and identify opportunities for improving the effectiveness of what you are doing. You may end up confirming that those approaches are right on target for your organization. On the other hand, you may find out that adopting some of my suggestions will allow you to greatly enhance the effectiveness of what you do.

All the pieces are described here: setting the context, defining staffing requirements, identifying and forecasting staffing availability, calculating staffing gaps and surpluses, and developing staffing strategies and plans that eliminate those staffing gaps and surpluses effectively and efficiently. Remember, though, that the successful implementation of a workforce planning/strategic staffing process does not depend only on how these basic components are defined. The "devil is in the details"—or (perhaps more appropriately in this case) the devil is in the implementation. It is not just the steps themselves that are important, it is how well they are developed, integrated, and implemented that counts. In addition to describing the components themselves, this book provides important tips to ensure an effective implementation of the processes I suggest.

One final note: Five years after publishing the first edition, I still meet HR professionals (some very senior) who do not consider staffing to be strategic in nature, especially when it defines specific plans and actions. I could not disagree more. To me, a business strategy that does not identify and address staffing implications is a strategy that cannot be implemented!

Good luck on beginning—or continuing—your journey!

Tom Bechet

1

Setting the Stage

CHAPTER

An Overview of This Book

This book describes pragmatic approaches for developing and implementing practical, effective, targeted strategic staffing/workforce planning processes. It includes process descriptions, actual examples and case studies, advice and hints, a series of spreadsheet templates that can actually be used to develop strategic staffing models, and PowerPoint presentations that can be used to communicate (and train others on) the strategic staffing/workforce planning process. Specifically, the book is divided into five sections.

Section 1: Setting the Stage

Section 1 sets the stage for effective strategic staffing. It provides an overview of the strategic staffing process and its objectives and describes the context in which strategic staffing works best. The section focuses on descriptions of specific nontraditional approaches to strategic staffing/workforce planning that have proved effective in a wide variety of organizations and industries. The section also includes a description of a new "hybrid" approach to strategic staffing/workforce planning that combines some aspects of a companywide approach with the focused, targeted process that I strongly advocate.

Section 2: Developing the Strategic Staffing/Workforce Planning Process

There are many approaches that can be used to organize and structure your strategic staffing/workforce planning efforts. Section 2 describes *in detail* an effective, practical approach that can be (and has been) implemented effectively in a wide variety of situations. This approach includes:

- A detailed description of the process itself (creating both long-term staffing strategies and short-term staffing plans)
- Specific examples of how required staffing levels can be determined (including actual, numeric examples with solutions)
- A discussion of various techniques that can be used to define useful staffing plans even when specific business plans are not complete or available
- A complete numerical example of a staffing strategy (and the staffing plans that result)
- Three detailed, "real-world" case studies, each of which describes the issues that an organization was facing and the staffing strategies and plans that the organization developed to address those issues
- A series of less detailed summaries of projects in which strategic staffing was implemented successfully

Section 3: Implementing and Supporting Your Strategic Staffing/Workforce Planning Process

Developing the right strategic staffing process won't help if that process is implemented incorrectly. Section 3 describes the context within which strategic staffing is best implemented. It includes:

- A framework that ensures effective implementation of the process
- A diagnostic tool that you can use to define the strategic context in which the process will be implemented in your particular situation
- A form that you can use to evaluate your company's current strategic staffing process and identify opportunities to improve its effectiveness
- Specific suggestions on how you can engage and involve line managers in the process, including an interview guide that can be used to help identify staffing issues and define staffing requirements
- A description of what might be included on a strategic staffing web site that could reside on your company's intranet
- A description of the HR functional structure that best supports strategic staffing/workforce planning (including some of the skills and capabilities the staff will need)
- Detailed suggestions and notes (almost a script) that you can apply when using the PowerPoint presentations that are available to you on the web site

Section 4: Beyond Staffing Plans: Analyzing and Applying the Results

One of the key deliverables of the strategic staffing process is a set of very specific staffing plans that should be implemented to address critical staffing needs. There are times, though, when a broader analysis of your results will be needed if you are to select the appropriate course of action. The fourth section of the book describes what those analyses might look like, including:

- A discussion on how strategic staffing/workforce planning can be used to identify and address the impacts of retirements on your organization

- A description of how some of the quantitative aspects of workforce planning can be used to strengthen your management succession and development process

- A case for including workforce planning ("talent planning") as a mandatory first step in any talent management process

- Specific suggestions on how to structure strategic staffing/workforce planning processes to support common business initiatives (e.g., opening a "green field" site)

- A description of how workforce planning concepts can be used to define and implement staff reductions more effectively

- A description of how to measure the effectiveness and efficiency of your staffing practices

- A discussion of how an analysis of staffing costs can be integrated into your strategic staffing process

Appendices

The appendices include a number of supporting materials that will help you implement an effective strategic staffing process. Specifically, the appendices include:

- Frequently asked questions (with answers, of course!)

- Specific instructions for modifying the generic spreadsheet staffing model templates (made available on the web site when you purchase this book) so that they can be used to support the development of your own staffing models, strategies, and plans

- Instructions for retrieving the computer files that come with this book

Summary

While no approach is foolproof, this book is designed to help you get an effective strategic staffing/workforce planning process up and running quickly and easily. If your organization is not yet creating staffing strategies, these tools will ensure that you will get off on the right foot and avoid many of the pitfalls that other companies have encountered. These tools can also be used to jump-start or improve the effectiveness of an existing strategic staffing process. If you are already developing staffing strategies, the approaches and tools provided in this book will help you improve the quality and effectiveness of your results. In either case, be forewarned: Many of the ideas in this book may differ from what you think strategic staffing/workforce planning is and what you think the process entails. Just read it with an open mind and be ready to consider alternative approaches—approaches that many organizations have found to be realistic and helpful.

2

CHAPTER

What Is Strategic Staffing, Anyway?

Definition

Strategic staffing is the process that organizations use to *identify* and *address* the staffing implications of their business strategies and plans. Notice that it includes both identifying and addressing—not simply one or the other. Some companies implement strategic staffing solely to help them to identify issues such as staffing gaps (where demand exceeds supply) or surpluses (where supply exceeds demand). While this identification is a necessary part of the process, it is by itself insufficient. Strategic staffing is effective only when the process also defines what the organization should do to eliminate or reduce those staffing gaps and surpluses most effectively.

I sometimes say that strategic staffing might better be defined as a process for identifying and addressing the staffing implications of *change*. To me, putting the emphasis on change indicates that staffing implications should be identified and addressed (or at least discussed) on a continuing basis (whenever changes to business plans are being considered), not just once a year as part of a set planning process.

Some companies use the term *workforce planning* to describe what I call strategic staffing. I think the phrase *strategic staffing* better communicates both the idea that the process has a longer-term business orientation (i.e., the *strategic* part of the phrase) and the idea that the results of the process are staffing *actions*, not just plans (i.e., the word *staffing* implies action, not simply planning). However, the term *workforce planning* (or even *strategic workforce planning*) is already in widespread use. I have used the terms *strategic staffing/workforce planning*, *strategic staffing*, and *workforce planning* interchangeably throughout this book. Don't worry too much about what you call the process—just be sure that you implement it effectively!

Objectives and Outputs

No matter how you define it, the strategic staffing/workforce planning process has one specific objective (described in more detail later in this chapter): to create a longer-term context within which shorter-term staffing decisions can be made most effectively. The process has two major outputs:

- **Staffing strategy.** A staffing strategy is a long-term, directional plan that describes what an organization is going to do over the course of its planning horizon (e.g., the coming four quarters or three to five years) to ensure that its supply of staff (both staffing levels and current capabilities) matches its demand for staff (i.e., the number of staff and the capabilities needed to implement business strategies and plans). Said another way, staffing strategies describe what an organization is going to do *across planning periods* to address its most critical staffing issues.

- **Staffing plans.** Staffing plans are short-term, tactical plans that describe what an organization will do in the near term (e.g., the current quarter or year) to address immediate staffing gaps and surpluses. Staffing plans describe specifically what the organization will do in a given planning period to support the implementation of their chosen staffing strategies.

Other Key Definitions

As you read through this book and begin to consider implementing some of the processes it describes, you will need to keep in mind my very specific definitions of some otherwise common terms. I am not suggesting that *you* need to use these terms this way, but you do need to understand how *I* am using them throughout this book. In some cases, my definitions are quite normal; in other cases, they may deviate significantly from your own definitions.

Staffing

I may have the broadest definition of *staffing* that you will ever hear. To me, staffing includes any action or movement that relates to getting people into, around, and/or out of an organization in a planned way—including retention. Staffing is not simply a process that is triggered by an opening, nor is it the internal equivalent of external recruiting (although both of these would be included in my definition of staffing). Staffing includes (but is not limited to) recruiting, hiring, transfers, promotions, redeployment, use of contingent and temporary staff, "decruiting" (i.e., the active management/movement of staff out of an organization), outsourcing of work (when done to eliminate the need for staff), retirements, terminations, and retention. I also include in my definition of staffing the development that is needed to support specific staffing plans (e.g., accelerated training needed to implement a rapid redeployment of staff) as well as staffing-related compensation changes (e.g., those needed to attract or retain key talent).

Issue

In staffing terms, an *issue* is simply a difference between the staff that will be required to support business strategy implementation at some point in the future and the staff that will be available at that same point in the future. This difference can be expressed in terms of staffing levels, required capabilities (type), or both. In some cases, an organization may have the wrong number of people and the people that it does have may not possess the skills that are required. In these situations, the company is sometimes said to be facing a staffing *mix* issue. Issues/differences can take the form of either gaps (where requirements exceed availability) or surpluses (where availability exceeds requirements).

An issue is not simply a subjective difference—it is both specific and measurable. In order to calculate a difference (and thus determine whether or not there is a staffing issue), an organization needs to define *in specific terms* both its staffing requirements *and* its staff availability. Unless both supply and demand are calculated, it is impossible to determine whether there is a critical staffing need. Supply and demand must also be defined in consistent terms (and at the same level of detail) so that they can be compared directly. It is very difficult to measure impact or progress (e.g., that staffing issues are actually being addressed) unless these specific differences are calculated.

Here is an example: Suppose an organization perceives that it has a "lack of management depth." Will the management pool become sufficiently deep if the organization develops and deploys five more qualified candidates? Ten more? Given the vague definition of the issue, it is just not possible to determine what the proper solution will be. Clearly, a definition of an issue that is based on a "gut feel" alone is inadequate. In order to determine whether or not this perceived lack of depth really is an issue, the organization should:

- Define its needs for management talent at a particular point in the future.

- Project the availability of qualified staff/candidates at that same point in time.
- Compare needs to availability to see if there is indeed a critical gap.

Strategy

Typically, a strategy is defined as a long-term, directional plan of action. I add one more element to that definition: A strategy (whether a staffing strategy or a business strategy) should define *how* an organization will achieve its objectives, not simply restate those objectives. Some organizations define a strategy that includes such items as becoming the low-cost producer of their product, or achieving specific growth or revenue targets (e.g., becoming a top five player in their market). These are objectives, not strategies. Although more specific than broad objectives, they still just describe *what* is to be accomplished, not *how* those things will be done.

Here is why I think this distinction is important in the area of strategic staffing: It is simply impossible to identify and address the staffing implications of business objectives. To define its staffing requirements, an organization needs to define what it plans to do throughout the planning period in order to achieve its objectives (e.g., to become the low-cost producer). Only when a plan of action to reduce costs sufficiently to meet that objective has been proposed or defined can you determine the numbers and types of staff that will be needed to fully implement that plan.

Here is an example: Suppose two manufacturing companies state that they intend to become the low-cost producer of their respective products. To do this, both companies need to reduce their operating costs. One company chooses to do this by relocating its manufacturing facilities to low-wage countries in Asia. The second decides to implement a more efficient production method in its existing domestic facilities that takes advantage of new production technology. Obviously, while both alternatives will reduce operating costs, the staffing issues and implications of these two approaches are quite different. It is impossible to determine staffing implications by looking at objectives alone. Two additional clarifications are necessary:

- Strategic does not mean "organization-wide" or "integrated." True, many strategies are broad and comprehensive in nature, and most effective strategies directly support the integration of functions and actions. However, just because a plan covers many organization units or provides overall solutions to common problems, it does not mean that it is strategic. It is quite possible to have broad, common approaches that are defined strictly for the short term (and thus lack the longer-term context of strategy).

• Strategic does not mean "innovative." There are many standard staffing practices that can be implemented in a very strategic manner. Conversely, many innovative staffing practices are implemented only in the short term (and thus are not strategic at all).

Data versus Information

One more definition or distinction might also be helpful: the difference between data and information. Data are facts, figures, charts, tables, graphs, and the like. Data that you use to make decisions are information. If you look at a table and decide to act or allocate resources differently because of what you see, then that table has become information. On the other hand, if you hear the results of an analysis and find those results "interesting" (e.g., "I never would have thought it was that big") but do nothing differently, then those results are merely "data." Many organizations spend an inordinate amount of time gathering and analyzing staffing data. Make sure that the analyses and reports you provide are information that drives critical decision making.

What Is the Objective of Strategic Staffing?

Let's start thinking differently about strategic staffing/workforce planning by defining a new, nontraditional objective for the process itself. In many cases, firms think that the objective of strategic staffing is to predict future staffing needs (usually with some degree of certainty) and then define the staffing actions that should be taken in the near term to eliminate problems that may (or may not) occur in the future.

At best, this is difficult to do well (and accurately); at worst, it proves to be an academic exercise that has little impact on the organization. Some companies give up on the process right away because managers lack the skills, understanding, or patience to forecast their long-term staffing needs reliably. In other companies, predictions are made and staffing plans based on those predictions are produced, but the plans are not implemented because the predictions they are based on are not perceived as accurate. Consequently, managers often view these long-term staff planning efforts as something that may be "nice to have," but not as a required, valued component of the overall business planning process.

Instead of thinking of strategic staffing as a way of predicting future needs and acting in the near term to avoid future problems, think of it as a way of creating a longer-term context (staffing strategy) within which the most effective near-term staffing decisions (staffing plans) can be made right now. Of course, this combination of long-term staffing strategies and short-term staffing plans is intended to allow your organization to address critical staffing issues as effectively and efficiently as possible.

Here is a simple example of how this process works (and why this new definition of process objective is valuable). Suppose you have a job category that is critical to the implementation of a new business strategy. Upon doing an analysis, you determine that by the end of the first year of your plan, you will experience a shortfall in that category of 10 full-time equivalents (FTEs). For the purposes of this example, assume that this gap of 10 FTEs is really going to occur. What staffing actions might you implement to address this need? Is recruiting the "best" answer? Promotion? Redeployment with development? The use of contractors or consultants? Outsourcing of work to eliminate the need for the additional staff? Which of these alternatives is the "right" one? Which would you choose?

Obviously, it would be impossible to choose the most appropriate option by looking only at a short-term need for 10 FTEs. Still, many organizations make all kinds of staffing decisions while looking only at short-term criteria. What is missing from such an approach is any long-term context. Suppose I were to tell you that your workforce plans showed that in that job, you would need 10 FTEs this year, 15 in year 2, 20 in year 3, and 25 in year 4. Armed with these new data, you would probably meet that initial need for 10 FTEs through recruiting, promotion, internal movement, development, or some other more "permanent" solution.

But what if you needed 10 additional FTEs in that job in year 1, were expecting to have 5 too many in year 2, forecast that you would have the "right" number in year 3, and expected to need 3 more in year 4? Given the fluctuation in needs (from gaps to surpluses and back again), it would make no sense at all to hire or promote to fill those openings in year 1. That would meet your needs in the short term, but it would also create even larger surpluses to deal with in future years. Instead, one of the temporary staffing options (such as using contractors) would probably be more appropriate. Temporary solutions such as these are also most appropriate when longer-term plans show that a near-term staffing need is merely a "blip" in the curve. Needs might also be created by scheduling problems, in which case rescheduling of work might be the most appropriate "staffing" option. In both these cases (in this admittedly simple example), we have used a long-term context (i.e., an understanding of what our needs would be in future years) to make an effective decision on how our needs should be met in year 1.

The relationship between long-term staffing strategies and short-term staffing plans is depicted in Figure 2-1. When staffing is done well, organizations will be operating in the shaded part of the diagram, where long-term staffing strategies and short-term staffing plans intersect. Looking at

Figure 2-1. Integrating Your Long-Term and Short-Term Staffing Processes.

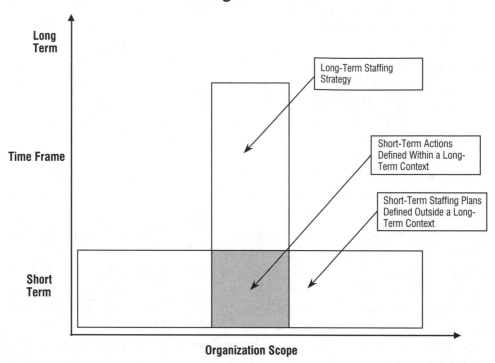

this diagram, we might be tempted to conclude that our objective should be to spread out the stem of the "upside-down T" so that it intersects the entire scope of our organization. After all, if creating this long-term context for short-term decision making is good for some parts of the organization, won't it be good for all parts of the organization?

Surprisingly, perhaps, the answer to this is a resounding no. Strategic staffing/workforce planning is a powerful process, but it demands lots of time and resources. Therefore, it should be used only to address issues that really require that strategic perspective. As a simple example, the process need not be applied to any job category where the supply of talent (internally or externally) is currently adequate and is expected to remain sufficient over the planning horizon being used. Figure 2-2 depicts the process when it is implemented correctly—strategic where it needs to be (each vertical bar), but not implemented across the entire scope of the organization.

Not only is defining this long-term context a more realistic objective for the process, but this approach might just engage your line managers in the strategic staffing process more than traditional long-range staff forecasting does. The idea of creating a context that allows better decisions to

Figure 2-2. Applying Strategic Staffing Selectively.

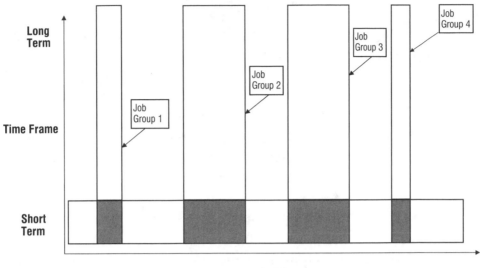

be made immediately might just capture the attention of those line managers who are being measured by and rewarded for achieving near-term objectives. This approach to strategic staffing allows them to manage their own current staff resources most effectively right now. Unlike what happens with the traditional approach, you are not asking them to manage differently (or expend resources) in order to help their successors avoid problems or achieve improved results in the future. Placing the focus on defining effective short-term staffing actions makes it more likely that the line managers making the staffing decisions will still be in place to reap the benefits of those decisions. A more detailed description of what can be done to engage and involve line managers in the strategic staffing/workforce planning process is included in Chapter 13.

An Overview of the Process

This book describes all aspects of the strategic staffing process in detail. From an overall perspective, the process usually includes the following steps:

- Identify and prioritize longer-term staffing issues and implications—those that arise from your business strategies and plans. A staffing issue usually involves a significant difference between the staff that will be available and the staff that will be needed to implement business strategies effectively. This might be a difference in skills, staffing levels, or both. It could also be a deficit or a surplus.

- Create a staffing model that calculates specific shortages and surpluses of talent. Such a model usually includes:

  —Defining the number (staffing levels) and types (capabilities) of
  employees that will be needed at a particular point in the future
  (or at several points in the future) to implement business plans
  effectively (often including how that staff should be organized and
  deployed)

  —Identifying the staffing resources that are currently available

  —Projecting the supply of talent that will be available at each future
  point for which requirements have been defined (e.g., factoring in
  the effects of turnover, retirements, planned movement, and other
  such factors)

  —Calculating specific differences between the anticipated demand
  for and the forecasted supply of talent

- Develop specific staffing strategies that address the most critical
  staffing issues most effectively in the long run. As defined earlier,
  staffing strategies are usually long-term, directional plans of action
  (spanning planning periods) that describe what will be done to address critical staffing issues.

- Define and evaluate near-term staffing alternatives within this strategic context, selecting and implementing those short-term (i.e., within
  a planning period) staffing actions (such as recruiting and internal
  placement) that best support the implementation of the staffing strategies.

By implementing this process, you can be sure that all staffing actions
taken in the short term will fully support the implementation of your organization's longer-term strategies.

Staffing Strategies

As stated previously, staffing strategies are long-term, directional plans
that describe what will be done over the course of the organization's planning horizon to address critical staffing issues. Therefore, staffing strategies usually span several planning periods (e.g., all three years of a three-
year business strategy); they are not developed for each planning period
individually. Staffing strategies should be specific enough to describe how
staffing needs are to be met, but not so specific that they describe individual staffing needs or actions. "Promote from within" is an example of a
simple staffing strategy. It describes, in directional terms, the approach
that an organization will take to meet certain staffing needs, yet it does
not specifically identify who should be promoted when. Those specific

descriptions are part of the organization's short-term staffing plans. Other examples of staffing strategies include:

- Meeting needs for management talent by blending hires and promotions from within
- Developing and retaining critical technical capabilities within the organization while contracting out noncritical skills
- Using accelerated development and redeployment to eliminate a major talent surplus in one area while meeting a critical need in another
- Building a full-time staffing base for minimum (or "foundation") workloads and using part-time employees to meet workloads that exceed those minimum levels

In almost every case, staffing strategies are (or at least should be) an integral part of the organization's business strategy. Business strategies might even include the specific staffing implications of those strategies and what will be done to address those implications.

Staffing Plans

Staffing plans describe the specific, near-term staffing actions that an organization is going to take so that it can best implement the staffing strategies that most effectively address critical staffing issues. Unlike staffing strategies, which span planning periods, these plans are usually fully implemented within a single planning period. They are detailed enough to define and guide individual staffing actions (e.g., stating clearly just how many employees need to be hired or promoted to fill identified openings). These plans specifically address:

- Recruiting
- Internal movement, including promotions, transfers, and redeployment
- Retention
- Use of contingent and part-time staff
- Use of overtime
- Outsourcing of work (when done to negate the need for additional staff)
- Planned losses

Summary

Strategic staffing is the process of identifying and addressing the staffing implications of business strategies and plans (or perhaps even of change).

The objective of the process is to create a long-term context (i.e., a staffing strategy) within which the most effective short-term decisions (i.e., staffing plans and actions) can be made. The strategic staffing process consists of four steps: identifying staffing issues, calculating differences (gaps and surpluses) between staffing requirements and availability, developing staffing strategies, and defining staffing plans.

As you read on, all of the ideas and concepts included in this overview will be described in detail. Most of these descriptions are supported with concrete examples to help you cement your understanding of those ideas and concepts. All are designed to allow you to develop and implement the strategic staffing/workforce planning process quickly, in a way that yields significant benefits.

3

How Should You Begin?

You are probably reading this book for one of three reasons. Some of you may work for organizations that have implemented strategic staffing/workforce planning processes in the past that just did not work or were not sustainable. Some of you may have workforce planning processes in place that are just not working as effectively as you might like. Others may be looking to develop and implement workforce planning for the first time.

This book is indeed meant to be a system and "tool kit" that will apply no matter which of these three groups you are in. The chapters in Section 2 are meant to provide specific guidance regarding what you should do either first (if you are just starting out) or next (if a process is in place or has been implemented previously). How should you go about your task of implementing or improving strategic staffing/workforce planning? Where should you begin?

Why Is Effective Strategic Staffing/Workforce Planning So Rare?

Before I describe "what works," let's discuss (and perhaps learn from) what has not worked in the past. One of the questions that I am often asked (and usually dread!) is this: "What companies do you think are doing a good job of strategic staffing/workforce planning?" Those asking the question probably expect me to be able to rattle off the names of many companies that are actively engaged in workforce planning in ways that are having a significant impact on business results. Often, my response disappoints them—the organizations that I know of that are effective users of workforce planning (using either the approaches described in this book or any other process) are few and far between.

Most companies understand at some level that strategic staffing/workforce planning can be valuable. Some truly believe that the process is required if they are to achieve their business objectives and implement their business strategies. Others have a "gut feel" that workforce planning can help, but are not really sure how. Still others might assume that workforce planning is a key component of a "well-managed" company. A few might have even identified the need to begin to use workforce planning as a result of some kind of benchmarking process. With all this interest in strategic staffing/workforce planning, why is the process not implemented effectively on a widespread basis? In fact, what has hindered your own company's strategic staffing efforts?

Common Impediments to Strategic Staffing

There are a host of reasons why strategic staffing/workforce planning efforts fail (or at least are not as effective as planned). Some of the more common ones are listed here. Do any of them sound familiar?

- **"We tried it once and it did not work."** Just because you attempted to implement workforce planning once and were unsuccessful does not mean that your organization does not need strategic staffing/workforce planning. Why did it not work for you? Perhaps you were trying to use a poorly designed or ineffective workforce planning process. Maybe you focused too much attention on implementing a process and not enough on adding value. Will managers give you a second chance? Perhaps, but only if you offer them an effective approach that quickly yields tangible results.

- **"Managers told us that the process took too much time."** Did managers really mean what they told you? When managers say that a process takes too much time or requires too much effort, what they usually mean is that the value they received from the process did not justify the work and resources that the process required. Managers will always find time for the things they feel are worthwhile. Are you certain that the workforce planning process you proposed was effective? Was there really a significant benefit, especially one that justified the work involved?

- **"We developed a comprehensive process, but there really weren't any results."** Comprehensive, organization-wide processes often yield few results. The commonality of these approaches virtually prevents the specific, valuable findings and recommendations that managers need and want. Further, some HR functions focus almost entirely on "rolling out" a process—not on achieving results, solving problems, or addressing critical staffing issues. How excited do managers really get about having to participate in a new process? Probably not very! How excited would they be if instead they found solutions to their most critical staffing issues?

- **"We don't have enough data about people."** Some organizations think that they cannot implement workforce planning unless they have *all* the data for *all* the people. They spend so much time gathering and managing data that they end up having no time left to use those data to support workforce planning. Why not implement the process in those areas where you do have data, or implement as much of the process as you can, given the data that are available? Is workforce planning really an all-or-nothing proposition? I don't think so.

- **"Things are changing too fast"** or **"We lack information regarding business plans."** Is there a time when strategic staffing/workforce planning is needed more than during periods of business change? If things are changing too quickly to develop and apply staffing strategies and plans, it is likely that the process you are trying to implement is inflexible, overly complex, or too comprehensive. Similarly, you will never have "complete" data regarding business plans. If your workforce planning process requires a perfect understanding of business plans, it is the wrong approach. Your process should allow you to come to valuable conclusions based on the data that are available, logical inferences, and scenario planning.

- **"Other initiatives are more important right now."** Is there really any HR initiative that is more important than one that ensures that an organization has the right number of people, with the right skills, in the right place at the right time? I don't think so. Those who think that other actions may be more important probably do not understand just how valuable the results of an effective workforce planning process can be. They may not understand the process well enough to see how it can address critical staffing issues. They might not realize that the outputs of workforce planning should actually *drive* decision making in other areas of HR.

What Should I Do?

What should you do to introduce (or reintroduce) strategic staffing/workforce planning to your organization if you are facing one or more of these impediments? What might you do to avoid some of these obstacles in the first place? The answer is not to somehow implement traditional workforce planning practices "better." That would just be doing the wrong thing more efficiently, and there is no benefit in that. Instead, you need to think about workforce planning from a nontraditional perspective. There are two things that you will need to do, whether you are improving the effectiveness of an existing process or implementing workforce planning for the first time:

- **"Tweak" the traditional workforce planning process to increase its efficiency.** The mechanics of the traditional workforce planning process are basically sound, but they can be very inefficient. There are a number of small changes that you can make to the process that will allow you to get good results with less time and effort. Chapter 5 describes that more efficient workforce planning process, including those efficiency-enhancing "tweaks."

- **Change the context within which you implement that process— perhaps drastically.** Even the most elegant process won't work if it is implemented within the wrong context. Implementing a one-size-fits-all approach to workforce planning that is applied to all jobs across the entire organization at the same time in the same way just won't work—no matter how well the process itself is designed. Chapter 4 describes a more focused context for strategic staffing/workforce planning. When used in this context, the process will always yield realistic, valuable recommendations and solutions that you will actually be able to implement to address the most critical staffing issues that managers are facing.

Because the changes in implementation context actually affect the design of the strategic staffing/workforce planning process itself, I have described them first. Read through the next two chapters carefully—they just might be the most important two chapters in this book. The nontraditional understanding of process and context described in those two chapters is the cornerstone on which many of my other thoughts and recommendations are built.

2

Developing the Strategic Staffing/ Workforce Planning Process

Placing Strategic Staffing/Workforce Planning in a New Context

As stated in the previous chapter, even the most elegant strategic staffing/workforce planning process can't be effective if it is implemented within the wrong context. As many processes fail because they are implemented incorrectly as fail because they were designed improperly. Yet many organizations with ineffective workforce planning approaches still try to change the process and not the implementation context. I truly believe that such companies will never achieve the results they desire. This chapter describes the implementation context within which I have found strategic staffing/workforce planning to work most effectively. And watch out—this is probably the most thought-provoking chapter in this book!

Traditional Approaches Just Aren't Effective

Many organizations that understand the value of strategic staffing/workforce planning create excellent processes, but then doom these processes to failure by implementing them incorrectly. Some organizations that attempt to implement a strategic staffing process follow a fairly traditional approach. Usually, these companies make staff planning a component of their annual business planning process. Often, they request that managers identify their future staffing needs for each year of the planning period (usually in terms of headcount, not required capabilities), using a common template or form. The templates are at a common level of detail and are based on common planning parameters (e.g., all units define requirements at a job-specific level for each of the coming three years). Once these templates are completed, they are often combined or compiled at various levels to create overall pictures of needs (e.g., unit plans are "rolled up" to a divisional level, and divisional plans are compiled to create a firm-wide view). The organizations then attempt to create meaningful staffing plans to address these overall staffing needs. Some organizations supplement these plans with a series of staffing-related reports and listings (e.g., a list of openings and how they were filled or a summary of turnover rates over time for various types of employees).

Unfortunately, these efforts rarely result in specific staffing and development plans that are actually implemented. Managers tend to see the process as being of limited value and complain loudly about the amount of work involved. In addition, managers are being measured and rewarded for achieving short-term objectives, and this is inconsistent with the longer-term view that strategic staffing requires. Forecasts of needs are often "hockey stick" projections that are inaccurate, unrealistic, and not grounded in business plans. Some managers (especially those in more volatile areas where business is changing rapidly) question the validity and value of processes that ask them to provide estimates of staffing needs for points in time that are well beyond their ability (or need) to forecast. Staff planning is also often incomplete—required staffing levels may be forecast, but required capabilities are not.

The staffing plans that result from traditional processes such as these often provide little valuable information and are rarely used to drive staffing decisions. Estimates of needs are imprecise and inaccurate. In many cases, the output from the process is too high-level and generic to drive recruiting plans, especially once the output has been rolled up to create that firm-wide view. Since required capabilities usually are not defined specifically, it is difficult (if not impossible) to create action-oriented development plans for individuals that address anticipated capability shortages. Some organizations do not even create staffing plans, opting instead to focus their "workforce planning" efforts almost entirely on compiling and reporting staffing information from the past (e.g., conducting detailed turnover studies and descriptions of recent staffing actions) rather than planning to meet future needs. In the end, much work has been completed, but few results are seen. The strategic staffing process then becomes solely staff-driven—or, worse yet, disappears completely.

More Effective Approaches to Strategic Staffing

Often, implementing a different, more pragmatic approach to strategic staffing can yield the high-quality results that organizations need and expect. Any approach to strategic staffing/workforce planning will include estimating staffing requirements, projecting staff availability, and calculating the difference between demand and supply. In more effective strategic staffing processes, this basic approach will not change, but the context within which it is applied will differ greatly from that of more traditional methods.

When searching for ways to improve (or initiate) your strategic staffing/workforce planning process, consider the options that follow.

Focus on Planning and Acting, Not on Analyzing and Reporting

Many organizations focus their workforce planning efforts on what I would call "workforce analysis." These companies usually spend a lot of time and resources on gathering and analyzing workforce-related data. They might perform in-depth analyses of internal or external demographics, or delve into the reasons for past turnover. They might carefully monitor, summarize, and report on past openings and staffing actions (e.g., "At the beginning of last month we had 26 openings, and at the end of the month we had 12"). They might conduct detailed statistical analyses to determine the causes of past turnover for different job categories. Are these activities producing data or information (as defined in Chapter 2)?

If the results of all these analyses are "business as usual" or even a group of raised eyebrows around a conference table, then those results are probably just data. If, on the other hand, the results are used as a basis for building staffing models, or developing staffing strategies, or defining staffing plans, then they are most likely viewed as information—and thus should be continued. If you do in fact create a workforce analysis capability, never forget that the purpose of strategic staffing/workforce planning is to identify and *address*—and not simply *analyze*—the staffing implications of your business plans and strategies.

Here are two specific (and very common) examples of staffing data vs. information:

- As mentioned previously, some organizations analyze past turnover patterns in depth. If this is done to help provide a foundation for making future projections of turnover rates to be included in a forward-looking staffing model, then those rates are definitely information, and those efforts should continue. If results are simply presented to managers, who accept them as "nice to know," but take no action, then the analysis is simply producing data and thus should be eliminated.

- Some organizations produce regular reports (e.g., monthly or quarterly) that detail staffing transactions. Some of these reports are quite extensive; their production requires significant resources and effort. Many such reports detail the number of openings at the start of a period, the number of openings created during that period, all the staffing actions that were taken during the period, and finally the number of openings that remain at the end of the period. Some of these reports even document how long each position remained vacant. What changes as a result of viewing and discussing these reports? If somehow they drive decision making, then they should be maintained. But if they just analyze "what was" or are viewed but quickly forgotten each month, they probably contain data and should thus be discontinued.

One more thought: The "workforce planning" staff in some companies spends most of its time "mining," reviewing, and updating employee data to ensure that they are consistent and accurate. This might include verifying that headcounts are exactly correct, standardizing reasons for turnover, or calculating turnover rates (using consistent measures that they have generated at great cost) to multiple decimal places. Is this level of perceived accuracy really required to support strategic staffing/workforce planning? I don't think it is. Given that staffing requirements are usually based on educated estimates (only some of which may turn out to be accurate), is there really any value in all those extra decimal places on the supply side?

In the end, make sure that your efforts are producing staffing information that affects decisions. Eliminate efforts that merely produce staffing data (no matter how "interesting" those data may appear to be) and redirect those resources to expanding your workforce planning process.

Address Staffing from a Proactive, Planning Perspective, Not Just as an Implementation Concern

It is no longer appropriate to consider staffing solely from an implementation perspective, or to create business strategies and plans that simply assume that qualified staff will be available whenever and wherever they are needed. It is not realistic for businesses to assume that all the staff needed to implement their plans will be readily available and can be recruited, developed, and deployed quickly and easily. In many cases, staffing constraints (e.g., an inability to recruit a sufficient number of individuals with critical skills within a short period of time) may actually restrict the company's ability to implement its business strategies and plans.

Consequently, staffing cannot be a process that begins only when an opening is identified. Staffing needs and actions must be defined on a proactive basis. Staffing issues and constraints should be identified and addressed as part of the planning process, not left as surprises to be uncovered when implementation begins.

Here is an example of a situation in which a staffing issue should have influenced a business strategy. In order to take advantage of population growth and migration, an HMO planned to expand into a geographic region of the state that it was not currently serving. The marketing and medical economics functions determined that four new medical centers would have to be built to meet projected member needs and realize the potential of this new market effectively and efficiently. Senior managers decided that these four new medical centers should be constructed simultaneously so that the HMO could enter this market quickly. As the buildings neared completion, staffing began in earnest. Unfortunately, the HMO found it extremely difficult to recruit physicians to the inner-city locations of the new medical centers. Consequently, the company could not attract enough physicians and medical technicians to staff the four new centers all at once, at least not without having a catastrophic impact on its existing facilities (e.g., as would be caused by a massive redeployment of talent from existing centers to the new ones). As a direct result of these staffing constraints, the newly constructed medical centers could be staffed (and thus opened) only one at a time, as a sufficient number of physicians and technicians were sourced and placed. This meant that some of the newly built medical facilities had to remain shuttered (some for many months) until they could be adequately staffed. Obviously, maintaining the unused facilities was quite costly. A review of available staffing *before* the construction decision was made would have shown that a sequential (not simultaneous) opening of the four medical centers would be more realistic and cost-effective.

From an even more positive, proactive perspective, a company may choose to implement some part of its business strategy (e.g., try to capitalize on a market opportunity) specifically because of the staffing levels and capabilities it has at its disposal. Here is an example of that. One huge international engineering and construction company had developed a large cadre of project management talent over the years, many of whom were expatriates and third-country nationals. Creating this cadre was not an explicit strategy; it was the result of the company's normal development process. However, this extraordinary pool of talent became a real competitive advantage, allowing the company to deploy qualified project management talent quickly and efficiently anywhere around the globe. This led to an explicit business strategy of bidding on projects where the quick deployment of project management talent was specifically necessary. Thus, business strategy was affected by staff availability.

Focus on Issues, Not Organizations

This suggestion may be the most significant of all those described in this section. It may also represent the largest departure from traditional workforce planning methodology. Many organizations feel that because staffing strategy is beneficial in one area, strategies should be created and implemented across the organization as a whole—that plans should be created for every unit, regardless of its situation. As we learned in Chapter 2, this type of process usually proves to be both ineffective and inefficient. Not every unit merits the detailed analysis that is typically needed to create and implement an effective staffing strategy.

Do not develop staffing strategies on a unit-by-unit basis or for units as a whole. Instead of creating models or analyses for every unit (regardless of need), focus your efforts on critical staffing issues—those areas or job categories in which longer-term staffing strategies are really needed. Then develop a series of separate staffing strategies that address each of these critical staffing issues. To put it explicitly, do not develop any staffing strategies that do not address critical staffing issues. Here are some examples of strategy development that address particular critical staffing issues:

- Build a staffing strategy that focuses solely on positions that are absolutely critical to business success.
- Create a strategy for a series of positions that are hard to fill or for which external competition for talent is great.
- Focus a strategy on a business unit that will experience significant change.
- Create a strategy that is concentrated on jobs for which the organization needs to tap new, nontraditional sources of key talent.

Chapter 5 provides more detailed examples of what these critical staffing issues may look like, along with a table that describes critical staffing issues that are often raised by specific business strategies. Simply stated, concentrating your strategic staffing/workforce planning efforts on specific, critical staffing issues will allow you to allocate your planning resources where they will have the most advantageous effect. You will not waste time and resources creating long-term plans where they really aren't needed.

Here is an example of this issue-oriented focus. To increase its staffing flexibility, the Department of Transportation of a state government was considering combining several separate job classifications (each of which required a particular set of skills) into a single category, "transportation worker," that included individuals with multiple skills. A staffing strategy was developed to define the impact that this change would have on classification (i.e., job evaluation), work scheduling, staff deployment, and training. Next, a staffing plan was developed that included transportation workers in all districts (because of bargaining unit considerations, the change had to be implemented on a statewide basis), but this plan focused

only on the positions that were affected by this combination of classifications. The strategy did not attempt to address any other staffing issues
that surfaced in the department (i.e., in positions other than the new class
of transportation workers). Where necessary, separate staffing strategies
were developed for such issues.

This focus on staffing issues does not mean that staffing strategies cannot span organizational units. In some cases, staffing strategies that cross
organizational boundaries are needed. These cross-unit staffing strategies
should be developed whenever an organization intends to manage key
talent across organization lines (e.g., managing information technology
[IT] staff, a pool of project managers, or entry-level engineering talent from
a corporate perspective). However, an issue orientation can still be maintained in these cases. When creating cross-unit staffing strategies, include
in the analysis only those positions that are to be managed from a broader,
cross-unit perspective (e.g., the project managers). Don't look at *all* jobs
across all units just because you need to look at *some* jobs that way.

Here is an example of a focused staffing strategy that spanned organizational units. A company was implementing a new nationwide data collection and analysis system that would support all of its regions (some of
which had their own such systems already). However, the company
needed to maintain its legacy systems while developing and implementing the new system. This raised numerous staffing issues. New talent
(with new IT skills) had to be acquired to support the development of the
new system, yet critical talent had to be retained in order to keep the old
systems functioning in the meantime. The organization could not simply
hire or contract for the new talent, since the skills of its existing talent
would then become obsolete (i.e., these people would understand and be
able to employ only the "old" technology needed to maintain the legacy
systems). The only sensible course was to address these critical issues from
a nationwide, cross-region perspective. The company developed a staffing
strategy that focused on the critical IT skills needed to support the transition—but only for the positions that required these specific skills. Additional plans (some strategic, some tactical) were developed for other
positions.

The identification of critical staffing issues (or the selection of specific
job categories to focus on) is perhaps the most important step in the strategic staffing/workforce planning process. Before going any further, let's
make sure that you have a good understanding of this concept. Here are
three mini-cases. In each of them, an organization is trying to implement
a particular change. Read each case and:

- Identify what is changing (and perhaps what is not).
- Define the job categories on which your strategic staffing efforts should focus.

A suggested solution is provided for each case.

Mini-Case 1. ABC, a commercial lines insurance provider in the United States, wants to become a "top 10" company (in terms of domestic revenue) within the next five years. ABC has determined that in order to do this, it must grow its revenues by 30 percent over that five-year period. The company does not expect to change its business focus or expand into new geographical areas. In what functions or units will staffing requirements change most? On what job categories would you focus your staffing strategies and plans?

Suggested Solution. In this case, it is important to define what is changing and what is not. It appears that ABC will attempt to meet its growth targets by doing more of the same in the areas it already serves. Given this, I'd start by looking at those functions that would be most directly affected by the change—probably the sales and marketing functions—and create specific staffing models for each of these functions. Once those were completed, I would then analyze the functions whose workloads would increase significantly if the sales efforts proved successful (e.g., underwriting, claims, and customer service), building staffing models where appropriate.

Mini-Case 2. XYZ Pharmaceuticals has just gained FDA approval to market a product for monitoring patients' blood sugar levels. Up until now, the company has primarily marketed its products directly to physicians, hospitals, and testing labs, but this new product could be sold directly to patients over the counter. What might the staffing implications be if XYZ continues to market the product only to physicians, hospitals, and labs? If it markets the product directly to patients?

Suggested Solution 1. If XYZ markets the new product to physicians, hospitals, and labs, what is changing? If the company is already selling its products to the same group that would buy the new product, this product may have a minimal impact on staffing requirements. It is likely that the current sales force will simply add the new product to its sample case; there might be a small increase in the required number of salespeople. In this case, an in-depth staffing analysis may not even be required.

On the other hand, if XYZ is going to market the new product to a new group of customers that does not currently buy its existing products (say a new set of specialists), then there will probably be a significant increase in the number of sales staff required. In addition, it is likely that both the number of marketing staff and the capabilities that they will need will also change. I'd build a staffing model that focuses on these two functions.

Suggested Solution 2. If the company moves from selling to physicians, hospitals, and labs to selling directly to patients over the counter (e.g., through pharmacies), this will be a major change that is likely to affect many job categories in XYZ. Clearly, the sales staff requirements will be different. Instead of a large sales force selling to a large number of relatively small customers (as is the case currently), XYZ will need to develop a wholesale sales force that will sell its products to a relatively small number of very large customers. Similar changes will also need to be made in marketing; it will have to move from a point of sale to a more broad-based approach. It may even be necessary for XYZ to create an entire distribution and logistics function from scratch, since it will no longer be able to distribute its products solely through its current network of sales staff. Again, I'd build models for the sales and marketing functions, but in this case I'd also build separate staffing models for each of the other areas that will be affected (e.g., distribution).

Mini-Case 3. TPB Corporation has developed a new technology that will allow the manufacturing of computer printers to be 25 percent more efficient. This new technique, which involves more automation and the use of some preassembled components, will be implemented on a line-by-line basis over the next four quarters. How will the required skills change? In what areas might required staffing levels go up? In what areas might they go down?

Suggested Solution. Again, let's look at what is changing—and what isn't. Clearly, production methods and roles will be changing, and this will probably affect the number and type of production workers that will be needed. In many cases, increases in production efficiency as a result of improvements in technology allow a company to use fewer production staff, but the staff that it does use will require a higher order of skills.

I'd focus the analysis on production staff. First, I would define the skills and staffing levels that will be needed to implement the change. Next, I would identify current staff that can be deployed to the new jobs (including defining any specific training and development gaps that would need to be addressed in order to make the redeployment success-ful). Finally, I'd determine the number of current production staff that may become surplus, identify opportunities to redeploy some of this sur-plus, and develop options for reducing the surplus that still remains (e.g., early retirement and layoffs).

It is important to note that in this case, nothing other than production technology is changing. There is nothing in the case that implies increased sales, different markets, or any other strategic shift that might affect staffing requirements. Consequently, there may be no need to build and run staffing models for any other area or function.

_____

Finally, don't attempt to resolve a second issue or problem until you have created (or at least are well on your way to creating) staffing strate-gies that fully address the first!

Tailor the Process for Each Issue

In a traditional workforce planning process, each business unit is typically asked to provide the same information regarding staffing, using a com-mon template, at the same time each year, for the same planning period/ time frame. While this approach may bring consistency, it also forces every unit to adopt the same process and set of planning parameters, and this may not always be appropriate. Rather than creating a one-size-fits-all process that is applied the same way everywhere, you should vary the planning parameters (e.g., the population to be included, the planning horizon, and the structure of the model itself) so that they are appropriate for each critical staffing issue that is being addressed.

Here is an example of this kind of tailoring: An engineering/construc-tion firm created a long-term staffing plan that addressed critical staffing needs in its IT unit. Given the rapid pace of technological change (and the fact that so little was known about the future of the technology), it was difficult to define staffing needs (whether in terms of capabilities or of staffing levels) beyond a 12-month period. Consequently, the staffing strategy for IT incorporated a one-year planning horizon. Even though the organization had a five-year business plan, it was perfectly appropriate for IT to develop staffing plans for the one-year horizon because so little was known about year 2 and beyond. If they had been asked to forecast needs past that first year, managers would simply be guessing at what the staffing requirements might be. A staffing strategy based on those guesses would have been of little value; the extra work would also have wasted management time and resources.

That same organization also found it necessary to increase the depth and breadth of its project management pool. Given the rate of change for the business as a whole (and the time needed to implement, observe, and measure any significant changes in project management capabilities), a three- to five-year staffing and development plan was developed. This, too, was an appropriate planning horizon for the issue being analyzed.

What would have happened if the two groups had had to use a single planning horizon? The use of a common horizon would probably have forced the IT function and the project management teams to use the same time frame, and this most probably would have resulted in ineffective plans for one or both groups. Would it have been appropriate to ask IT to create staffing plans for years 2 and 3, even though the managers knew that information beyond year 1 would not be useful (and therefore probably would not be applied)? Alternatively, would it have been appropriate to ask the project management unit to plan its talent needs for just a one-year time frame, given that it would take several years to address the identified issues regarding the depth and breadth of staffing? Clearly, the answer to both questions must be no. Would it have been possible to compromise and have each group prepare a two-year plan? I don't think so— that would probably result in a process that was ineffective for both groups. The only approach that makes sense is to allow IT to use a one-year horizon while allowing managers to use a three- to five-year horizon when addressing the project management issue.

Similarly, the level of detail of these two analyses also needed to vary. When defining IT capabilities, the organization needed to focus on a relatively small number of very specific technical skills (e.g., specific programming languages and/or platforms) that varied widely from job to job. In contrast, the analysis of project management would probably focus on a much larger number of broad, core skills (perhaps even extracted from a competency model) that were common among project management jobs. It certainly would have made no sense to force the IT analysis to include generic core management skills, but neither would it have been appropriate to ask those involved in the project management analysis to define specific technical skills for project managers. What makes most sense is to allow each group to use the capabilities—and the level of detail—that it thinks are most important (and are the best differentiators when it comes to evaluating candidates).

In these cases (and many others like them), it is only sensible to vary planning horizons, populations, and levels of detail, allowing each group to define a staffing plan that is appropriate for its particular needs. Obviously, this tailoring of parameters is viable only when separate staffing strategies are defined for each critical issue. The typical one-size-fits-all approach simply doesn't allow for this needed variation.

Focus on Particular Positions, Not All Positions

Some organizations attempt to develop staffing strategies that include all jobs. As discussed in Chapter 2, this is simply not required. Include in your process only those positions for which a strategic perspective is needed. It simply isn't necessary to address all jobs from a strategic perspective. For example, it is rarely necessary to develop a long-term staffing strategy for a job that can be filled relatively quickly from known internal sources or relatively abundant external pools. Because the development of effective staffing strategies requires a great deal of work and significant resources, it is at best unrealistic (and at worst a waste of effort and resources) to include each and every position in the analysis. Including all jobs in the strategic staffing/workforce planning process (including those for which a strategic perspective is not required) simply bogs down the process and spreads limited resources even thinner, making the process even more inefficient.

It is usually most effective to focus your strategic staffing efforts on two types of positions or situations: those where the organization needs to be proactive, and those where the organization needs time to respond.

The Organization Needs to Be Proactive. A longer-term perspective is usually required in areas where an organization is trying to be proactive in meeting staffing needs. Suppose, for example, that the organization is staffing and training a customer service unit so that it is fully functional before a new product is launched. Which jobs will be staffed just before launch? Which will be filled a month or two before launch in order to build continuity and teamwork? Which senior management/leadership positions should be filled a year (or more) in advance in order to set direction and strategy? A proactive staffing plan that addresses these questions will ensure a smooth implementation. The same proactive approach is also appropriate when an organization is opening a new plant or facility.

Here is a specific example of a situation in which a more proactive response was necessary. After conducting a demographic analysis of the external workforce, an oil company discovered that, from a recruiting and staffing perspective, it was particularly vulnerable in the area of geoscience. Competition for graduate geologists and geophysicists was intensifying, and the company anticipated that attracting the number of recruits it thought it needed would be much more difficult than it had been in the past. Given the critical nature of the need for this talent, the company wanted to be proactive in its staffing efforts. It created a staffing model and staffing strategy that focused solely on these hard-to-fill categories. The company decided to develop contacts and relationships with graduate students well before they entered the job market (e.g., through presentations and internships) to develop "ties" between the company and these individuals. This was expected to increase the possibility that these individuals would work for the organization upon graduation—thus meeting future staffing needs.

The Organization Needs Time to Respond. Strategic perspective is needed when an organization determines that its staffing needs can be best met in ways that require some advance preparation. This would include cases in which new sources of talent must be identified because the current channels have become less productive and cases in which talent needs will be met through longer-term development and promotion from within, not through short-term hiring. If a future need is to be filled from within, what internal movement must take place to fill the expected openings? What plans for development should be created and implemented so that these planned promotions and redeployments will be realistic and successful? If you are to develop new relationships with alternative sources of talent (e.g., new schools, geographically distant talent pools, or search firms), it will take time to identify such sources and develop possible partnerships with them.

Here is an example of a situation in which the company needed time to respond. In an insurance company, the traditional career path to branch manager passed through the underwriting function. Most branch managers began as trainees, became underwriters, were then designated "managers in training," and subsequently were named branch managers, usually in smaller offices. Experienced branch managers from smaller offices would then be selected to fill openings in larger offices. This process typically took eight to ten years.

Because of a rapid business expansion, a large number of new branch offices were to be opened. The traditional career path simply could not provide a sufficient number of qualified candidates in a timely way. Because of the length of time required to move along the traditional path, the company was forced to find alternative sources of branch manager candidates. It developed a staffing strategy that helped it to define the appropriate mix of targeted recruiting and accelerated development to meet its growing need for management talent. Since implementing these solutions required time, openings had to be identified well in advance of need.

———————

Long-term staffing strategies may not need to be created for any other type of position, and they certainly do not need to be developed for all positions. Remember that I am suggesting that you limit the number of jobs included in your *strategic* staffing process. It may be necessary to include more jobs (perhaps even all jobs) when you are defining required staffing in the near term (e.g., to specifically support headcount justification or budget preparation).

Keep Plans Separate and Detailed, Not Consolidated

In many cases, organizations prepare staffing plans that include all jobs, at all levels, at all units, for the same planning periods in order to roll these plans up into some kind of consolidated plan (perhaps even displaying the results "on one sheet of paper"). Common templates or forms are often used to gather staffing data in order to facilitate just this type of consolidation.

While on its face this summarizing might seem to be helpful, the process of consolidation actually creates two separate problems:

- **Consolidation can hide or mask significant staffing issues.** If one unit has 20 software engineers too many and another unit has 20 too few, a consolidated staffing plan would make it appear that there is no problem. The surplus of 20 and the gap of 20 would cancel out, implying that there are no issues that need to be addressed. However, if the units are not co-located (or if transferring individuals between their locations is not financially feasible), there may actually be 40 staffing issues to address—reducing a gap of 20 at one location and alleviating a surplus of 20 at another.

- **Consolidation often squeezes out of the plan the very detail that makes the plan most useful.** It is difficult (and sometimes actually impossible) to develop specific, implementable staffing plans to address consolidated, summarized staffing needs. Effective staffing plans may vary greatly in detail depending on circumstances and situations. For example, a consolidated staffing plan might describe an overall need for 150 "technical specialists." The staffing actions required to fill 150 such openings in one unit, location, or job might be completely different from those needed to fill a single such opening in each of 150 separate units or locations. The consolidated category might actually include jobs with the same title but vastly different skill requirements. The actions needed to fill 150 openings for one type of specialist would be quite different from those needed to fill 150 openings for different types, yet in a consolidated plan, all of those positions might be lumped together into the one classification of specialist. Similarly, it would be difficult (and perhaps even impossible) to define recruiting plans based on a strategy that consolidated various engineering disciplines (or even subdisciplines) into a single engineering category. Key differences in required capabilities would need to be considered if effective recruiting plans were to be developed for different disciplines, and these differences would be lost if all engineering needs were combined into a single, more generic category. In these and many other cases, it is unlikely that the information needed to create realistic, focused staffing plans could be discerned or inferred from summarized or compiled data.

When you create staffing strategies, keep the plans separate and distinct. This is especially important if you have developed plans that address separate issues, using different planning parameters. Create plans that are at the same level as your probable solution. Don't roll up data as a matter of course. Create a corporate view only if the staffing issues that can be identified should be addressed at a corporate level (and even then, include only the jobs that will actually be managed across organization lines). If an integrated plan is required in certain cases (e.g., to manage IT across, not within, organizational units), create a stand-alone model that spans those units but includes only those jobs.

When it comes time to summarize (and develop that one-sheet overview), don't combine the numbers into a summarized chart. Instead, create a page that highlights the most critical staffing issues you have defined and summarizes the strategies you plan to implement to address those issues. Figure 4-1 shows what this summary might look like for the bank described in a case study in Chapter 10. If more detail is requested, provide the relevant staffing data and the specific staffing plans that you relied on in coming to these conclusions as attachments.

Define Issues on an Ongoing Basis; Don't Create an Event

As stated in Chapter 2, strategic staffing can be thought of as defining and addressing the staffing implications of *change*. Thus, whenever business changes are being discussed or anticipated, the staffing implications of those changes need to be defined. If your organization discusses and considers changes to its business plans and strategies just once each year, then an annual staff planning process may be appropriate. However, if your organization discusses, considers, and implements changes throughout the year (as most do), then an annual strategic staffing/workforce planning process alone is probably insufficient. A discussion of the staffing implications of changes in business plans should be conducted each and every time such changes are discussed or anticipated—not at some set time during each planning period (or, worse yet, just once a year). Ideally, staffing issues should be identified and addressed as part of the ongoing business planning process. Assuming that change is constant, business plans will be reviewed and updated throughout the year. This requires

Figure 4-1. Example of a One-Page Strategic Staffing Summary.

ABC BANCORP
Summary of Strategic Staffing Issues and Recommendations

Critical Staffing Issues for the Unit

- Staff in the economic, education, and operations job streams are being asked to play the generic role of project manager and are not effectively applying the specialized expertise for which they were hired.

- Since they can't afford individual experts, many smaller regions have created positions that span or combine functional areas (e.g., education, health, and social programs), resulting in a general "lowering of the bar" regarding technical expertise.

- The company lacks sufficient high-level policy expertise to support the implementation of a more strategic focus.

- Current staffing programs are ineffective:

  —Most staffing efforts begin only after specific openings are identified.
  —Staffing programs are not specifically needs-based. In many cases, "promotions" were position upgrades based on performance; they do not "fill" actual openings.
  —The company tends to implement one-size-fits-all approaches to staffing, not targeted, as-needed processes.

Staffing Strategies to Be Implemented

- Differentiate job streams to support needed specialization.

- Position and develop the corporate unit as a "center of functional excellence."

- Recruit and develop high-level policy development expertise.

- Improve the effectiveness of staffing practices so that they are:

  —Proactive
  —Needs-based
  —Tailored to address specific user needs

Note: The detailed staffing models and analysis on which these conclusions are based are available.

that strategic staffing/workforce planning also be an ongoing process that is implemented and updated throughout the year, not a once-a-year event.

Here is an example: An engineering/construction company used an annual staff planning process that was driven by the budget cycle. However, rapid changes in competitive situations and quickly emerging opportunities meant that the company needed to mobilize and reallocate its staffing resources quickly, throughout the year—a process that could not be supported by the once-a-year staff planning process. As a result, the company now discusses the staffing implications of change at every management committee meeting (i.e., on a biweekly basis). Further, it has developed a performance expectation for managers that any proposal that requires additional resources (e.g., a new project or a change in technology used) has to include an analysis of staffing issues and a high-level staffing plan.

Solve Problems; Don't Just Build Capability

Line managers want answers to their staffing problems and solutions to their issues. Yet some human resources functions focus their efforts on developing and supporting a standardized process, system, or tool that managers can use to develop staffing strategies, not on meeting the managers' need for action and answers.

The best deliverable of strategic staffing isn't a process, a tool, or a model—it is a solution to a critical staffing problem (i.e., a qualified individual filling an opening).

Generally, the development of a process, tool, or model, while necessary in many cases, is by itself insufficient. A process or tool must be applied effectively to identify and address critical staffing issues. A staffing model is merely a component of an effective approach and is usually of little value by itself. Managers must be trained (perhaps by human resources staff) to use the process or tool effectively and apply the results analytically. Make sure that implementation of your process or tool results in specific, implementable staffing plans (i.e., what will be done to address staffing shortages and surpluses), not just a better definition of the needs themselves.

Think of Strategic Staffing/Workforce Planning as a Function That Feeds Other HR Functions

Some HR functions create units (perhaps even units of one individual) that focus on strategic staffing/workforce planning. In many cases, this unit is just one among many in HR—in effect, a peer of Recruiting, Staffing, Training and Development, Executive Development, Compensation, Benefits, and other traditional HR functions. As a peer, Strategic Staffing/Workforce Planning is expected to work hand in hand with these other functions on an ongoing basis. In some cases, workforce planning provides recommendations on what should be done in those functional areas; in other cases, the functions plan and implement without (or perhaps while ignoring) the recommendations of the workforce planning group.

When HR is organized in the most effective way, Strategic Staffing/

Workforce Planning is not simply a peer of the other HR functions. Instead, this function should lead the other functions in some significant ways. The outputs of the strategic staffing process (i.e., staffing strategies and plans) provide critical direction and inputs to decision making in other HR functions. Are there critical staffing issues that can be addressed solely by one HR function, or are most issues cross-functional in nature? Can Recruiting define all its objectives and plans without the input and direction provided by staffing strategies and plans? Can Staffing, on its own, identify all redeployment opportunities? Can Training and Development really determine its strategies without knowing the role that development will play in addressing the company's most critical staffing issues? Can Executive Development create helpful, realistic succession and development plans if it doesn't employ workforce planning tools and techniques? Can one HR business partner in one business unit go about addressing a critical staffing issue while ignoring the fact that another business unit is also facing the same issue?

I believe that the answer to all of these questions is no. Strategic Staffing/Workforce Planning clearly needs to partner with other functions to develop and implement realistic solutions to staffing problems, but it also must take the lead and provide specific direction to these other functions, not simply rely on peer relationships, partnering, or influence. Only when this direction is provided can an organization be sure that it is implementing the staffing strategies that will address its most critical staffing issues. This will just not happen if the Strategic Staffing/Workforce Planning function is operating strictly on a peer-to-peer basis with other HR functions.

Summary

If your organization understands the benefits of creating a staffing strategy but has had little or no success to date implementing a traditional process, consider the alternatives described in this chapter and summarized in Figure 4-2. Think of strategic staffing as creating a longer-term context within which more effective short-term staffing decisions can be made. Integrate staffing into business planning; don't think of it solely in terms of implementation. Create strategies that focus on particular issues, and vary planning parameters accordingly. Include only those jobs for which a longer-term perspective is really needed. Keep plans separate and distinct. Update staffing plans whenever significant changes in business plans are being considered. Work to provide managers with information, not data. And, most important of all, develop staffing strategies and plans that solve staffing issues and problems; don't just build a new tool or system.

Figure 4-2. Consider New Approaches.

Instead of:	Consider:
Focusing on analysis and reporting	Focusing on planning and acting
Thinking of staffing as an implementation concern	Addressing staffing from a proactive perspective
Focusing on organization units	Focusing on critical staffing issues
Defining a one-size-fits-all process	Tailoring planning parameters to fit each staffing issue
Including all positions	Focusing on positions where you need to be proactive or need time to react
Compiling results across units or groups	Keeping results separate and detailed
Planning on a set schedule	Defining issues and developing strategies whenever change occurs (or is discussed)
Building models or creating processes	Solving problems, addressing issues, and answering questions
Thinking of Workforce Planning as a function that "feeds" of other HR functions	Thinking of Workforce Planning as a function that "feeds" other HR functions

5

Designing Your Strategic Staffing/ Workforce Planning Process

Now that you understand the context within which the process can be implemented most effectively, you can begin to develop your own strategic staffing/workforce planning process. The process described here incorporates the tweaks to the traditional approach (mentioned in Chapter 3) that increase its efficiency. By following this approach within the context described in Chapter 4, you can ensure that your process will also be effective.

An Overview of the Strategic Staffing/Workforce Planning Process

Before describing the process, let's review some of the key concepts that were introduced in Chapter 2. Strategic staffing/workforce planning is a process that organizations use to help them identify and address the staffing implications of business plans and strategies. By implementing this process, organizations can ensure that they will have the right number of people, with the right capabilities, in place at the right time. When implemented effectively, the process results in two major outputs or deliverables: staffing strategies (which describe what will be done in the long term, across planning periods, to address critical staffing issues) and staffing plans (which describe specific, short-term tactical plans and staffing actions to be implemented in the near term—within a given planning period).

These two components can be developed in many ways, but I have found one process to be particularly effective. This strategic staffing process has four steps:

1. Define critical staffing issues/areas of focus. As you learned in the previous chapter, your strategic staffing efforts will be effective only when they focus on a relatively small number of particularly critical staffing issues or job categories—not on entire business units or organizations. The first step of the process, then, is to identify and prioritize your most critical staffing issues and select those for which specific staffing strategies are required.

2. Define staffing gaps and surpluses. Once you have selected an issue (or an area on which your analysis will focus), the next step is to develop a staffing model to address that issue that defines staffing requirements, forecasts staff availability, compares demand to supply, and calculates staffing gaps and surpluses for each job category for each period in your planning horizon. The design of the model will be specific to the issue that you select.

3. Develop staffing strategies. The next step is to review the preliminary staffing gaps and surpluses, as calculated by your model, across all the planning periods in your planning horizon. Create a series of long-term, directional plans of action that describe what your organization should do to address those critical staffing issues most effectively (i.e., how to best align staffing demand and supply) across all planning periods, throughout the entire planning horizon. At this point, do not focus your efforts on any one planning period.

4. Define staffing plans. After you have developed staffing strategies that span all planning periods, go back and examine the specific staffing needs for each period. Following the concept of the "upside-down T" (described in Chapter 2), use the staffing strategies developed in the previous step as a long-term context and define the specific staffing actions that will allow you to meet the staffing needs effectively and efficiently in each planning period. Make sure that those actions are consistent with and fully support the staffing strategies that you developed in the previous step.

Finally, you will need to fully implement the plans, measure your results, and adjust your staffing strategies and plans as needed to reflect changing business conditions.

This chapter describes each step of the strategic staffing process in detail. Remember that while the process itself is relatively straightforward, it should be applied within the more focused context described in Chapter 4. It should be applied selectively, not to all units within an organization in a one-size-fits-all manner.

Step 1: Define Critical Staffing Issues

The identification of critical staffing issues is one of the most important steps in the strategic staffing process. As discussed in Chapter 4, I strongly believe that staffing strategies should focus on critical staffing issues, not on organizations or business units. These staffing issues can be thought of as especially critical categories of jobs that warrant—and require—special attention (e.g., positions that are especially critical to effective strategy implementation or jobs that are traditionally hard to fill). To define critical staffing issues, it is necessary to understand the longer-term business context and define the staffing issues you will address.

Understand the Longer-Term Business Context

The identification of staffing issues requires a full understanding of your business objectives and plans as well as a mastery of the strategic staffing/workforce planning process. Begin your search for possible staffing issues by reviewing in detail what your organization is trying to accomplish in the long term and how those things are to be done. Ideally, your company will have a well-defined business strategy that you can refer to. There may also be other components of the planning process that will deepen your understanding of the future direction of the business (e.g., definitions of mission, vision statements, and sets of strategic objectives). You may also be involved in discussions of possible business strategies or changes in business direction. Any of these might be sources of critical staffing issues.

It is not enough for you to simply be an expert in the staffing process. Those who are responsible for developing staffing strategies must also know as much about the business as the business unit heads do. It is not sufficient to have some knowledge of the business and in-depth expertise in the area of staffing—an in-depth understanding of both is needed.

Do you really understand your company's business plans and strategies well enough to serve as a true business partner and develop effective staffing strategies and plans? Some HR professionals do have a full grasp of their company's business strategies, but others may not understand the business as well as they need to (or think they do). These people must gain a more robust understanding of these strategies before they can initiate or support a strategic staffing process. Here is a test that you can use to determine whether you do indeed understand your company's business strategy well enough. Suppose that on a Friday afternoon, you were suddenly named to head up a business unit in your company (e.g., to run a plant if you are in a manufacturing company, or to be general manager of a region if you are in a service company), starting the following Monday. Would you welcome such an assignment? Do you think that you would be fully prepared to function in the new position when you reported to work on Monday morning? Just before you fell asleep that Friday night (when you are really fairly honest with yourself), would you think that you knew enough about the business to be successful on your own? If the answer is yes, you probably know enough about the business. If the answer is no, however, you may need to improve your understanding.

If you determine that you need a better understanding of your company's business objectives and plans, here are some low-cost, nonthreatening things that you can do to learn more:

- Review the company's business strategies, plans, and proposals (e.g., unit, financial, marketing, technical, and functional plans) on your own and ask unit managers for clarification of or expansion on points that you don't understand.

- Examine planned capital investments, identifying what resources are to be invested, where, and why.

- Identify industry, competitive, and other external factors affecting the business and think about the impact that these will have on your company and its plans.

- Ask to meet with a planner or line manager, saying that you need a better understanding of business plans in order to determine the staffing implications or to develop realistic staffing plans.

- Where specific plans are not available, create your own "what-if" business scenarios that you can use as a foundation for strategic staffing.

Identify Staffing Issues Raised by Business Plans

First, identify (at least in a preliminary way) the particular aspects of your business plans that have (or may have) significant staffing implications. Identify key business initiatives, plans, and actions that may have a significant impact on required capabilities, staffing levels, or both. Identify specific, critical job categories that will need the special attention that strategic staffing provides. You might choose to focus your analysis on staffing issues/implications such as these:

- Job categories that are critical to strategy implementation
- Job categories in which significant changes in required capabilities will be needed
- Job categories in which required staffing levels need to change significantly (e.g., additions are needed to support significant growth, or reductions are necessary because of a downsizing)
- Positions that are expected to be hard to fill
- Positions that have long learning curves (and thus should be filled well in advance of actual need)

- Emerging skill sets, especially those that you have not looked for previously
- Skill sets for which there is intense competition externally
- Areas in which specific staffing plans are needed (e.g., when identifying opportunities to redeploy surplus staff rather than resort to layoffs)

While this list of possible staffing issues is not exhaustive, it is a good place to start.

When you are identifying staffing issues and their implications, it is often helpful to focus on what will be changing in your organization (i.e., not just what is to be done, but what is to be done differently). In many cases, business strategies describe very specific changes that are to be implemented; often, these changes have an impact on required staffing levels, required capabilities, or both.

It may be helpful to think of these various changes as "staffing drivers," since they drive changes in required capabilities and staffing levels. These staffing drivers are really just categories of change that your business may be implementing. Staffing drivers might include:

- Changes in business focus, objectives, or activities
- Business expansion or contraction
- Changes in markets or customer base
- Major projects or capital expenditures
- Changes in technology
- Changes in product mix
- Productivity improvements and cost containment efforts
- Changes in competitive positions
- Changes in organization structure

Since they are somewhat generic categories (rather than specific changes), many of these staffing drivers can be identified in advance. Create a list of the staffing drivers that typically affect staffing in your organization. Then use this list as "crib notes" when identifying staffing implications. When you read a business plan, highlight (perhaps literally, using a marker) the parts of the plan that describe the kinds of changes that are included on your list of staffing drivers. Remember that these changes are often described in financial sections and tables, so don't just read the text. Consider these highlighted sections to be rocks to look under—you will need to go back to them later and dig deeper to identify what the potential staffing issues or implications really are.

If you are participating in planning discussions (rather than reviewing written plans), staffing drivers can also be helpful. As planning discussions progress, specifically listen for the changes described on your list of drivers. When they are described, politely stop the conversation to ensure that the staffing implications of these changes are also discussed.

Figure 5-1 includes a table that identifies some of the critical staffing issues that typically arise from given business changes.

Figure 5-1. Identifying Potential Staffing Issues.

Specific Staffing Issues Driven by Business Changes

Business Change	Common Staffing Implications
Change in business focus, objectives, or activities	• Changes in required skills • Changes in staffing "mix" (both skills and staffing levels simultaneously)
Business expansion or contraction	• Changes in required staffing levels
Changes in product mix	• Changes in required skills and staffing levels (e.g., in sales and marketing)
Changes in markets or customer base	• Changes in required skills and staffing levels (e.g., sales and marketing)
Major capital expenditures/projects	• Changes in staffing levels to support new projects • New skills to support new technology • Reductions in staffing levels where old systems are phased out
Changes in production technology	• Changes in staffing levels to support new projects • New skills to support new technology • Reductions in staffing levels where old systems are phased out
Changes in competitive positions	• Reduced staffing levels (e.g., to reduce staff cost) • New skills and additional staffing required to support new products and approaches
Productivity/Quality improvements	• Changes in staffing "mix" (e.g., fewer, but more highly skilled, staff)
Changes in organization structure	• Redeployments • "Harmonization" issues (e.g., same position titles but different levels)
Merger and Acquisition activity	• Integration of two workforces • Potential surplus staff (e.g., overlapping sales accountabilities, redundant staff positions)

Figure 5-1. (Continued)

Generic Staffing Issues

Staffing Issues Driven by Business Changes	Staffing Issues Driven by Potential Solutions
Significant changes in required skills	Positions that will be hard to fill
Significant changes in required staffing levels	Positions with long learning curves
Specific positions or job families that will become critical	Positions with skills not previously required
Redeployments spurred by reorganizations	Positions where competition for required talent is intense
Workforce integration issues raised by L&A activity	

In some cases, business plans just don't provide the richness of detail that is needed to define critical staffing issues. In these cases, interviews with line managers and planning staff may provide the additional information that you need. Prepare for such an interview by learning all you can about that manager's business. Identify possible staffing issues or areas of concern. Define the manager's current staffing resources, in terms of both requirements and staffing levels. When conducting the interview, verify current staffing, talk about business plans and changes, and discuss the impact that those changes might have on required skills and/or staffing levels. A suggested format for such an interview (and an interview guide) is included in Chapter 13 of this book.

Another caution: Don't limit your analysis and efforts to the staffing data that might be included in the business strategy (if there are any) or the human resources section of your business plan (if your business plan includes such a section). In many cases, those plans and projections are inaccurate and unrealistic. They are simply management's best guess regarding staffing requirements. Create your own staffing plans instead, using the tools and techniques described in this book.

Identify Other Potential Staffing Issues

It is quite possible that your organization may be facing significant staffing issues that are not driven by business plans or changes. Significant retirements (whether in terms of large numbers of losses or the departure of specific individuals with critical skills or experience), for example, could severely hamper your company's ability to implement its strategies even if there are no real changes in the objectives, scope, or direction of those strategies. As an example of the latter, one company I worked with determined that the retirement of a particular marketing executive would not be a problem because an adequately skilled successor had been developed. Unfortunately, while the successor was skilled, he lacked the intimate knowledge of each customer that the previous incumbent had acquired over the years. This created a major issue that was not directly related to any specific change in the business itself. Other issues that are not driven by business plans might include a lack of management depth, chronic shortages of key talent, or an ongoing lack of needed workforce diversity.

Select the Staffing Issues You Will Address

Once you have identified your potential staffing issues (both those that are raised by business plans and those that are not), review the list and select those that you will address. Usually, it is not possible to address all the issues that you identify. Set priorities and select those issues for which staffing strategies will be developed. In some cases, the order in which you address issues will be based on need (i.e., you first address those that are most critical). In other cases, it may be necessary to address issues in a particular sequence (i.e., less critical issues must be addressed first because they provide input that is needed in order to address more critical issues). Finally, you need to clearly document and define the staffing issues that you are going to address.

Step 2: Define Staffing Gaps and Surpluses

Once you have identified the staffing issues to be addressed, the next step is to define, for each issue, the staffing gaps and surpluses that must be eliminated (or at least alleviated) if that issue is to be addressed fully (and thus your business strategies implemented effectively). In order to create staffing strategies, you must first define the staffing gaps and surpluses that are expected during each planning period of your planning horizon. These gaps are specific, quantifiable, and objective. There are three kinds of differences that you might identify:

- **Staffing levels.** You may have too many staff (a surplus) or too few staff (a gap or deficit) in some job categories to implement the company's business plans effectively.

- **Capabilities.** It may be that you have the right number of staff, but that these individuals lack particular capabilities that will be needed to implement the company's business strategies.

- **Mix.** It may be the case both that you have the wrong number of staff and that the staff you have lack critical capabilities. I call this a staffing mix problem.

In order to define these differences in sufficient detail, you will need to create a staffing model that allows you to define staffing requirements, forecast staff availability, and compare requirements to availability. Step 2a describes the overall approach that should be used to structure the staffing model process. Step 2b describes the steps involved in developing and implementing a specific, detailed staffing model. A separate staffing model will be required for each staffing issue that you are going to address.

Step 2a: Define Your Overall Staffing Model Process

To define staffing strategies and plans for each staffing issue, you will need to develop a staffing model that includes a definition of staffing requirements (in terms of both skills and staffing levels), a projection of staff availability, and the calculation of specific gaps and surpluses for each of your planning periods. At the core of the strategic staffing process is a fairly traditional quantitative model that defines required staffing levels (demand), identifies available staffing (supply), and calculates the gaps between supply and demand (net needs). Figure 5-2 shows this process at its simplest.

The simple (and often used) process shown in Figure 5-2 is rarely appropriate. It applies only when there are no changes in available staffing between "now" (whenever current staff availability was determined) and "then" (that point in the future for which demand has been calculated). In most companies, many actions that affect staff availability will occur between now and then (especially when you consider that my broad defini-

Figure 5-2. The Traditional Approach.

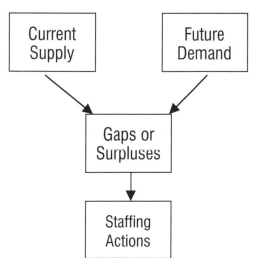

tion of *staffing* includes all movement into, around, and out of an organization). People will leave the organization through turnover, through retirement, and for other reasons. Those who stay may change jobs, be promoted, or be redeployed. New people may join the organization. There is simply no way to account for these actions in the simplistic model described in Figure 5-2, so a different version of the model is necessary.

A better process for defining staffing gaps and surpluses is one in which you first define how many people you have now, then use that information as a foundation for projecting the number and types of people you think will be available at the point for which requirements have been defined. To do this, you need to make assumptions regarding the losses, additions, and movement that you think will occur between "now" and "then." By using this technique, you can compare supply and demand at the same point in time and get a meaningful estimation of staffing gaps and surpluses. Figure 5-3 shows what this process looks like.

You will still start by determining future requirements (both required

Figure 5-3. A Better Approach.

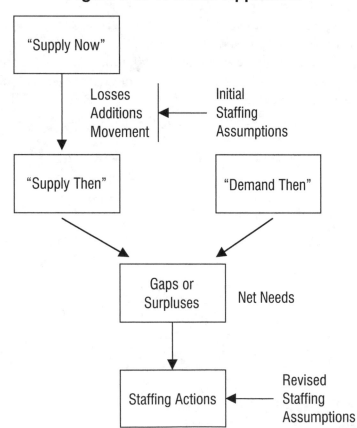

skills and required staffing levels) at a particular point in time ("demand then"), but in this version of the process, the supply side has two steps. Once you have determined demand, you then define the current staffing levels and capabilities, just as you did in the traditional approach depicted in Figure 5-2. What follows is different, however. Next, you make specific assumptions about the staffing actions that you think are likely to occur between now and then. Make your "best-guess" assumptions about the number of people you think will make any kind of staffing move (e.g., leave voluntarily, retire, be promoted, be redeployed, or be hired). Once you have made (and documented) these staffing assumptions, you apply them to the current population to see what staff will be available if all these staffing actions actually take place. Take the following steps:

- Subtract from your current population the number of people you think will leave each job category (e.g., through voluntary turnover, retirements, and other planned losses).

- Add in the number of people that will be hired into each job (or added from sources not included in your model).

- Account for promotions and other movement (e.g., redeployment) by subtracting that number of people from the jobs they are leaving and adding them to the jobs they will be entering.

Chapter 9 includes a specific example of what these calculations might look like. Once you have applied all your assumptions, you will end up with a "snapshot" or forecast of the numbers and types of employees that will be available at that point in the future ("supply then"), given that all the staffing actions you assumed really do take place.

Now compare "supply then" to "demand then" and calculate staffing gaps and surpluses. Finally, define the staffing actions needed to eliminate these gaps and surpluses. This process usually entails a revision of the staffing assumptions you made initially. For example, if you assumed that some hiring would take place, but there are still some gaps, you may need to hire even more people. Alternatively, you may need to promote or redeploy additional people to meet that need. Conversely, there may be surpluses in jobs where the number of people you assumed would be hired or promoted was greater than the number actually needed. In these cases, you might need to reduce the number of people you assumed would be hired or promoted. In other cases where there are surpluses, you may need to assume that more people will leave than you projected in the first place (e.g., through layoffs or early retirement). In the end, your objective is to create a set of staffing assumptions (actions) that most effectively matches supply and demand.

While this approach is certainly better than the first one (because it factors in the staffing changes that will occur between now and then), it too can be improved. The problem with this version is that it is iterative in nature: You make assumptions regarding the staffing actions that are needed and then test those assumptions to see if in fact the staffing gaps and surpluses are eliminated. If they are, you have arrived at a good solution. If, however, there are still differences between supply and demand (a scenario that is quite likely), you must revise your staffing action assumptions and recalculate the gaps and surpluses. It may be necessary to repeat this process (perhaps many times) until an acceptable solution is reached. Thinking of it another way, the staffing "assumptions" that you make when using this particular approach are often just guesses. You guess at a solution, try it, and if it is not correct, you guess again—and just keep guessing until you arrive at an acceptable solution. For example, you may not know the actual number of people that need to be promoted from one job to another, so you guess at that number (calling it an assumption, of course), plug in your guess, and see if you were right. If you weren't, you need to revise your promotion assumptions (in fact, guessing again) until you get supply to equal demand. While you will eventually arrive at the right answer, the process is very iterative and is not very efficient.

By making a relatively small change in our model, we can largely eliminate the guesswork. The difference lies in the nature of the assumptions that are made. This third, "best" version begins the same way as the second version (see Figure 5-4). With this approach, you start by defining "demand then" and "supply now," just as you would have done in the previous processes. This time, however, you make assumptions only about the staffing actions that you really can't control—that is to say, those staffing actions that are likely even if you do nothing. You might wish to think of these actions as those that will happen no matter what you do. Usually, these "uncontrollable" actions include:

- Voluntary turnover
- Normal retirements
- Seniority- or tenure-based promotions
- Completion of hiring plans that are already in motion (e.g., openings that will be filled during the period by candidates who have accepted offers but have not yet started work)
- Returns or losses resulting from planned leaves of absence (e.g., because of military service or health-related issues)

Create your first version of "supply then" by considering *only* uncontrollable actions like these. At this point, specifically do not make any as-

Figure 5-4. The "Best" Approach.

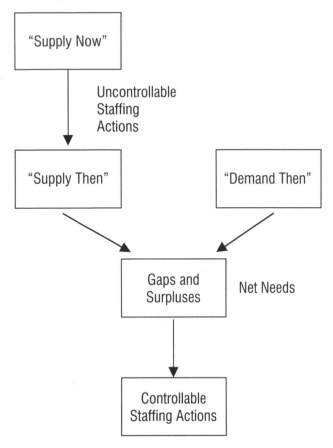

sumptions regarding other staffing actions. Compare this preliminary "supply then" to "demand then" to determine the preliminary gaps and surpluses that result.

Now you can begin to define the "controllable" staffing actions that you will take to eliminate these gaps and surpluses. Consider at this point all of the various types of staffing actions that you can choose to implement in order to eliminate the preliminary gaps and surpluses you just identified. Controllable staffing actions are all those that happen because you make them happen—they would not happen otherwise. Controllable staffing actions include virtually all:

- Hiring
- Promotions
- Transfers and redeployments
- Planned staff reductions
- Use of temporary or contingent staff

- Use of overtime
- Planned losses

Each of these staffing actions is a specific move that is made in an intentional way to meet a particular need that has been identified. The advantage of this approach is that it completely eliminates the guesswork (and thus all the iterations) that is part of the second approach described previously. For example, rather than guessing how many promotions to a particular job will be needed, first determine the number of openings that will be created as a result of uncontrollable actions and then decide how many of those openings can and should be filled through promotion. Similarly, don't estimate the number of new hires at first. Instead, use this technique to figure out how many openings are expected, then determine how many of those openings can and should be filled with new hires. In fact, this technique allows you to identify talent surpluses from which employees might be redeployed, eliminating the need for some hiring or promotion. With this process, there is no need to guess, test, and guess again until you arrive at an acceptable solution. Instead, you get that solution in a single iteration. All these controllable staffing actions form the basis of your near-term staffing plans and thus should be carefully documented. Table 5-1 includes a list of typical controllable and uncontrollable staffing actions.

In summary, it is typically most effective to adopt an overall approach to strategic staffing that takes into account the staffing actions that are anticipated between the current time and that point in the future for which demand has been calculated. The efficiency of the process can be improved (and the guesswork eliminated) by first considering the uncontrollable staffing actions and then determining the mix of controllable staffing actions needed to eliminate the resulting gaps and surpluses.

Step 2b: Create a Detailed Staffing Model

Using the approach described in Figure 5-4 as your road map, you will now need to develop a detailed staffing model for your critical staffing issue that will calculate specific staffing gaps and surpluses and help you define the staffing actions that best eliminate those gaps and surpluses. A separate model will be needed for each staffing issue that you will focus on. Again, Chapter 9 includes a worked-out example of this process. Here are the steps in the process.

Define Staffing Model/Planning Parameters

Once business plans have been defined and understood, you should begin to define and quantify staffing requirements and availability. As discussed

Table 5-1. Examples of Uncontrollable and Controllable Staffing Actions.

Staffing Action	Uncontrollable	Controllable
Recruiting	• Positions for which candidates have accepted offers but are not yet working • Positions for which candidates are being actively considered and the openings will be filled in the planning period	• Any opening for which specific candidates have not been identified • Openings that have been "approved" but for which no candidate will be placed • Most openings that are to be filled by implementing the staffing plans you are preparing
Promotions, transfers, and other internal movement	• "Lock step" promotions (e.g., those defined by labor agreements) • Seniority- or tenure-based promotions that are not at the discretion of management • Any move where an employee has been selected but not yet placed (assuming that the placement occurs during the planning period in question)	• Any opening for which specific candidates have not been identified • Most openings that are to be filled by implementing the staffing plans you are preparing
Losses	• Voluntary turnover • Normal retirement • Temporary/contingent staff whose contracts will expire during the planning period	• Early retirement programs • Termination for cause • Layoffs or reductions in force • Temporary/contingent staff whose contracts will be terminated prematurely

earlier, it is usually best to build a separate model for each issue, so that you can vary the planning parameters accordingly. For every model that you build, you must define three sets of parameters: the time frame/planning horizon, the population, and the model structure.

Time Frame/Planning Horizon. This parameter has two components. The first, the *planning horizon*, describes how far out you will plan (e.g., the coming three years). The second, the *planning period*, describes how frequently you will plan or update within your planning horizon (e.g., annually or quarterly). Each of these two components should be appropriate (and may differ) for the particular staffing issue that you are addressing.

It is important that you match the planning horizon to the staffing issue that you are addressing. As discussed in Chapter 4, there is no need to force every unit to use the same time frame, nor is it necessary to use the time frame and planning horizon of your strategic planning process "just because." If you are looking at jobs in which requirements and technology change quickly, you might use a one-year time frame, creating plans for each of the four quarters in that year (it is likely that you would update a plan like this each quarter). If you are analyzing management depth, you might need to use a three- to five-year planning horizon (it will take that long to get any measurable results), updating the plans annually within that framework.

Never create a staffing plan that has a planning horizon longer than your management's ability to provide reasonable forecasts or its willingness to allocate resources. If managers cannot estimate staffing requirements more than three years in the future, why ask them to do so for years 4 and 5? If managers won't act on the longer-term results of your work, why create such a long-term plan in the first place?

Here is an example of how planning horizons might be determined. Suppose that your managers were willing to change resource allocations to avoid an issue that was two years out but would do nothing more than cast a watchful eye on issues that were three years away. What would be the proper planning horizon? At first glance, a two-year plan would seem appropriate, since that matches management's proclivity to act. However, remember that the objective of a staffing strategy is to create a longer-term context that can be used to guide short-term decision making. How would you determine the best staffing plan for year 2 without creating a plan for year 3 as well? I would create a three-year plan, using year 3 as the context for defining the right actions for year 2. However, I would share only the first two years of that plan with managers, given that they would probably be unwilling to implement the plan for year 3.

Population. What jobs/staff should be included in your plan? Remember that there is no need to create a single model that includes all jobs or all people. Instead, you need to include in each model only those positions (or staff) that are directly affected by the issue you are addressing. When you build a model, you should include three groups of people/jobs:

- **The target population:** those positions or individuals who are directly affected by the issue you are addressing
- **Sources:** those jobs that might be likely, significant, realistic sources of talent if there is a need in your target population. Are there other jobs in the organization that require similar skills and capabilities from which you might draw talent?

- **Uses:** those jobs that might be significant users of talent if there is a surplus in the target population. Are there other areas of the company that might need people with these skills and capabilities?

Once you have determined the job categories to be included from an overall perspective, try to separate the specific positions that must be addressed strategically from those that can be addressed primarily from a tactical perspective. Include in your model only those jobs that must be analyzed from a strategic perspective—those for which staffing needs must be addressed proactively or those for which it will take considerable time to address staffing needs.

If you are unclear as to whether or not a job category should be included in your strategic staffing process, think about the nature of the staffing actions that you would be likely to apply if a gap in that area were to be defined. Consider each of the four categories of staffing action and try to reach a consensus as to whether the job is more strategic or tactical in nature. As you review each category, think about the following questions:

- **Recruiting.** If you were to rely on recruiting to meet the need, could you wait until an opening occurs and just react (e.g., simply posting the job on an Internet job board will identify a sufficient number of qualified candidates)? If so, it's likely that this job can be addressed tactically, and it may not be necessary to include it in your process. On the other hand, would you really need to anticipate that opening and be more proactive (e.g., where competition for people with those skills is intense and the number of qualified candidates is relatively low)? If so, it's likely that a more strategic approach will be needed.

- **Internal movement.** Think about filling an opening in this job category through normal channels or career paths. Does there tend to be a relatively large pool of qualified candidates available when openings occur? If so, a tactical approach may be sufficient. If that pool is not usually large enough, or if the candidates require additional development before they can be placed, then the opening should be addressed from a strategic perspective.

- **Redeployment.** Will it be possible to meet staffing needs in this category through redeployment? Are there qualified candidates available (allowing you to be tactical), or would such redeployment require advance planning or significant development (requiring you to be more strategic)?

- **Development.** Think about closing a staffing gap in this category by providing existing staff with the required skills. How large are the skills gaps? Can these gaps be dealt with through training in the time available? Is it possible that the missing skills can be developed after the job moves are made? If so, then a tactical approach is probably adequate. On the other hand, if development needs are substantial, involve core/strategic capabilities, and/or cannot be met in a short-term time frame, then it's better to include these jobs in the strategic category.

Following is a worksheet that you can use as a guide to help you determine whether a job should be addressed strategically (and thus should be included in your model) or tactically (and thus can be excluded). In each cell of the worksheet, jot down likely staffing actions, whether strategic or tactical. Review your probable actions and determine whether you are more likely to implement the strategic options or the tactical options. Indicate your choice in the fourth column.

Worksheet
Should a Job Be Included in the Strategic Staffing Process?

Job Category: _____

Staffing Action	Strategic	Tactical/Operational	Most Likely Option
	Need time to respond? Need time to be proactive?	Can you respond quickly? Can you be reactive?	
Recruiting			☐ Strategic ☐ Tactical
Internal movement			☐ Strategic ☐ Tactical
Redeployment			☐ Strategic ☐ Tactical
Development			☐ Strategic ☐ Tactical

Model Structure. You will now need to create some kind of model structure or framework to keep track of and organize your data. Usually, a two-dimensional matrix works well. Try using the columns of the matrix to capture "big-picture" concepts like organization units, functions, job groups/families, or locations. Use the rows to differentiate levels of experience or accountability.

Remember that whatever matrix you build, you will be using it to structure each component of your model. Use the same matrix format to capture required staffing ("demand then"), current staffing ("supply now"), losses (e.g., voluntary turnover for each category), hiring, transfers in and out, and future availability ("supply then"). When you compare "supply then" to "demand then" (as described later), you will end up with a gap, a surplus, or zero in every cell of this matrix. Don't forget to capture capabilities information (both supply and demand) for each cell of your matrix (at an appropriate level of detail), using this very same row/column framework.

When defining model structure, don't limit your choices to those titles and levels that exist currently. I often find it helpful to define various roles that individuals play. Frequently, technical or functional areas can be defined using just three roles: senior (those with especially deep experience in a particular area), individual contributor (those who have some specific capabilities and can function independently), and entry level (those who have basic capabilities and aptitudes, but no significant expertise or experience). Usually, a vast number of individual position titles can be combined into a very small number of roles. Not only is this a more realistic way to describe the work that is being done (or needs to be done), but it has the added benefit of keeping the size of the model manageable.

There may also be cases (such as those where required capabilities are expected to change significantly) in which it is necessary to create categories for jobs that are expected to exist in the future but that do not exist currently. If this is necessary, include both old and new job categories in your matrix. However, it is likely that there will be no staff that currently have all the skills that will be necessary in the future; further, it is just as likely that you will need no one in the future that has only the skills that are needed now. Later on in the modeling process, your "supply now" matrix will probably include those with the skills that are currently required but will include no one with the skills needed in the future. Conversely, your "demand then" matrix will document your requirements for the new skills, but will define no requirements for the obsolete skills now available. Figure 5-5 is a simple example of what that type of matrix might look like for just two job families.

Sometimes it is necessary to keep track of more than two dimensions (e.g., it may be necessary to define staffing needs by function, location, and level of experience). Often, a two-dimensional model can still be used to track three (or more) variables. Suppose that there are three locations (e.g., New York, Chicago, and Los Angeles), four functions (e.g., Manufacturing, Sales, Finance, and HR), and three roles (e.g., manager, senior, and individual contributor). First, create a column for each location. Next, create a separate row for each combination of function and level (e.g., HR/manager, HR/senior, HR/individual contributor, Sales/manager, and so

Figure 5-5. Example.

Supply Now

Role	Networking (Current Skills)	Data Management (Current Skills)	Networking (Future Skills)	Data Management (Future Skills)
Team Leader	5	10	0	0
Individual Contributor	25	21	0	0
Entry-Level	15	6	0	0

Demand "Then"

Role	Networking (Current Skills)	Data Management (Current Skills)	Networking (Future Skills)	Data Management (Future Skills)
Team Leader	0	0	7	12
Individual Contributor	0	0	30	27
Entry-Level	0	0	18	10

on). In this way, you can create a model that uses a two-dimensional format to track three variables. While this is a little unwieldy, it is usually preferable to somehow creating a three-dimensional array or spreadsheet. Figure 5-6 shows one way in which that model might be structured.

Define Staffing Requirements

Once you have defined all three sets of parameters, you can begin to build and load your staffing model. While you can start with either the supply side or the demand side, I almost always start with demand for the following reasons:

- In virtually every case, it is more difficult to define the required capabilities and staffing levels than it is to describe the anticipated supply. If you start with demand, you will get the hard part done first.

- Usually, less information is available about demand, and the information that is available is at a more "macro" level than that available for the supply side. If you start with the supply side, it can be easy to develop a very detailed model, if only because a human resource information system usually contains a lot of detailed data. Rarely, however, is that same level of detail available for future plans (e.g., longer-term forecasts or business volumes). Since the model can be built only to the lowest level of detail available on both the supply

Figure 5-6.

Function/Role	New York	Chicago	Los Angeles
Manufacturing/Manager			
Manufacturing/Senior			
Manufacturing/Individual Contributor			
Sales/Manager			
Sales/Senior			
Sales/Individual Contributor			
Finance/Manager			
Finance/Senior			
Finance/Individual Contributor			
HR/Manager			
HR/Senior			
HR/Individual Contributor			

and demand sides, it is more likely that the level of detail on the demand side will become the design parameter. Thus, any time spent or resources expended on gathering additional detail will be wasted.

- Most managers are more interested in requirements than they are in availability. If you are trying to build interest in and credibility for the strategic staffing/workforce planning process, start by defining requirements.

You will need to define both the capabilities and the staffing levels that will be needed in each job category (or cell of your model/matrix) in order to implement the business plan. It is not possible to define staffing levels until you have determined the roles and capabilities that will be needed, so start there. Don't try to identify all the capabilities that are required in each category. Instead, try to focus on a very small number of capabilities (usually five to ten) that are really important, including:

- Those that are especially critical (e.g., those that are needed to win, not just to play the game)
- Those that differentiate one job, category, or level from another (and thus one row of your model from another)
- Those that are changing (e.g., newly emerging capabilities that might need to be developed quickly)

If your company uses competency models or some kind of skills database, use this as your starting point. Remember to select only those skills that are absolutely critical, however. If you choose skills from a predefined list, you are apt to choose too many.

Once you have identified the required capabilities, define the required staffing levels. There are many techniques that can be used to do this, including statistical techniques, staffing ratios, project-based staffing, and staffing profiles. Rather than describe these techniques here, I've provided detailed descriptions of each (including specific examples with solutions) in Chapter 7 of this book.

It may be necessary to combine several of these techniques in order to create a complete picture of the requirements. For example, when defining staffing requirements for new bank branches, you might combine the following techniques:

- The number of branch managers might be constant (e.g., one per branch).
- The number of loan officers might be determined by a staffing profile (e.g., ten officers for a large branch and six for a small branch).
- The number of tellers or personal bankers might be defined using staffing ratios (e.g., relating the number of tellers or officers to the anticipated number of customers or transactions).

Regardless of the technique you use, you will end up with a definition of the critical capabilities and required staffing levels for each cell of the matrix/model you have developed.

Forecast Staffing Availability

Once you have defined the demand, the next step is to forecast the anticipated supply of staff. First, define the number and types of staff that are *currently* available in each job or category (i.e., each cell of your model/matrix). Where possible, first document the overall existing capabilities in each category/cell. Capture the common or core skills of the group as a whole (i.e., by cohort), not the specific capabilities of each individual in that group. Individual skills and capabilities are not helpful at this point (although they may be later on when you identify the specific individuals who will be promoted, redeployed, and so on).

The information you need in order to produce this "supply now" component can usually be extracted from your human resource information system (HRIS). Access the system to determine the number of individuals you currently have in each job category (i.e., each combination of row and column headings). It may be necessary to "map" the HRIS data into the categories you have created (e.g., to define a role that you are using as consisting of several actual titles or a given experience level as a group of salary grades).

Next, forecast the number of staff that you think will be available at that point in the future for which you have calculated demand. Make assumptions regarding the staffing actions involving current staff that will occur between the current time (now) and that point in the future for which demand has been calculated (then). Remember to consider only those staffing actions that are uncontrollable. In this context, which staffing actions should be considered controllable and which are uncontrollable? It may be helpful to think of the difference this way:

- **Uncontrollable staffing actions** are those that are likely to occur anyway (i.e., whether or not your organization creates and implements staffing strategies and plans).

- **Controllable staffing actions** are those that you will define and implement specifically to meet the staffing needs that your strategic staffing process identified.

Again, Table 5-1 lists some common examples of both uncontrollable and controllable staffing actions.

Calculate the number of staff that will be available in each category if your assumptions concerning uncontrollable actions actually occur, including:

- Subtracting out anticipated turnover, retirements, transfers out, and other planned losses

- Adding in anticipated hires and transfers in

- Adjusting for preplanned promotions and movement (i.e., subtracting from the source jobs and adding that same number to the target jobs), including retirements, internal movement, hiring, and other staffing actions that are anticipated between now and then

- Adjusting for additions and losses resulting from planned leaves of absence

Don't forget to document changes in capabilities, too. If, for example, you have a major development initiative that will be completed between now and then, capture the new skills that you assume the group will gain as a result of the training that is to occur.

What role do historical rates (e.g., turnover rates and promotion patterns) play in making these assumptions? The objective here is to develop a realistic set of assumptions that reflects what you think will actually happen between now and then as defined by your model parameters. If considering historical rates helps you to develop realistic assumptions about the future, feel free to calculate and use them. If, however, you think the future will be different from the past, make new assumptions that reflect what you think will occur—don't simply rely on past patterns that probably won't recur in the future. If, for example, the average voluntary turnover rate for the last five years has been 5 percent, and you think that that trend will continue, assume the same turnover rate for the future. However, if you think that changing economic conditions will affect that rate (e.g., times will get better and turnover will increase somewhat) or that competitive activities will increase (e.g., a growing competitor might attract more of your experienced staff than usual), use the rate that you think will occur, not the historical rate.

Don't try to forecast promotions based on historical data. Promotions are usually controllable and thus should not be considered at this point anyway. Furthermore, a historical promotion rate from one job to another of 10 percent probably reflected the way in which the organization chose to fill openings at that point in the past. Since it is unlikely that a similar number of openings will be filled in that manner in the future, it would be better to make new assumptions regarding promotions (between now and then) that show what you think will occur. Don't blindly assume that past trends will continue.

In forecasting the number of retirements, two approaches are particularly helpful:

1. Calculate the average retirement age, and then actually count the number of individuals in each job category that will reach that average age in each planning period.

2. Forecast retirements based on actual eligibility. Access the data in the HRIS to determine the individuals in each job category who will become eligible for retirement (e.g., based on a "rule" such as age plus service equals 80). Next, create a series of assumptions that describe how many of those who are eligible will actually retire in each planning period. Here are three possible assumptions:

- All will retire as soon as they are eligible. Under this assumption, simply count the number of people that become eligible to retire in each planning period and assume that they all will leave during that period.

- Spread retirements evenly over a set number of years (e.g., five years) following eligibility, with an equal percentage of staff retiring in each year (e.g., 20 percent in this simple case). Thus, if 20 employees become eligible to retire in period 1, assume that 4 of them (i.e., 20 percent of the 20) retire in period 1, 4 more in period 2, and so on for the five periods.

- Spread the retirements out unevenly over a set number of years (e.g., 20 percent of those eligible will retire as soon as they can, 15 percent will stay one year longer than they need to, 10 percent will stay two years longer, and so on).

When using a process similar to that described for the second and third assumptions, remember to add up all those who are projected to retire across all eligibility distributions. Look at the third assumption. Let's suppose that for the jobs in question, 20 percent of those who become eligible in year 1 will retire. In year 2, 15 percent of those in that same category who became eligible in year 1 will retire, along with 20 percent of those who first become eligible in year 2. Similarly, retirements in period 3 will be the sum of 10 percent of those who became eligible in year 1 plus 15 percent of those who became eligible in year 2 plus 20 percent of those who first become eligible in year 3. This logic continues for each year. A separate spreadsheet can easily be developed to model these retirement scenarios and calculate the total number of people in each job category that will retire in each planning period. Figure 5-7 is a sample of what that might look like for a given job (the results of the calculations have been rounded to the nearest whole number).

Your HRIS may include valuable data that you can use to develop these assumptions. You may be able to calculate historical voluntary turnover rates that you can use as a foundation for estimating future rates. Your HRIS can also provide retirement eligibility data. Ask the HRIS staff to produce a listing of employees by retirement eligibility date (based on your actual criteria). Make sure that the listing also includes the information you need in order to identify the job category (in your staffing model) that each employee is in currently (i.e., row and column headings). Then simply count the number that become eligible in each of your planning periods and enter that number in the appropriate cell of your model.

Here is a quick example of how "supply then" might be calculated for a given job category. Suppose that there are 40 people in a job right now. Suppose also that the following uncontrollable staffing actions are expected:

- The voluntary turnover rate for this job is 5 percent.
- Two people are expected to retire.
- One person will be promoted from this job to a higher level (a move based on seniority).

Figure 5-7. Sample Retirement Projection.

Percent retiring in the first year of eligibility: 20 percent

Percent retiring in the second year of eligibility: 15 percent

Percent retiring in the third year of eligibility: 10 percent

Percent retiring in the fourth year of eligibility: 25 percent

Percent retiring in the fifth year of eligibility: 30 percent

Model Year	Number Becoming Eligible	Retire in Year 1	Retire in Year 2	Retire in Year 3	Retire in Year 4	Retire in Year 5
Year 1	50	$0.20 \times 50 =$ 10	$0.15 \times 50 =$ 8	$0.10 \times 50 =$ 5	$0.25 \times 50 =$ 13	$0.30 \times 50 =$ 15
Year 2	60		$0.20 \times 60 =$ 12	$0.15 \times 60 =$ 9	$0.10 \times 60 =$ 6	$0.25 \times 60 =$ 15
Year 3	40			$0.20 \times 40 =$ 8	$0.15 \times 40 =$ 6	$0.10 \times 40 =$ 4
Year 4	55				$0.20 \times 55 =$ 11	$0.15 \times 55 =$ 8
Year 5	35					$0.20 \times 35 =$ 7
Total Retiring		10	20	22	36	49

- One person has accepted a job offer and will join the company in two weeks.

What is "supply then" in this case? Your calculation will look like this:

"Supply now"	40	
Minus voluntary turnover	− 2	(i.e., 5 percent of the 40 staff)
Minus retirements	− 2	
Minus promotions to other jobs	− 1	
Plus planned hires	+ 1	
Equals "supply then"	36	

This calculation assumes that no other uncontrollable staffing actions will take place and that all controllable staffing actions will be defined and applied later in the modeling process. A similar calculation would be made for every cell of your model/matrix.

Define Staffing Gaps and Surpluses for the First Period

For each cell of your model, compare staffing requirements (demand) to staffing availability (supply) and calculate gaps (where demand exceeds supply) and surpluses (where supply exceeds demand). When you make this comparison, subtract demand from supply. If you use this convention, staffing gaps will be defined as negative numbers and staffing surpluses will be defined as positive numbers. For example, if you will have 10 staff in a job category that will require 12, you will have a gap of 2 people. On the other hand, if you will have 15 people in a job that will require 10, you will have a surplus of 5 staff. Figure 5-8 shows a simple example of what this might look like. Remember to identify capability gaps as well, not just differences in staffing levels.

Define Staffing Gaps and Surpluses for All Remaining Periods

After you have calculated gaps and surpluses for period 1, you might be tempted to try to define the staffing actions needed to eliminate those gaps and surpluses. As discussed in Chapter 4, you should not do this at this point. Doing so would mean that you were meeting staffing needs while considering only a short-term perspective. Resist this temptation and instead calculate gaps and surpluses for subsequent planning periods. To do this, use your "supply then" matrix from period 1 as the "supply now"

Figure 5-8. Example.

Demand Then

	Project 1	Project 2
Engineering Manager	10	12
Engineer	25	40

Supply Then

	Project 1	Project 2
Engineering Manager	11	10
Engineer	23	43

Expected Staffing Gaps/Surpluses

	Project 1	Project 2
Engineering Manager	11 − 10 = +1	10 − 12 = −2
Engineer	23 − 25 = −2	43 − 40 = +3

matrix for period 2. Calculate "supply then" for period 2, factoring in any uncontrollable staffing actions that you think will happen during period 2. Compare the result to staffing requirements for the end of period 2 (which obviously could be different from the requirements for period 1) and calculate the staffing gaps and surpluses that you expect in each job category for the end of period 2. Repeat this process for all remaining planning periods, always remembering to:

- Use "supply then" from the previous period as "supply now" for the subsequent period.
- Define and include the uncontrollable staffing actions that you think will occur during the period you are analyzing.
- Define a new set of staffing requirements for each period.

These gaps and surpluses are preliminary, of course, because they do not take into consideration the staffing plans that you will implement (i.e., the controllable staffing actions that you will take). They are a necessary interim step, however.

Note that this approach represents a significant departure from common practice. Usually, the staffing actions needed to address gaps and surpluses are defined for a given period before the analysis for the subsequent period begins. This practice precludes any longitudinal view of staffing needs (i.e., analyzing needs across periods), and this longitudinal view is absolutely required if effective staffing strategies are to be developed.

Step 3: Develop Staffing Strategies

Staffing strategies are longer-term, directional plans of action that describe what an organization is actually going to do to address staffing needs across all planning periods throughout its planning horizon. Examples of staffing strategies include:

- Meet needs at senior levels through a 75 percent/25 percent blend of promotion from within and external recruiting.
- Focus recruiting and development on core positions that generate significant competitive advantage.
- Meet short-term needs for specific technical skills by using contractors.
- Redeploy individuals who are surplus in one area to a different area, providing accelerated development as required.

- Reorganize work to better utilize the available talent.
- Initiate intern programs at local high schools to develop pools of qualified technicians to meet long-term future needs.

By definition, an effective staffing strategy can be defined only across planning periods (e.g., across all five years of a five-year business strategy). Consequently, meaningful staffing strategies can be developed only after the initial differences between staffing supply and demand have been defined for *all* planning periods in the planning horizon. The best staffing strategy can be developed only after you have developed a full understanding of the staffing gaps and surpluses that are expected in *each* period in your planning horizon and analyzed those needs from an integrated, holistic perspective.

Once you have calculated gaps and surpluses for each period, review your needs in each model category *across* those periods (as opposed to looking at each period by itself) and develop staffing strategies that will most effectively eliminate or reduce those particular staffing gaps and surpluses in the long run. Don't simply choose an action that seems to meet a need in a particular planning period. Instead, review the needs across all periods and define the actions that will best eliminate staffing gaps and surpluses when all planning periods are considered.

There are two main reasons why such a specific definition of staffing needs must be completed for all planning periods before staffing strategies can be developed:

1. **Staffing strategies must address actual needs.** While staffing strategies are long term and directional, they are not simply general approaches that seem to make sense. The strategies that you choose to develop and implement must be those that address your actual staffing needs most effectively. Consequently, it is not possible to develop staffing strategies until staffing needs have been defined in very specific terms. At a minimum, needs must be defined in terms of what (i.e., particular capabilities and staffing levels), where (i.e., function or location), and when (i.e., a given period of your planning model). If you do not define your staffing needs at this level of detail, it will not be possible for you to develop the specific, targeted staffing strategies that will meet those needs most effectively.

2. **Staffing strategies span planning periods.** Staffing strategies define what will be done throughout your planning horizon, across all planning periods. It doesn't make sense to develop a strategy that addresses needs in a single period; instead, you must determine the staffing ap-

proach that works best when all planning periods are considered. A staffing action that seems to make sense within the bounds of a single period may actually prove to be inappropriate when staffing needs in subsequent periods are considered. Here are some examples:

- A plan for hiring in period 1 may seem to be a good alternative if analyzed by itself, but its effectiveness needs to be evaluated in light of the needs of later periods. It makes no sense to hire individuals into full-time roles to meet a gap in period 1 of your plan if those individuals are not also required in periods 2 and beyond.

- It may also be possible to balance staffing needs by moving work from one period to another. This is especially the case in a project environment. If there is a shortage of a particular skill in period 1 and a surplus of that skill in period 2, it may be best to move some of the work from period 1 (thus reducing the need for that skill during that period) into period 2 (thus eliminating the surplus in that subsequent period). This kind of cross-period change in work allocation allows needs to be met without staffing changes of any kind. However, such a reallocation cannot be considered if staffing needs and plans are defined for one period at a time.

- It may be that a staffing gap in a critical role (e.g., one of the core roles that provide competitive advantage) in a future period (e.g., period 4) can best be met by redeploying current employees. However, some of those to be redeployed may have particular training or development needs that must be addressed before such movement is possible. A staff plan that addressed only period 4 might have indicated that, because the required talent was not available internally, external hiring was the only option.

Here is an example of how this approach might work. Suppose that a staffing analysis for period 1 identified several staffing needs in a job category that is normally contracted out. Looking at period 1 alone, it seems reasonable to continue to contract for those services, and if only period 1 were considered, that staffing action would probably be the one selected. However, when gaps and surpluses were calculated for periods 2 through 4, it was determined that there would be several openings in that category in each period. Though contracting made sense when period 1 was analyzed by itself, it was no longer the most appropriate option when the needs in all four periods were viewed longitudinally. When staffing needs were viewed across all four periods, it made more sense to hire full-time staff than to continue to pay a premium to contractors. It would simply be cheaper to hire full-time staff. In addition, the continuity that full-time staff allows would result in a significant competitive advantage. Furthermore, full-time hires would probably be of higher quality than contract staff. Regardless of the reasons, the staffing actions defined when all four periods were considered differed significantly from what would have been done were the needs defined and met one period at a time.

As this example shows, it is quite possible that the particular strategy that best meets staffing needs in a particular planning period may not be the most effective approach when needs are viewed across all periods. Here are four examples of staffing strategies that might be developed after reviewing staffing gaps and surpluses across multiple periods:

1. An organization is expecting a staffing gap in a critical job category in the first planning period. Given that the required capabilities are indeed critical, it would seem to make sense to fill these first-period openings with full-time hires. Suppose, though, that this need was expected to disappear in subsequent periods as demand for the services provided by these people lessened. If the jobs were filled through hiring in the first period, these new employees would become surplus in period 2 and beyond. Consequently, it might make more sense to contract the work out in period 1 so that the company can avoid the payroll expense of carrying these unneeded employees in periods 2 through 4. The flexibility in meeting fluctuating staffing needs is well worth the short-term premium paid to those contractors.

2. A need for a "commodity" type of skill in the first planning period is identified. Normally, these skills are contracted out. However, a review of periods 2 through 4 shows that these skills will be needed in each period. While in general the strategy is to contract out commodity skills, it may make more sense in this case to hire these people full-time, since the need is ongoing (i.e., to provide continuity and lower costs).

3. A surplus is defined in a particular job category in the first planning period. A deficit in this same category is forecast in period 3. If these skills can be obtained easily, it might be acceptable to lay off these people at the end of period 1 and hire new staff at the beginning of period 3. However, if the skills are difficult to find (or if competition for people with these skills is intense), it might be better to retain these individuals at the end of period 1 so that they will be available in period 3:

- It may be cheaper to maintain the employees on the payroll than it is to pay them severance and incur the additional expense of hiring new people.

- If people with these skills really are hard to find, the company may not want to take the risk that it will not be able to find and attract individuals with the needed skills at the beginning of period 3.

4. In a project-based environment, a company forecasts that there will be a deficit in a technical area in the first quarter of a four-quarter model and a surplus of that very same capability in the second quarter. Hiring to meet this need in period 1 would only increase the surplus in the second period. Using contractors in the first period would also eliminate the deficit, but it would do nothing to alleviate the surplus that is expected in period 2. The best staffing strategy in this case might be to identify a project in period 1 that requires these skills and defer it to period 2. This action would meet both needs.

It may take more than one strategy to address a given issue. For example, if you determine that your company lacks sufficient management depth, you may need to develop and implement a strategy that integrates succession, development, and targeted recruiting (where any of those strategies alone would be necessary but insufficient). Obviously, these strategies will provide the context within which you can define effective near-term staffing plans.

Step 4: Define Staffing Plans

The final "take-away" or deliverable of the strategic staffing process is usually a set of well-documented staffing plans that define all the staffing actions that must be implemented in each planning period if supply is to equal demand for all periods. Once you have defined particular staffing needs and developed your overarching staffing strategies (following steps 2 and 3), you will be able to define specific staffing plans for each planning period within your planning horizon.

Regardless of its particular format, any staffing plan must provide a list of specific actions to be implemented to eliminate staffing gaps and surpluses for a given planning period. This is actually where the rubber hits the road—without such plans, it is unlikely that your strategic staffing/workforce planning process will drive any significant changes. Since they define exactly what you will do, in very specific terms, staffing plans may actually be the most important component of the strategic staffing process. The following process can be used to create staffing plans.

Define Required Staffing Plans and Actions

I usually define staffing *plans* in terms of the numbers and types of moves to be made (e.g., 10 individuals should be promoted from Senior Sales to

Sales Manager) and staffing *actions* as the names and faces (e.g., identifying the 10 specific individuals who will actually be promoted during the period). First, define the specific staffing plans that will most effectively eliminate the staffing gaps and surpluses that you have identified. Remember that the plans and actions that you develop must be consistent with, and fully support, your staffing strategies. Staffing plans might include:

- Redeployment that eliminates a gap in one area while also reducing a surplus somewhere else
- Promotions
- Lateral moves
- Hiring to reduce a gap
- Accelerating internal movement (and defining the development that such movement entails) to reduce a future gap
- Using contractors
- Increasing or decreasing the use of overtime
- Encouraging turnover or early retirements to reduce a surplus
- Reductions in force (or other planned losses)

Once the staffing plans are completed (on a tentative basis), staffing actions can be defined (i.e., specific individuals can be identified). This level of detail requires more in-depth information on the skills and capabilities of the individuals being considered. Staffing actions give your efforts teeth. It is impossible to implement a plan that simply says that someone should be promoted—you need to identify which person that is. The definition of staffing actions can also ensure that your staffing plans are realistic.

Here is an example: A staffing plan might state that a staffing need should be met by promoting 10 people from one job to another along traditional career paths. This might appear to make sense, but it would be impossible to implement such a plan if all the individuals in that source pool happened to be recent hires who lacked the required skills or experience. This important distinction could not be made if you were operating only at the level of staffing plans (i.e., the numbers).

Here is another hint: If your model is hierarchical (e.g., if more senior positions are at the top of a column), create your solution by starting at the top of each column and working your way down. Determine the staffing actions needed to address gaps and surpluses at the most senior level. Next, work down a level. Continue the process until you resolve staffing issues at the lowest level of your model (usually through hiring, since there are rarely other sources of qualified talent at the entry level).

Here is an example of how gaps and surpluses might be translated into a staffing plan. Suppose that your analysis yielded the following gaps and surpluses:

	District A	District B
Managers	− 4	+ 2
Engineers	− 8	− 1

Start by addressing the gap of 4 managers in District A. Let's say that we could redeploy the 2 surplus managers from District B to District A (assuming that there are 2 qualified individuals who would be willing to make such a move). This would eliminate the surplus of managers in District B (a surplus of 2 less the 2 that are moved = 0) and reduce the deficit in District A to 2 (the gap of 4 plus 2 transfers in = a gap of 2). One way of addressing that gap of 2 would be to promote 2 engineers in District A to manager. This would eliminate the gap in District A managers (gap of 2 plus 2 promoted in = 0) but would increase the deficit at the engineer level to 10 (− 8 less the 2 that were promoted). The gaps of 10 engineers in District A and 1 engineer in District B occur in separate, distant districts. Therefore, they would probably be addressed though hiring.

Thus, your final staffing plans would show that the following staffing actions should be taken in District A during the planning period in question:

- A redeployment of 2 managers from District B to District A
- The promotion of 2 engineers from District A to manager positions in District A
- The hiring of 10 engineers into District A and 1 engineer into District B

Document Your Plans

Document your staffing actions in detail. Consider creating a table to capture this information. The columns can capture key information on each action; each type of action is a row on the table. If you have created a model, use the row and column headings to describe the needed moves. Note the number of staff making each move and the type of move. Further, make sure that you note the date by which the action is to take place and the individual(s) responsible for making it happen.

Figure 5-9 is an example of what a staffing plan using this format might look like.

Figure 5-9. Sample Staffing Plan.

Type of Action	Number of Staff	From		To		Completion Date
		Row	**Column**	**Row**	**Column**	
Promote	10	Senior	Sales	Manager	Sales	12/31/08
Promote	5	Staff	Sales	Senior	Sales	12/31/08
Hire	8			Staff	Sales	12/13/08
Promote	3	Supervisor	Project 1	Manager	Project 1	4/15/09
Redeploy	6	Supervisor	Project 1	Supervisor	Project 2	4/15/09
Promote	2	Staff	Project 1	Supervisor	Project 1	4/15/09
Promote	3	Staff	Project 2	Supervisor	Project 1	4/15/09
Transfer	9	Staff	Project 2	Staff	Project 3	4/15/09
Lay off	6	Staff	Project 2			12/31/09

Define Supporting Actions

Remember also to define and document any actions that support or are directly related to required staffing. Such actions might include:

- Development needed to support accelerated promotions or redeployment
- Changes in compensation needed to increase the company's ability to attract outside hires
- Changes in relocation policies or practices to support redeployment
- Changes in staff or resources in the recruiting infrastructure
- Identifying new sources of talent and proactively finding sources of skills that were not previously needed
- Developing or improving relationships with outside suppliers of talent

Define Accountabilities and Time Frame

Define who is responsible for implementing or completing each staffing action that you define. Determine when each action needs to be completed (in most cases, the time frame will be defined in terms of the planning period of your model).

Define Support Activities and Infrastructure

Once your plans are completed, review the volume of required staffing actions and define the support and infrastructure that will be needed to implement those plans. Make sure that you have the number of recruiters you need in order to source, contact, and evaluate a sufficient number of qualified candidates. Ensure that your training department has the staff and resources required to provide the development needed to support accelerated promotions and redeployment.

A Note About Staffing Plan Integration

When staffing plans are defined, it sometimes becomes obvious that several business units are looking to implement similar solutions. For example, several facilities in a region might be trying to recruit similar talent. You don't want to create a situation in which these facilities end up competing against one another for qualified talent, so some integrated approach to recruiting is probably warranted. This type of integration is facilitated by a review of staffing plans across units, even when different or separate models were created and used. In some cases, needed integration is better achieved by creating models that span units in the first place (e.g., creating one integrated model that includes all project management talent, across locations) rather than trying to identify and integrate staffing plans after separate models are run.

Repeat

All of the components of step 4 must be completed for each period of your analysis. For example, if you are developing a three-year plan, these steps must be completed for each of those three years. Once you have defined the appropriate staffing plans and actions for period 1, enter that information into your model and calculate a new set of staffing gaps and surpluses for period 2. Define the staffing plans and actions that best address the staffing gaps and surpluses that remain. Remember to keep your plans and actions consistent with the staffing strategies that you developed. Document the plans, actions, accountabilities, time frame, supporting activities, and infrastructure, just as you did for period 1. Then repeat this process for all remaining planning periods.

Review Plans and Progress

Once plans have been prepared for all periods, they must of course be implemented if the gaps and surpluses are to be reduced as expected. Carefully track your plans to ensure that the required staffing actions are actually taking place and that the anticipated gaps and surpluses are being addressed. Follow up as quickly as possible on actions that do not occur. Similarly, identify and amend those actions that have not had their desired effect (e.g., specific recruiting plans that have been implemented, but that have not attracted and retained key talent).

6

Strategic Staffing/ Workforce Planning at 30,000 Feet

Striking a Balance Between Consistency and Flexibility

In Chapter 3 I clearly defined two approaches to workforce planning: a traditional approach that is typically applied in a consistent way across an organization, and a more tailored approach that is applied only as needed to address critical staffing issues.

When I first developed the targeted approach, I saw it as a complete alternative to the organization-wide approach. I saw little commonality between the two, and I tried to build a case that the more focused, targeted approach was the only methodology that would yield effective results.

Some of the organizations I worked with struggled to define an appropriate level of consistency when developing and implementing a focused approach to workforce planning. They realized that a common process that was implemented identically throughout the organization just would not work, especially when it was driven to the level of detail needed to define specific staffing plans and actions. Further, they realized that managers often resist these one-size-fits-all processes because they are not all that helpful—especially since with these approaches, planning parameters cannot be tailored to what those managers perceive to be their own unique situations. On the other hand, the focused, issue-oriented approach does not necessarily provide the desired consistency in process. While focusing on critical staffing issues is indeed a very effective approach, it is selective in nature and might leave large components of the organization untouched by workforce planning. Furthermore, allowing managers to develop and implement their own approaches to workforce planning would make it nearly impossible to create the consistent, organization-wide workforce plans that many HR professionals desire.

The answer to this apparent dilemma is what I call "workforce planning at 30,000 feet." With this approach, companies mandate common workforce planning processes and parameters up to a point (i.e., that 30,000-foot level), but allow managers flexibility in how they develop, implement, and apply workforce planning below that level. This hybrid approach ensures that workforce plans are developed in a consistent way across the organization, yet allows managers to tailor the process so that the workforce plans they create address what they perceive to be their most critical staffing needs.

The "Common" Part

With workforce planning at 30,000 feet, some, but not all, of the components of the workforce planning process should be common among all units and applied consistently across the organization. Here are six examples of what should be consistent above that 30,000-foot level:

1. Develop a consistent definition and set of objectives for workforce planning. Define from an overall perspective what the workforce planning process is and what it should accomplish, but don't define the process to the nth level of detail or specify exactly how it must be implemented. As described in Chapter 2, I define workforce planning as the process an organization uses to both identify and address the staffing implications of its business strategies and plans. The objectives or "deliverables" of the process should be both long-term staffing strategies (that span planning periods) and short-term staffing plans (for each planning period).

2. Clearly define and communicate that workforce planning is a management accountability. Make sure all managers understand that as part of the normal business planning process (however it has been defined by the organization), they are expected to identify and address the staffing implications of their business strategies and plans. This should be done from both strategic and short-term perspectives. Of course, HR staff will need to make sure that managers have the skills needed to do this type of staffing analysis in addition to understanding that they need to do it in the first place.

3. Mandate output and results, not process. Hold managers accountable for identifying and addressing their most critical staffing issues, but don't force them to use a particular one-size-fits-all process to do that. Instead, make sure that they develop the staffing strategies and plans that best address their most critical staffing issues, using whatever process they find most effective. If managers can create (or are already using) processes that result in effective staffing strategies and plans (processes that are different from the one developed corporately), let them continue to use those processes.

4. Clearly show what you think the workforce planning process should look like. While you should not force managers to use a particular approach to workforce planning, it is usually a good idea to provide them with a realistic, well-defined option that they can implement if they choose (e.g., if no other process is available). This suggested process should include alternatives for each step of the workforce planning process, enabling managers to identify critical staffing issues and develop the staffing strategies and plans that best address those issues. This will give managers a prototype or model to follow and will allow them to see at least one example of what an effective workforce planning process "looks like."

5. Provide tools and support that are consistent with the approach you are suggesting. Develop and distribute a wide variety of tools, templates, forms, and other resources that managers may use to support their workforce planning efforts—provided, of course, that they are doing it "your way." Provide process outlines and diagrams, "helps" for identifying the critical staffing issues that are inherent in their business plans and strategies, examples of staffing strategies, spreadsheets that can be used to define staffing gaps and surpluses, completed examples of staffing plans, workbooks and resource guides, and easy access to workforce planning web sites. However, don't require managers to use these resources. Instead, allow them to use whatever resources they find to be necessary or most helpful. Remember that the objective of the process is to develop the proper outputs (i.e., staffing strategies and plans), not simply to use the tools and complete the forms. Provide ongoing, tailored internal consulting help that directly supports the development and implementation of the workforce planning process.

6. Develop corporate staffing strategies only where absolutely necessary. Strategic approaches to staffing are absolutely required for some staffing issues—but not all staffing issues. Create coordinated staffing strategies where needed, but don't assume that there needs to be one coordinated, integrated "plan" that addresses all the staffing issues a company is facing. Think about how staffing resources will actually be managed, and create strategies that span units only when staff will actually be managed that way. As an example, create a corporatewide staffing strategy for project management talent only if that talent will actually be moved across business units on a regular basis. No corporate strategy is needed if project managers will most likely be managed within business units.

The "Tailored" Part

You should indeed mandate definitions, objectives, and outcomes, but at the detailed level, don't try to implement a single approach to workforce planning. Don't force consistency for consistency's sake. Instead, allow managers the flexibility that they need in order to develop and implement the staffing strategies and plans that they think address their most critical staffing issues most effectively, while following the mandates described earlier. Here are six examples of the flexibility that managers should be afforded below that 30,000-foot level:

1. Develop separate strategies where necessary. As described so often throughout this text, develop staffing strategies on an issue-by-issue basis, focusing on those staffing issues that are most critical. Do not mandate that any detailed workforce planning process be created or implemented for an organization unit as a whole.

2. Allow managers to define what staffing issues are most critical. Let managers identify the staffing issues that are most critical, and thus warrant the time and effort required to apply the workforce planning process. Don't force them to apply the process everywhere or to address staffing issues that can be addressed effectively through the normal course of business.

3. Let managers select the jobs to be included in the process. Even when focusing on staffing issues, not all jobs are so critical that they should be included in a truly strategic workforce planning process. When done correctly, workforce planning usually requires a lot of time and effort. Allow managers to select those positions that require this high level of scrutiny and for which comprehensive workforce planning is warranted.

4. Allow managers to define critical planning parameters. Different units will be facing staffing issues that have different rates of change and varying levels of detail. While mandating that a long-term view is required, don't define what the length of that view must be. For some units that are facing rapidly changing conditions (e.g., IT or any area where new technologies are constantly being implemented), "long term" might be 18 months; in other areas that are facing less change (e.g., issues related to executive succession and development), "long term" might be three to five years. Allow for this flexibility—don't force a common time frame across all units. Similarly, don't try to set one level of detail to be used by all units. In that IT area, for example, a small number of specific technical skills may adequately define staffing requirements, while a longer list of more generic management competencies might be appropriate at senior levels in another part of the organization. Note that the planning horizon is dictated by the nature of the issue being addressed. At no time should the planning horizon be defined to match that of the organization's strategic plan "just because" (unless, of course, that time frame is indeed appropriate for the staffing issue being addressed).

5. Engage managers in staffing strategy development. Don't expect HR to be solely accountable for developing staffing strategies and plans across the organization. Instead, engage and involve managers in the process when staffing strategies and plans are developed. This allows for the development of solutions that are appropriate for each unit and increases the chances that managers will support and implement those solutions. When managers are allowed to determine where and how strategic staffing should be applied, they are more likely to be engaged; when they are provided with an array of tools and resources, they are more likely to become involved. This topic is discussed in more detail in Chapter 13.

6. Provide customized support. Where feasible, work with individual managers to give them the specific support they need in order to implement workforce planning. Some may require help in identifying critical staffing issues, but no help at all in developing staffing strategies and plans for addressing those issues. Others will be able to identify the issues, but may need help in implementing workforce planning to address those issues. Still others might need assistance in the more quantitative aspects of workforce planning, such as calculating staffing gaps and surpluses. Whatever assistance is needed, keep the focus on addressing critical staffing issues, not on simply following a given process by rote.

An Example, Part 1

A health insurance company was implementing new IT platforms to support customer service efforts. In fact, the organization was moving from having five separate platforms to having two common ones. Clearly, this change would have a major impact on the numbers and types of IT staff that would be needed, and the company decided to use workforce planning as the tool to identify and address these staffing implications.

This health insurance company chose to implement the issue-oriented approach described in Chapter 4, but added an interesting twist. A specific workforce planning process was indeed developed and implemented to address the staffing issues raised by the platform change. Clearly, as a part of this effort, it was necessary for the company to develop workforce planning processes, tools, and other supporting materials. However, instead of developing these things to support only the initial IT project, the company made a conscious effort to develop all the things that would be necessary to implement the workforce planning process anywhere in the company at any time, on a repeatable basis. Each process and tool was developed to support the first IT application, but each was then generalized so that it could be used again, at different times and under different circumstances. In effect, the health insurance company was creating a generic workforce planning at 30,000 feet approach at the same time it was developing a targeted solution to a critical, specific set of staffing implications raised by the IT platform changes. Its version of workforce planning at 30,000 feet included:

- **Detailed process descriptions and documentation.** The workforce planning process that the company developed was "translated" into traditional process documentation that described each step, each decision, and each alternative outcome. In fact, several levels of documentation, with greater and greater levels of detail, were created. As described earlier, the process that was documented applied specifically to the IT project, but it was also applicable to any workforce planning opportunity that might arise anywhere in the organization at any point in the future.

- **Process instructions.** Specific instructions for developing and implementing the workforce planning process were developed. These instructions described what was necessary to complete each and every step of the process. Specific examples and "helps" were developed to support each process step.

- **Spreadsheet templates.** The core of any workforce planning process includes a methodology for calculating staffing gaps and surpluses. For this implementation, this capability was delivered through a series of spreadsheet templates that could be customized to support a wide variety of staffing issues and organization units. As an example, for the IT project, specific row and column headings were chosen; for the generic version, reusable row and column headings were used (e.g., Row 1, Row 2, Col 1, Col 2). In addition to the templates themselves, the organization created a set of instructions that detailed what needed to be done to customize and use the spreadsheet templates to address any staffing issue.

- **Suggested roles and responsibilities.** Suggested roles to be played by line managers, HR staff, and workforce planning professionals were defined for each step of the process. The skills needed to play those roles were also defined. Where possible, direct links were drawn between these skills and the training and development that was already being offered.

- **Frequently asked questions.** As the workforce planning process was being developed, the project team kept track of the questions that users asked most frequently. Answers to these questions were formulated and made available to all users.

- **Examples and supporting materials.** The project team provided examples of staffing issues, sample staffing plans, examples of completed spreadsheets, suggestions regarding how required skills and staffing levels might be determined, interview guides that HR staff could use to gather data from managers, and a host of other tools to help users to better understand and implement the workforce planning process.

- **A workforce planning web site.** Creating all the necessary workforce planning tools and resources is the first challenge; making all that material available to large numbers of managers in a huge organization is the second. As the various tools and resources just described were created, they were posted to an internal web site that could be accessed by any manager or HR professional. The site was designed in layers. Users could access the various materials (such as process documentation) at an appropriate level. If additional understanding or information (e.g., more detailed descriptions of various process steps) was required, users needed only to click on the item to access the detail that was required. A more detailed description of this type of web site is included in Chapter 14.

Clearly, this HMO defined what it thought belonged above the 30,000-foot level and provided a wide array of assistance to managers to help them develop and implement workforce planning processes. Yet it also allowed managers the latitude to apply those processes to address those staffing issues that they thought were most critical—a true example of workforce planning at 30,000 feet.

An Example: Part 2

As the generic, focused approach to workforce planning was being rolled out, several senior managers still thought that some form of the process should be implemented for all positions, not just critical staffing issues. These managers felt that this type of process was needed, if only to help managers plan for and justify budgeted staff headcounts. Some approach to doing this had to be developed that would not have a negative impact on the issue-focused approach to workforce planning that had already been developed.

A good compromise approach was created and implemented. A form of workforce planning would be implemented for all positions, but the focus and objectives of that process would differ significantly from those of a more traditional approach to workforce planning. Instead of being used to define specific staffing actions, this more general process would simply require managers to identify planned staffing requirements and headcount changes at a "macro" (e.g., organization unit) level and come to one of two conclusions:

1. Those headcount changes could be implemented fully by relying solely on "normal," readily available HR processes (e.g., the recruiting and development practices that were available on an ongoing basis).

2. The changes were more significant, and so the focused approach to workforce planning (described earlier) should be applied to create tailored, more strategic solutions (e.g., staffing strategies and staffing plans). These solutions might involve normal HR practices, specifically developed staffing strategies and plans, or some combination of the two.

Once each manager had defined the required headcount changes and determined whether normal HR practices or the more focused workforce planning methodology was required, the results were "rolled up" to the next level. The manager at that next level would review the work of the subordinate, approve headcount changes, and verify which approach to workforce planning would be required. If the manager had questions (or did not agree with the subordinate's conclusions), then the work was passed back to the originator and a consensus reached.

Again, this approach proved to be another good application of workforce planning at 30,000 feet. An organization-wide approach was in fact created, but this approach did not call for performing gap analyses and defining specific, required staffing actions; instead, it was used only to verify headcount changes (i.e., approve headcount requirements) and determine "next steps" regarding the need for a more detailed approach to workforce planning.

Conclusion: Strike the Right Balance

When implementing workforce planning, you need to strike the right balance between "common" and "tailored." By following these guidelines, an organization will develop workforce plans that are adequately consistent across units. Yet by allowing for tailoring—and thus ensuring that the value of managers' time and effort is maximized—companies will produce workforce plans that are effective and realistic. They will also engage managers directly in the process, instead of dragging them along kicking and screaming!

7

CHAPTER

Defining Required Staffing Levels

Defining staffing requirements is often the most difficult and time-consuming part of the strategic staffing/workforce planning process. There are many techniques that can be used to estimate or project the numbers and types of staff that will be needed to support business plans and strategies. Some are quantitative and at least somewhat objective (especially those that focus on staffing levels); others are primarily qualitative (including most of those that address required capabilities) and rely primarily on the subjective judgments of managers. This chapter describes several of the more common techniques and provides an example of each (including the solution).

Remember that when you are trying to estimate staffing requirements, you are not trying to predict the future with certainty. You are simply trying to define the staffing levels (and capabilities) that will probably be needed to implement your company's business strategies and plans. In the final analysis, this will be your "best guess." Sometimes your guess will be "spot on"; in other cases it might turn out to be fairly inaccurate. If you know what all of the staffing requirements are, you can define them specifically and create staffing plans accordingly. If you are certain about some portion of those requirements, you should create specific plans for the portion you are sure of and contingency or "what-if" plans for the remainder.

Finally, when it comes to estimating requirements, do the best job you can with the data that are available. Don't try to find, or wait to get, full, complete data on staffing requirements—they probably don't exist. Instead, make full use of the data that you do have, even if they address only part of an issue. It's far better to address only part of an issue completely than to do nothing at all. Specific techniques for defining staffing needs when business plans are uncertain are discussed in Chapter 8.

There Is No "Magic Bullet"

Wouldn't it be great to find an easy, objective way to define required staffing levels? Many organizations think that there must be a "magic bullet" out there somewhere. Isn't there a software package I can buy that will tell me what my staffing requirements will be? Isn't there a model I can build or buy that I can just plug some numbers into and obtain staffing level forecasts?

There is not, and there never will be, such a magic bullet. The definition of required staffing levels will be difficult, but the rewards for doing this well will be many. There is a possible corollary to this: Any vendor that tells you that it has such a model or package simply does not understand the realities or nuances of your business.

The closest thing we have to that magic bullet isn't a specific software package, model, or process. Any magician will tell you that the secret to magic lies in preparation, hard work, and practice. When it comes to defining required staffing levels, the "magic" is the result of a carefully crafted combination of effective staffing processes, in-depth business knowledge, keen insight, and hard work.

Preparing the Right Foundation

Before you even start to define required staffing levels, make sure that your managers and you have a common understanding of what you are actually trying to accomplish. Without such a common perspective, most efforts will fail. Here are some basic elements that should be part of that understanding:

- **Clearly define why you are defining staffing requirements.** The definition of required staffing levels is a critical, necessary component of any staff or workforce planning process, but it is only a component. It is not the objective. To add value, you can't simply define what the required staffing levels will be. You must also develop a combination of long-term staffing strategies and shorter-term staffing plans that will allow your organization to reach those required staffing levels.

- **No single, common approach to defining required staff levels can be used across companies or business units.** The definition of required staffing levels is as unique and different as one company or unit is from another. No one technique applies, even within business units. In almost every case, the definition of staffing levels will require a coordinated approach that integrates multiple quantitative and qualitative processes.

- **Not all definitions of required staffing levels can be completely objective.** Some can be, such as where staffing levels are directly related to work output or task time. In other cases, quantifiable relationships between staffing levels and work simply do not exist, and looking for such relationships is a waste of time.

- **Required staffing levels should rarely, if ever, be driven by the amount of financial resources that are available.** Organizations need to define the staff that will be required to implement business strategies and plans; define the resources needed to obtain, develop, and deploy those staff; and build a coherent business case for obtaining and allocating those needed resources.

- **Don't worry about being exactly correct.** The definition of required staffing levels is equal parts art and science. Your yardstick should not be, "Is my forecast exactly correct?" Instead, make sure that you are simply adding value. If you develop and implement staffing strategies and plans based on requirements forecasts that are off by 15 percent, will you be better off than if you did nothing at all?

Finally, remember that when defining staffing requirements, you must identify the required skills and capabilities in addition to the staffing levels. Some organizations put too much emphasis on defining required staffing levels and ignore the definition of required skills. It is difficult, if not impossible, to define required staffing levels until the organization has first defined the required roles and, second, identified the required capabilities.

Defining Required Staffing Levels: An Overview

From an overall perspective, there are several steps that you should take to define required staffing levels:

- **Fully understand your business.** In order to define requirements, you must be able to identify what is really driving changes in staffing levels at your company. To do this well, you must fully understand your business and its strategies and plans. Just understanding the staffing process well is insufficient.

- **Identify what is driving staffing needs.** Identify what is truly creating or changing your staffing needs, whether they are defined in terms of skills or staffing levels. Staffing requirements are often driven by changes in business activity (up or down), shifts in product/service mix, geographic expansion, improvements in service levels, and similar factors (a list of common staffing drivers is included in Chapter 5).

- **Identify constraints regarding staffing.** In addition to defining staffing drivers, also identify the "limiting factors" regarding the required staffing levels. As an example, suppose that Marketing forecasts that product sales are to increase by 20 percent in the coming year, and that sales levels drive the number of sales reps that are needed. At first glance, you might think that an increase in the number of sales reps would be appropriate. However, if manufacturing capacity is "maxed out" currently and is to remain unchanged for the coming year, it is unlikely that any additional product can be produced. If this happens, sales cannot increase as forecast, and additional sales reps will not be needed.

- **Start by defining changes in roles and positions.** Before you attempt to define required staffing levels, you will need to first identify the changes in roles that will be needed to implement business plans and strategies. You can define staffing levels in a meaningful way only after you have figured out what people need to be doing. Next, define changes in skills and capabilities that will be needed to perform these roles. Define required staffing levels only after roles and required skills have been defined.

- **Apply a combination of quantitative techniques.** First, understand where quantitative techniques apply and where they don't. Quantitative approaches are appropriate where there are direct, measurable relationships between staffing levels and/or task times. Staffing ratios (e.g., number of patient hours per nurse) or time-based ratios (e.g., if an average call requires 6 minutes, a customer service rep can handle 10 calls per hour) can be set based on actual values or desired changes (e.g., to reflect productivity improvements). Where the past is prologue, statistical techniques such as regression analysis may be helpful in determining the relationships between various staffing drivers and the required staffing levels. When defining the required staffing levels for a unit, use a combination of approaches tailored to each of the positions within that unit. Don't try to create a single, one-size-fits-all process. Finally, verify that the quantitative relationships that you have defined are based on information that is actually available in business forecasts. It will do you no good, for example, to create a staffing ratio based on sales of a particular product if business objectives and plans don't define how much of that product is to be sold during the planning period.

- **Supplement quantitative approaches with qualitative ones.** In many cases, quantitative relationships simply cannot be defined. To define the required staffing levels in these cases, conduct structured interviews with managers. Provide each manager with a snapshot of current staff (both staffing levels and skills), discuss how the business will be changing during the planning period, and define the impact that those changes will have on required staffing. Usually these changes are defined in incremental terms (e.g., if sales are expected to increase by 15 percent and productivity by 10 percent, about 5 additional sales representatives will be needed).

- **Learn as you go.** Don't worry about getting it exactly right the first time. Do the best you can, but determine which parts of your analysis worked well and which did not. Hone your understanding of the factors that truly drive staffing requirements, and focus your future efforts on those factors. Adjust staffing ratios so that they produce more accurate results. Apply qualitative approaches when quantitative approaches just don't yield predictable results. The process will become more effective and efficient with each iteration.

The balance of this chapter discusses several very specific approaches for defining staffing requirements. These are not the only methods available, but they are the ones that I have found to be most helpful. Note that the examples of each method have been included with the computer files that you can access (e.g., if you wish to use them as handouts during a presentation) at www.amacombooks.org/go/StrategicStaff2E.

Regression

Traditionally, statistical techniques, including regression analysis, have been used to define required staffing levels. With these techniques, statistical analyses are used to define the historical relationships between staffing levels and other variables (e.g., developing an equation that relates actual sales volume achieved to the number of sales staff employed). The use of regression requires historical data on both the independent variable(s) (e.g., sales, number of products produced, number of customers served) and the dependent variable (usually staffing levels or full-time equivalents). There are several types of regression analysis, including the following:

- **Simple, or single.** This technique defines a straight-line relationship between one independent variable and one dependent variable (e.g., relating sales to the number of sales staff).

- **Multiple.** This technique defines a straight-line relationship among two or more independent variables and the dependent variable (e.g., relating both total sales and the number of accounts served to the number of sales staff).

- **Curvilinear.** This technique defines nonlinear relationships between independent and dependent variables. Because of its complexity, it is less commonly used (and won't be discussed here).

To develop a single regression model, create a table that captures actual historical data for each variable. Each row of the table should include the value of the independent variable (e.g., actual total sales) at a particular point in time and the value of the corresponding dependent variable (e.g., the number of staff actually on board and supporting that work) at that same point in time. An eight-quarter model would thus include eight rows or data points. Here is what a simple one might look like:

Quarter	Total Sales ($000)	Number of Sales Staff
1Q 2006	2,000	5
2Q 2006	2,125	5
3Q 2006	2,403	6
4Q 2006	2,599	6
1Q 2007	2,680	6
2Q 2007	2,598	7
3Q 2007	2,821	7
4Q 2007	3,011	8

Next, enter these data into a program that includes a regression routine. Most spreadsheet programs usually include such routines, and virtually all statistical packages include a regression capability as well. Many business-oriented calculators also have simple regression capability.

The output of the analysis is an equation that describes the best fit between your independent and dependent variables. In the case of single regression, the equation is of the form:

$$y = ax + b$$

where y is the dependent variable (e.g., staffing levels), x is the independent variable (e.g., sales), and a and b are values determined by a regression analysis. A regression analysis of the simple eight-quarter model given here produces this equation:

Number of Sales Staff = 0.0027896 × Sales (in thousands) + 0.8067036

To use this equation to forecast staffing levels, you simply obtain projections for the future values of the independent variables you have used (e.g., get projected sales levels from sales forecasts), enter these in the equation you have created, and calculate the required staffing level. In this simple example, if expected sales for the coming quarter were projected to be $3,000,000, then the expected number of sales staff needed to support that level of activity would be 7.56 (i.e., 0.0027896 × 3,000 − 0.8067036).

Multiple regression is similar, but it includes more than one independent variable. If there are two independent variables, the regression equation is of the form:

$$s = ax + by + z$$

where s is the dependent variable (e.g., staffing levels), x and y are the independent variables (e.g., total sales and number of accounts), and a, b, and z are values determined by the regression analysis. Again, spreadsheet programs can often be used to produce multiple regression analyses, and most statistical packages include multiple regression routines as well. To develop a multiple regression model, again create a table that captures actual historical data for all variables. Each row of the table should include the value of each independent variable (e.g., actual total sales and actual number of accounts) at a particular point in time and the value of the corresponding dependent variable (e.g., the number of staff actually on board and supporting that work) at the same point in time. A 12-quarter model would thus include 12 rows. To use a multiple regression equation to forecast staffing levels, simply obtain projections for the independent variables you have used, enter these in the equation you have created, and calculate the staffing that will be needed.

Suppose, for example, that your equation was in this form:

Number of Sales Staff = [0.100 × Sales (in millions)] +
(0.01 × Number of Accounts) + 2

In this example, if expected sales were $100 million and the number of accounts was 200, then the expected number of sales staff needed to support that level of activity would be 14:

Number of Sales Staff = (0.100 × 100) + (0.01 × 200) + 2 = 14

All regression techniques have limitations. First, they work only in situations in which "the past is prologue"—that is, those situations in which the expected work and conditions in the future resemble those of the recent past. If you think the future will differ significantly from the past, don't use this approach. A second caution is also in order: Technically speaking, regression relationships (and thus regression models) are valid only within the range of the data that were used to construct the model in the first place. Regression equations should be used to forecast required staffing levels only if the sales projections fall within the range of sales that has actually been observed in the past. For example, suppose you built a regression model that related actual sales for a quarter to the number of sales staff that supported that volume. If the lowest level of quarterly sales actually observed was $20 million and the highest was $40 million, the model would be valid only for this particular range of quarterly sales. It should not be used to forecast the number of staff that would be needed to support anticipated sales of $50 million (or $10 million, for that matter).

Regression is best applied where there are direct relationships between the amount of work that is done and the number of staff doing that work. Further, you must be able to define the work or output in quantifiable terms. The technique should also be applied primarily to job categories that have relatively large numbers of staff doing substantially similar work.

There is another situation in which regression works quite well. Instead of building a historical database for a given unit, you can use the process to analyze staffing across units at a given point in time. Suppose that your organization has branch offices of various sizes that are handling different workloads. Regression can be used to define the relationship between staffing and workload across branches or locations. Once the regression equation has been developed, it can be used to define the "ideal" staffing level for any given workload for any branch. Figure 7-1 defines the problem; Figure 7-2 provides the solution.

Staffing Ratios

It is often possible to define simple, specific numerical relationships between work volumes or output and the number of staff required to do that work or produce that output. Usually, these relationships are expressed as a ratio of volume or output per person (e.g., 270 policies per underwriter or 10,000 barrels of oil refined per petroleum engineer). Not surprisingly, ratios that directly relate work to required staffing levels are called *direct ratios*. Once the ratio has been defined, it can be applied to the projected output or workload to define the number of staff that would be needed to support that effort. For example, if each underwriter can handle

Figure 7-1. Regression

The Packer Insurance Company would like to determine the number of additional underwriters that will be needed to support the acquisition of a "book of business" that is being spun off by a competitor. Packer has determined that the number of underwriters needed is most dependent on the mix of auto, home, and life polices. Over the last ten quarters, the following data have been reported:

Quarter	Number of Auto Policies	Number of Home Policies	Number of Life Policies	Number of Underwriters
1	2,123	1,722	991	45
2	2,241	1,821	1,003	47
3	2,302	1,901	1,098	52
4	2,605	2,011	1,187	53
5	2,771	2,198	1,251	55
6	2,803	2,347	1,376	57
7	3,009	2,290	1,434	60
8	3,107	2,401	1,563	63
9	3,229	2,551	1,479	70
10	3,398	2,612	1,501	71

The new book of business is expected to include 2,200 auto polices, 1,851 home policies, and 1,434 life policies. How many underwriters will be needed?

Figure 7-2. Solution to Regression Problem

First, we need to determine the equation that defines the relationship between the number of underwriters and the various types of business. Because there are three different types of policies to be considered, we will need to use multiple regression. Using any available statistical package, we determine the regression equation for these data. That equation turns out to be:

$$\begin{aligned} \text{Number of Underwriters} = \ & (0.01504)(\text{Number of Auto Policies}) \\ & + (0.01344)(\text{Number of Home Policies}) \\ & - (0.01042)(\text{Number of Life Policies}) \\ & - 0.1642 \end{aligned}$$

To obtain an estimate of the number of underwriters needed to support the given book of business, we need to insert into this equation the number of each type of policy that is to be supported (i.e., 2,200 auto policies, 1,851 home policies, and 1,434 life policies, as stated at the end of Figure 5-1). Entering our data, the equation becomes:

$$\begin{aligned} \text{Number of Underwriters} = \ & (0.01504)(2,200) \\ & + (0.01344)(1,851) \\ & - (0.01042)(1,434) \\ & - 0.1642 \\[4pt] = \ & 42.86 \text{ Underwriters} \end{aligned}$$

Thus, 42.86 underwriters (if full-time equivalents) or 43 underwriters (if whole bodies) would be needed to support Packer's anticipated book of business.

270 policies in a month, and 2,700 policies are expected to be in force in a given month, then 10 underwriters would be needed (i.e., 2,700 policies divided by 270 policies per underwriter). Usually, it will be necessary to define a separate, distinct staffing ratio for each job category in your model (at least those to which staffing ratios will be applied).

There are also cases in which the required staffing in one area relates not to the amount of work being done, but to the number of workers in another area. These ratios are called *indirect ratios*. Span of control is an example of an indirect ratio. Span relates the required number of supervisors not to the amount of work being done by those supervisors but to the number of staff being supervised (e.g., 1 supervisor per 10 staff). To define indirect ratios, first apply the appropriate direct staffing ratios to determine the number of staff of the first type that are required (e.g., 1,000 engineers are needed). Next, apply the indirect ratio (e.g., 1 supervisor per 10 engineers) to determine the required number of staff of the second type (e.g., 1,000 divided by 10 equals 100 supervisors).

When using this technique, you must first determine what is actually driving staffing in each job category. Different jobs will have different drivers. Here is an approach that you can use to define staffing drivers:

- Make a table that has two columns. In the first column, simply list the job categories or titles for which staffing ratios are to be determined. Give each job category a separate row.
- Analyze each job category separately, on a row-by-row basis. For each job, identify all the inputs, work activities, and outputs that may drive staffing levels. Document these possible drivers in the second column. List as many as you can think of that may have a significant impact on staffing.
- Review the list of drivers for each job and identify those for which information is available. Cross off your list any drivers for which data either are not available or are too difficult to gather and maintain on an ongoing basis.
- Develop staffing ratios for those drivers that remain on your list. Start by gathering data for each driver at a particular point in time. Then, for each job category, determine the number of staff that were employed in that job category at that same point in time. Calculate an initial ratio by dividing the value of the driver by the number of staff. Finally, use future data or management judgment to modify this ratio (if necessary) so that it can be applied on a looking forward basis (e.g., raise the ratio of driver to staff to account for productivity increases). You may want to talk with line managers and supervisors in each area to fine-tune your estimates.

Figure 7-3 shows examples of possible staffing relationships that were proposed in a manufacturing environment. Each of the possibilities included in Figure 7-3 (along with some others) was considered. After some detailed analysis, the best relationship was identified and a specific staffing ratio was determined for each job category. In a few cases, required staffing levels were a function of two staffing ratios. For example, with production workers, it was necessary to develop one ratio linking staffing to the number of production runs and a second ratio linking staffing to the number of production slots, and then summing the results. Data for the drivers came primarily from production plans and schedules; additional information came from other planning systems and the company's human resource information system.

The staffing ratio technique works best where specific relationships exist (or can be inferred or determined) between staffing and workload (e.g., in sales, manufacturing, production, and customer service). Ratios can be based on history (what the ratios have been in the past), current

Figure 7-3.

Job Category	Possible Staffing Drivers
Production workers	Number of production runs by type Number of slots
Facilities workers	Number of work orders Number of projects Number of critical systems Number of noncritical systems Number of operating production lines Number of shut down production lines Number of shutdowns Number of changeovers
Equipment cleaning crews	Number of operating production lines Number of shut down production lines Number of changeovers
Project managers	Number of projects by type and complexity Project duration
Other management	Number of staff Number of shifts Number of work centers
Administrative	Number of staff Number of managers Number of work centers

practice (what they are now), or desired future performance (future target ratios that reflect needed increases in productivity).

Here is a simple example of how staffing ratios are applied: An insurance company needed to forecast the number of claims adjusters, support staff, and supervisors that would be needed to support its workload of claims. The company had a performance or productivity target of 200 claims per adjuster per month. It used an indirect ratio to determine the required number of support staff (i.e., 1 support staff per 5 claims adjusters). The desired span of control was 1 supervisor per 6 staff (of all types). The company expected that there would be 2,000 claims in the last month of the fourth quarter. Applying staffing ratios, we would estimate required staffing as follows:

- **Adjusters.** This involves a direct ratio. Divide the expected value of the driver at the desired point in the future (i.e., 2,000 claims) by the ratio (i.e., 200 claims/adjuster) to determine the required number of adjusters (2,000/200 = 10 adjusters).

- **Support staff.** This involves an indirect ratio. Divide the required number of adjusters (i.e., 10) by the indirect ratio (1 support staff per 5 adjusters) to determine the required number of support staff (10/5 = 2 support staff).

- **Supervisors.** Calculate total staffing (i.e., 10 adjusters plus 2 support staff = 12 total staff) and divide this by the desired span of control (1 supervisor per 6 staff) to define the required number of supervisors (12/6 = 2 supervisors).

This technique is particularly appropriate for determining staffing levels in call centers. Define the overall operational parameters for the centers (e.g., the hours that the center will be open), key volume parameters for the center (such as number of calls expected and average length of call), and quality indicators (e.g., answer within x rings; keep caller on hold for no more than y seconds). Next, define the relationships among these parameters. Keep developing and linking these relationships until you determine the number of staff that will be needed to meet your standards. As a simple example, suppose your call center will be open 24 hours per day and you expect that on average it will field 4,800 calls per day. That means that on average you can expect 200 calls per hour (this is just an example, of course; it is unlikely that in reality calls will be spread evenly over the whole 24-hour period). If each call lasts 10 minutes, then you will need 2,000 staff minutes per hour (i.e., 200 calls times 10 minutes per call) to handle that volume of calls. Given that each customer service representative works 50 minutes per hour (factoring in break time), you will need

40 staff members on duty each hour (i.e., 2,000 staff minutes divided by 50 minutes per staff member). This calculation assumes that all the customer service reps are busy all the time and that call volume perfectly matches staffing patterns. Since this is unlikely, you will probably need to adjust staffing levels upward, based on the quality standards that you set (e.g., more staff will be needed if callers are to be kept on hold for no more than five minutes than will be needed if the standard is ten minutes).

I have both led and participated in many strategic staffing projects over the years. Quite possibly, staffing ratios is the technique that has proved to be most valuable when defining required staffing levels. It is direct and simple, yet it is not simplistic. The technique is easy to use, understand, and explain to others. It is flexible and can easily be tailored to reflect the specific needs of individual jobs or organization units. When appropriate, it can be based on historical data, but it can also easily reflect "what needs to be" rather than "what has been." While it can't be used in all cases, it is especially useful in those cases where it can be applied. Figure 7-4 gives the facts of the problem, and Figure 7-5 gives the solution.

Figure 7-4. Staffing Ratios

To increase revenues and improve service to its members, Blair Healthcare (formerly known as Blair General Hospital) is considering opening a second full-service facility in the suburbs, twenty-five miles from its present urban location. By opening this facility, Blair expects to attract new members as well as to better serve existing members who are moving out of the city. Currently, Blair has 50,000 members.

The Medical Economics group expects that this move will increase membership in Blair Healthcare significantly. In fact, the group expects that Blair will add as many as 30,000 new members in the first year and an additional 20,000 in the second.

Based upon an analysis of historical and desired future staffing levels, Blair developed the following staffing ratios:

Job Category	Ratio
Family practice physicians	1:2,000 members
Cardiologists	1:15,000 members
Psychologists	1:8,000 members
Physical therapists	1:10,000 members
RNs	(# of physicians) $\times$ (0.8) $\times$ (0.5)
LPNs	(# of physicians) $\times$ (0.8)
Lab staff	1:25,000 members
Appointment clerks	(# of family practice physicians) $\times$ (0.6) + (# of specialty physicians) $\times$ (0.4)

James Kildare, the CEO, recently stated that 40,000 new members must be added next year if revenue projections are to be met. Consequently, the marketing targets have been set at this level, and programs are under way to try to attract these new members.

Define the required staffing levels for each of the above job categories for the coming year.

Figure 7-5. Solution to Staffing Ratios Problem

First, we need to define the scenario we are analyzing. There are two possibilities:

- We can determine the staffing needed to support the projections of the Medical Economics group (i.e., 50,000 current members plus the increase of 30,000 members that is expected, for a total of 80,000 members).
- We can determine the staffing needed to meet the targets the CEO set in order to meet revenue projections (i.e., 50,000 current members plus an increase of 40,000 members, for a total of 90,000 members).

If we know which one of these two scenarios is actually going to be implemented (or is more likely), we will probably define only the staffing requirements for that scenario. In some cases, however, it may make sense to define the staffing requirements for each scenario. By defining each, we will be able to:

- Analyze the difference in staffing requirements between the two (e.g., determine whether one is more effective or less expensive than the other).
- Define the lower of the two and create:

  Foundation staffing plans that define what should be done to obtain and deploy the minimum number of staff

  Contingency staffing plans, defining what could be done to obtain and deploy the additional staff needed to support the more aggressive strategy

The following solution assumes that total membership will be 80,000. The process will simply be repeated, using 90,000 members in place of 80,000, if the staffing requirements of the second scenario are needed.

Now we can define the staffing needed to support this number of members. The solution requires a combination of direct and indirect staffing ratios:

- For all direct ratios (e.g., the number of family practice physicians), simply divide 80,000 by the appropriate ratio.
- For all indirect ratios (e.g., the number of LPNs), first define the number of each type of physician that will be needed (using a direct ratio), then calculate the total number of physicians required (by adding up the results for each type) and apply the appropriate ratio.

Our solution would look like this:

Category	Required Number of Staff
Family practice physicians	$80,000/2,000 = 40$
Cardiologists	$80,000/15,000 = 5.33$
Psychologists	$80,000/8,000 = 10$
Physical therapists	$80,000/10,000 = 8$
RNs	$(40 + 5.33) \times (0.8) \times (0.5) = 18.13$
LPNs	$(40 + 5.33) \times (0.8) = 36.26$
Lab staff	$80,000/25,000 = 3.2$
Appointment clerks	$(40 \times 0.6) + (5.33 \times 0.4) = 26.13$

Project-Based Staffing

Sometimes you need to know the total number of staff of a particular type that will be needed (e.g., a particular category of engineers), but the information that is available defines the required staffing on a project-by-project basis (the number of engineers that are needed for a given engagement). Often this staffing information is defined in project proposals or plans. Complicating the issue further is the fact that the projects start and finish at different times.

The project-based staffing technique simply aggregates the required staffing for each job group for each project, at a particular point in time, across all projects to determine overall staffing requirements. There are two approaches, the zero-based approach and the incremental approach.

Regardless of which of these approaches is used to define staffing changes, the basis of this technique is simply to determine the number of staff of each type needed to support each project and aggregate those estimates across all projects to determine the total number of staff needed.

The Zero-Based Approach

This approach is used when project plans typically define the total number of staff of each type that are required at various points in time, independent of how many such staff are currently working on that job (e.g., 10 apprentice-level engineers will be needed on a particular project at the beginning of the second quarter). To use this technique, take these steps:

- Identify the points in time for which you are defining staffing requirements.
- Determine which projects will be underway at each point.
- Define the staffing required for each project at each point in time.
- Sum the requirements for a given point in time across all projects to determine total requirements.

This approach works best when projects are starting from scratch and when project managers have a good understanding of the staffing that will be required. Figures 7-6 and 7-7 provide an example of this approach.

The Incremental Approach

With this approach, staffing requirements are defined in terms of increments above or below current staffing (e.g., four more apprentice-level engineers will be needed, over and above the six that are already working on that project). The incremental method is especially helpful where no information regarding required staffing exists.

As with the zero-based approach, you will need to take these steps:

- Identify the points in time for which you are defining staffing requirements.

Figure 7-6. Project-Based Staffing: Zero-Based

Nelson Motorsports is currently staffed effectively; that is, the current staffing will allow the firm to complete all the assignments it has "in house" for the remainder of the year (i.e., Projects 1, 2, and 3). The current headcount is as follows:

	Team A	Team B
Engineering managers	15	14
Engineers	30	40
Apprentices	30	25

Next year, the following work plan is anticipated:

- Project 1 will continue and will require

    5 engineering managers on Team A and 3 on Team B
    12 engineers on Team A and 8 on Team B
    15 apprentices on Team A and 10 on Team B

- Projects 2 and 3 will be completed in the current year and will require no staff.

- Project 4 is a new project that will require

    4 engineering managers on Team A and 4 on Team B
    10 engineers on Team A and 9 on Team B
    8 apprentices on Team A and 11 on Team B

- Project 5 is also a new project and will require

    6 engineering managers on Team A and 2 on Team B
    9 engineers on Team A and 10 on Team B
    9 apprentices on Team A and 8 on Team B

What will be the staffing demand for Nelson Motorsports in the coming year?

Figure 7-7. Solution to Zero-Based Staffing Problem

In this example, we need to identify the staffing requirements for each project in each of the six categories (i.e., the three job categories for each of the two teams). The data that we need are provided in the case. In a "real-life" situation, this staffing information would probably be extracted from a project plan or unit business plan. It might also be provided by a manager through some kind of structured interview. Note that since this is a zero-based technique, the starting headcounts that are provided are not relevant and should be ignored.

For each of the six categories, we simply need to define the needs for each project and sum the requirements across all projects.

Category	Team A		Team B	
Engineering managers	Project 1:	5	Project 1:	3
	Project 2:	0	Project 2:	0
	Project 3:	0	Project 3:	0
	Project 4:	4	Project 4:	4
	Project 5:	6	Project 5:	2
	Total	**15**	**Total**	**9**
Engineers	Project 1:	12	Project 1:	8
	Project 2:	0	Project 2:	0
	Project 3:	0	Project 3:	0
	Project 4:	10	Project 4:	9
	Project 5:	9	Project 5:	10
	Total	**31**	**Total**	**27**
Apprentices	Project 1:	15	Project 1:	10
	Project 2:	0	Project 2:	0
	Project 3:	0	Project 3:	0
	Project 4:	8	Project 4:	11
	Project 5:	9	Project 5:	8
	Total	**32**	**Total**	**29**

- Determine which projects will be underway at each point.
- Define how many more (or fewer) staff will be needed in each category than are currently available.
- Define the staffing required for each project at each point in time, adjusting staffing levels by the increments just defined.
- Sum the requirements for a given point in time across all projects to determine total requirements.

One advantage of this technique is that it can be used even if the staffing information you require is not readily available (e.g., specific project plans either do not exist or do not define staffing requirements explicitly). When you use this method, follow a structured interview format (you may find the interview guide in Chapter 13 helpful here). Define current staffing levels and capabilities before you meet with each manager. When you meet with a manager, review this information first. Next, discuss how the business is expected to change during the planning period (e.g., expansion, contraction, implementation of new technology, introduction of new products or services). As you discuss these changes, work with the manager to define how current staffing levels will be affected (e.g., there will be a need for more staff, fewer staff, or staff with different capabilities). Figures 7-8 and 7-9 provide an example of this technique.

Figure 7-8. Project-Based Staffing: Incremental

The current headcount for Nelson Motorsports is as follows:

	Team A	Team B
Engineering managers	15	14
Engineers	30	40
Apprentices	30	25

Based on interviews with senior managers, the following changes are expected in Team A:

- GT Motorsports will continue to run Ford engines and will need additional staff, including 1 engineering manager, 3 engineers, and 4 apprentices.

- Drew Racing will begin to use Ford's Zetec engine. To support the team, Nelson Motorsports will add 2 engineering managers, 4 engineers, and 6 apprentices

- The Schumacher team has decided to use Ferrari engines, thus freeing up 3 engineering managers, 10 engineers, and 15 apprentices.

The following changes are expected in Team B:

- Project A will expand and will require additional staff of 1 engineering manager, 4 engineers, and 2 apprentices.

- Project B has proved unrealistic and will be dropped, resulting in a reduction of 2 engineering managers, 5 engineers, and 3 apprentices.

- Project C has been reengineered; it will require 1 additional engineering manager but 2 fewer engineers and 3 fewer apprentices.

Calculate all staffing requirements for the coming season.

Figure 7-9. Solution to Incremental Staffing Problem

Because this technique is incremental (rather than zero-based), the starting populations in each category are relevant—in fact, they are the foundation of our calculations.

First, define current staffing levels for each category. Next, identify the changes that will occur in each category (based on the information provided in the case) and sum the totals across projects.

Here is the solution:

Category	Team A		Team B	
Engineering managers	Initial headcount:	15	Initial headcount:	14
	GT Motorsports:	+1	Project A:	+1
	Drew:	+2	Project B:	-2
	Schumacher:	-3	Project C:	+1
	Total	**15**	**Total**	**14**
Engineers	Initial headcount:	30	Initial headcount:	40
	GT Motorsports:	+3	Project A:	+4
	Drew:	+4	Project B:	-5
	Schumacher:	-10	Project C:	-2
	Total	**27**	**Total**	**37**
Apprentices	Initial headcount:	30	Initial headcount:	25
	GT Motorsports:	+4	Project A:	+2
	Drew:	+6	Project B:	-3
	Schumacher:	-15	Project C:	-3
	Total	**25**	**Total**	**21**

Staffing Profiles

In some cases, a series of "profiles," or templates, can be developed to estimate the staffing that a unit (or a project) will require given certain combinations of parameters (such as project size and type). Each such profile will include the same rows and columns that you included in your staffing model. A different profile is created for each unique combination of parameters. Taken together, these different profiles form a set or "reference library" that can be used to define the staffing needed to support business plans. Once the profiles are developed, you take these steps:

- Review business plans and strategies to identify the projects that will be underway.

- For each project described in the plans, identify the actual values for the key parameters that you have used to differentiate profiles (e.g., project size and type).

- For each project, select from your library of profiles the one that corresponds to each of the projects described in the plans. Similar projects (e.g., those of a similar size and type) might use the same profile.

- Sum the staffing across all projects to determine the required staffing for each job category.

Here is a simple example that describes how profiles can be used to define the required staffing for a bank. First, the critical parameters that drive the bank's staffing are identified. For this example, let's assume that the bank has determined that branch staffing for tellers and loan officers depends primarily on branch size (i.e., small, medium, or large, expressed in terms of assets) and type of lending (i.e., primarily retail or primarily commercial). Next, the institution will develop six staffing profiles, one for each unique combination of size and type (small/retail, medium/retail, large/commercial, and so on). Each profile will specify the number of tellers and loan officers needed in that environment (e.g., a small/retail branch requires two officers and three tellers, a large/commercial branch requires six officers and six tellers, and so on). The profiles might look like the matrixes in Figure 7-10.

The institution will now review its business plans to see how many branches of each combination of size and type it expects to operate in the coming year (e.g., five small/retail, eight large/commercial, and so on). To determine the required staffing, the institution will:

- Define the total number of branches of each size and type that will be operated.

- Select the profile that corresponds to each combination of size and type (e.g., in this example, the profile for small/retail shows that two officers and three tellers are needed).

- Multiply the staffing requirements defined in each profile by the number of branches of that size and type to be operated.

- Calculate the total needs for officers and tellers by adding up the needs for each category across all types and sizes of branch.

Figure 7-10.

Retail Branch Staffing

Job Category	Small Branch	Medium Branch	Large Branch
Officers	2	2	3
Tellers	3	4	5

Commercial Branch Staffing

Job Category	Small Branch	Medium Branch	Large Branch
Officers	3	4	6
Tellers	4	5	6

Suppose there were to be four branches in a region in the coming year:

- One small/retail
- One large/retail
- Two medium/commercial

To calculate the staffing needs across all four branches, select the three appropriate profiles, determine the staff required from each, and sum the results:

- Officers: $2 + 3 + 2(4) = 13$ staff
- Tellers: $3 + 5 + 2(5) = 18$ staff

Staffing profiles are particularly applicable to retail establishments (e.g., where staffing is determined for each of three standard store sizes/ "footprints") and to engineering/construction projects (e.g., where projects of a given size, complexity, and type might typically require a certain number of project managers and technical staff).

The example in Figures 7-11 and 7-12 uses profiles generated for an oil company, where the number of geologists and engineers needed depends on a project's type (i.e., offshore or onshore), size, and stage (i.e., initial exploration versus testing for commercial viability). Based on past performance and desired future effectiveness, the company defines a series of profiles, one for each unique combination of type, size, and stage. For example, if there are 27 unique combinations there would be 27 separate staffing profiles.

To use these profiles, the company defines the actual type, size, and stage for each project (or proposed project). Based on these, the company

Figure 7-11. Staffing Profiles.

The McLaughlin Oil Company is involved in oil exploration and production. The company is preparing a staffing strategy and needs to determine the number of geologists and engineers that will be required. It has been determined that staffing of exploration projects depends on:

- The size of each project (i.e., the potential number of barrels to be found)

- The stage of each project (i.e., the degree to which each phase has been completed)

- The type of the project (i.e., whether the project is onshore or offshore)

McLaughlin has created a series of staffing profiles that define the required staffing levels for geologists and engineers for various combinations of these variables. These profiles are shown on the following pages. Business plans call for the following activity:

Figure 7-11. (Continued)

Project	Size	Stage	Type
Exploration Project 1	350	1	
Exploration Project 2	190	2	
Exploration Project 3	460	3	
Production Project 1	270	3	Onshore
Production Project 2	150	2	Offshore
Production Project 3	360	1	Onshore
Production Project 4	420	2	Offshore

Your analysis should assume the following structure:

	Geology	Engineering
Manager		
Technician		
Trainee		

The profiles that follow also use this format. What is McLaughlin's total need for geologists and engineers, across all projects?

Exploration

Profile 1
Stage 1

	Geol	Engr
Mgr	10	8
Tech	20	14
Train	20	16

(<200)

Profile 2
Stage 2

	Geol	Engr
Mgr	8	10
Tech	10	18
Train	12	20

Profile 3
Stage 3

	Geol	Engr
Mgr	2	14
Tech	5	20
Train	5	24

Profile 4
Stage 1

	Geol	Engr
Mgr	10	9
Tech	22	16
Train	24	19

(200 to 400)

Profile 5
Stage 2

	Geol	Engr
Mgr	9	12
Tech	11	21
Train	13	25

Profile 6
Stage 3

	Geol	Engr
Mgr	3	16
Tech	6	24
Train	6	30

Profile 7
Stage 1

	Geol	Engr
Mgr	12	10
Tech	24	17
Train	28	20

(>400)

Profile 8
Stage 2

	Geol	Engr
Mgr	9	13
Tech	13	22
Train	16	26

Profile 9
Stage 3

	Geol	Engr
Mgr	3	18
Tech	7	26
Train	8	32

Onshore Production

<200

Profile 10 — Stage 1	Geol	Engr
Mgr	8	10
Tech	14	20
Train	16	20

Profile 11 — Stage 2	Geol	Engr
Mgr	10	8
Tech	18	10
Train	20	12

Profile 12 — Stage 3	Geol	Engr
Mgr	14	2
Tech	20	5
Train	24	5

200 to 400

Profile 13 — Stage 1	Geol	Engr
Mgr	9	12
Tech	16	22
Train	19	24

Profile 14 — Stage 2	Geol	Engr
Mgr	12	9
Tech	21	11
Train	25	13

Profile 15 — Stage 3	Geol	Engr
Mgr	16	3
Tech	24	6
Train	30	6

>400

Profile 16 — Stage 1	Geol	Engr
Mgr	10	12
Tech	17	24
Train	20	28

Profile 17 — Stage 2	Geol	Engr
Mgr	13	9
Tech	22	13
Train	26	16

Profile 18 — Stage 3	Geol	Engr
Mgr	18	3
Tech	26	7
Train	32	8

Offshore Production

<200

Profile 19 — Stage 1	Geol	Engr
Mgr	10	8
Tech	16	18
Train	18	18

Profile 20 — Stage 2	Geol	Engr
Mgr	12	6
Tech	20	8
Train	22	10

Profile 21 — Stage 3	Geol	Engr
Mgr	16	2
Tech	22	5
Train	26	5

200 to 400

Profile 22 — Stage 1	Geol	Engr
Mgr	11	10
Tech	18	20
Train	21	22

Profile 23 — Stage 2	Geol	Engr
Mgr	13	7
Tech	23	9
Train	27	11

Profile 24 — Stage 3	Geol	Engr
Mgr	18	3
Tech	26	6
Train	32	6

>400

Profile 25 — Stage 1	Geol	Engr
Mgr	12	10
Tech	19	22
Train	22	26

Profile 26 — Stage 2	Geol	Engr
Mgr	15	7
Tech	24	11
Train	28	14

Profile 27 — Stage 3	Geol	Engr
Mgr	20	3
Tech	28	7
Train	34	8

Figure 7-12. Solution to Staffing Profiles Problem

First, we need to find the staffing profile that corresponds to each of the seven projects to be completed (i.e., the proper combination of project type, size, and stage).

Exploration Project 1:   Size = 200–400, Stage = 1 (Profile 4)
Exploration Project 2:   Size = <200, Stage = 2 (Profile 2)
Exploration Project 3:   Size = >400, Stage = 3 (Profile 9)
Production Project 1:   Onshore, Size = 200–400, Stage = 3 (Profile 15)
Production Project 2:   Offshore, Size = <200, Stage = 2 (Profile 20)
Production Project 3:   Onshore, Size = 200–400, Stage = 1 (Profile 13)
Production Project 4:   Offshore, Size = >400, Stage = 2 (Profile 26)

Next, add up the staffing requirements for the seven projects (three exploration and four production) in each of the six job categories:

Position	Geology		Engineering	
Manager	Exploration Project 1:	10	Exploration Project 1:	9
	Exploration Project 2:	8	Exploration Project 2:	10
	Exploration Project 3:	3	Exploration Project 3:	18
	Production Project 1:	16	Production Project 1:	3
	Production Project 2:	12	Production Project 2:	6
	Production Project 3:	9	Production Project 3:	12
	Production Project 4:	15	Production Project 4:	7
	Total:	**73**	**Total:**	**65**
Technician	Exploration Project 1:	22	Exploration Project 1:	16
	Exploration Project 2:	10	Exploration Project 2:	18
	Exploration Project 3:	7	Exploration Project 3:	26
	Production Project 1:	24	Production Project 1:	6
	Production Project 2:	20	Production Project 2:	8
	Production Project 3:	16	Production Project 3:	22
	Production Project 4:	24	Production Project 4:	11
	Total:	**123**	**Total:**	**107**
Trainee	Exploration Project 1:	24	Exploration Project 1:	19
	Exploration Project 2:	12	Exploration Project 2:	20
	Exploration Project 3:	8	Exploration Project 3:	32
	Production Project 1:	30	Production Project 1:	6
	Production Project 2:	22	Production Project 2:	10
	Production Project 3:	19	Production Project 3:	24
	Production Project 4:	28	Production Project 4:	14
	Total:	**143**	**Total:**	**125**

selects the staffing profile for each project that corresponds to that combination of parameters. This profile defines the staffing needed to support that project. The results can then be summed across projects to determine overall staffing requirements.

Case Study: Combining Approaches

As discussed earlier, it is often necessary to combine various approaches for defining demand in order to determine the staffing requirements in a given situation. Here is a simple example that combines several of the approaches for calculating demand that were just described.

A restaurant chain was analyzing its needs for management staffing. Each restaurant requires general managers, assistant managers, and management trainees. Because restaurant capacity and design are standardized, a management staffing profile can be created. Here are some critical assumptions:

- The restaurant is open for business from 11 a.m. to 10 p.m. Monday through Friday, 11 a.m. to 12 a.m. Saturday, and 11 a.m. to 9 p.m. Sunday.
- Prep work and cleanup require two hours before opening and another two hours after closing.
- There must be one general manager on site at all times.
- There must be one assistant manager on the floor and a second in the kitchen at all times for a restaurant that seats 200 people.
- On average, general managers and assistant managers each work 53 hours per week.
- Three management trainees can be accommodated in a restaurant of this size.

How many managers and trainees are needed to support 10 restaurants?

The solution to this case requires both staffing ratios and staffing profiles. First, create the staffing profile for each restaurant. Calculate the total amount of time that the restaurant is open (including prep and cleanup time):

Monday–Friday:	15 hours/day
+ Saturday:	17 hours/day
+ Sunday:	14 hours/day
	106 hours/week

Given that there must be a general manager on duty at all times, the required number of general managers for each restaurant is 2 (106 hours/week divided by 53 hours/week/general manager). Because there must be one assistant manager in the kitchen and another on the floor at all times, there must be 4 assistant managers per restaurant (106 hours/week divided by 53 hours/week/assistant manager for the kitchen and an identical number for the floor). The number of management trainees is set according to restaurant capacity and is 3. Thus the standard management staffing profile for the restaurant would be:

Job Type	Number Required
General manager	2
Assistant manager	4
Management trainee	3

Given this profile, 10 new restaurants would require 20 additional general managers, 40 additional assistant managers, and 30 more management trainees.

Up until now, this restaurant chain has operated only inside upscale shopping malls. To build business and increase visibility, the chain is planning to build new, stand-alone facilities in mall parking lots. Because rents are much cheaper in the lots, the chain plans to double the seating capacity of these restaurants (to 400 diners). What will the staffing profile be for each new facility?

First, we need to determine the impact of increased capacity on staffing. Because the required number of general managers did not depend on restaurant size, the required number per restaurant remains the same. We also still need one assistant manager for the kitchen. The number of assistant managers on the floor will be different, however. If one assistant manager could handle 200 diners (e.g., visiting each table, each party, each visit), two will be needed to provide that same level of service to 400 diners (the new capacity of the larger restaurant). The number of management trainees will also change. If a restaurant that seats 200 can support three trainees, a facility that seats 400 can support six. Thus, the new staffing profile for the parking lot–type restaurant will be:

Job Type	Number Required
General manager	2
Assistant manager	6
Management trainee	6

How many assistant managers will now be needed to support 10 new facilities? This is really a trick question. If all 10 facilities are of the large, parking lot type, then 60 will be needed (6 assistant managers per location times 10 locations). If all are small, inside-mall locations, then only 40 will be needed (4 assistant managers per location times 10 locations). If there will be 5 large restaurants and 5 small ones opened, then 50 will be needed (5 times 6 for the large plus 5 times 4 for the small).

Summary

The definition of staffing requirements is a critical component of the strategic staffing process. There are many ways in which staffing requirements (both capabilities and staffing levels) can be determined, several of which are described in this chapter. In many cases, you will need to mix and match approaches; rarely will a single approach be appropriate for all job categories in your model.

But what do you do if staffing requirements are not well defined? Chapter 8 describes how staffing requirements can be determined even when business plans are uncertain.

Defining Staffing Requirements Where Plans Are Uncertain

Sometimes we need to create staffing strategies in situations where you lack perfect, complete information regarding business strategies and plans. In some cases, business strategies may be unclear or may describe only strategic objectives. In other cases, business plans may describe several possible outcomes or approaches, but do not specifically define which ones will be implemented. Sometimes the business plans are clear, but information on the staffing levels and capabilities needed to implement those plans is sketchy at best.

If the missing data can be uncovered and documented within a realistic time frame by expending a reasonable amount of effort, by all means go get those data. But what do you do if that full set of data doesn't exist or is just too difficult to gather? The answer in these cases is not to try to get those missing data or (worse yet) to wait around until the data become available. Instead, you should forge ahead with your strategic staffing/ workforce planning efforts and do the most you can with the data that you do have. In virtually every case, you will find that you know more than you think you do about staffing requirements; in most cases, there will be plenty of data that you can use to create some helpful staffing plans. Remember, a complete solution to part of a problem is better than no solution at all.

This chapter describes various approaches that can be used to develop staffing strategies and plans that maximize the value of the information that *is* available.

Alternatives to Perfect Data

Even when you don't have all the information you think you need in order to develop a staffing strategy, you probably have access to at least some good information. The objective here is to create staffing plans that are helpful and that maximize the value of the information that is available. Here are some specific examples of approaches you might take to create helpful staffing strategies, even if business plans seem unclear or incomplete.

Fully Solve Part of the Problem

Often, you won't have all the information for all the units or job categories in your plan, but you will have most of the data for some of the units. In these cases, create staffing strategies and plans for those units for which you have sufficient data. Don't be concerned that you are excluding parts of the organization. Don't "do nothing for anyone" just because you can't "do everything for everyone."

Here is an example—of what *not* to do. I once worked with a company that was developing a kind of skills inventory. Our workforce planning efforts at the time were focused on IT, one of the units for which the new skills inventory was relatively complete. However, HR staff in that area prevented us from using those skills data simply because similar data were not yet available for *all* employees. Their perception was that it would not be "fair" to use this type of information to manage some employees but not others. Thus, we would be able to use that skills inventory to support workforce planning only when the inventory was "complete"—that is, we could not use any of the data until HR had gathered all the data. I could not have disagreed more with their conclusion, but I could not influence the decision in any way.

If you have *all* of the data for some of the jobs in your units, create staffing plans for the jobs for which the data are available. Don't hold up work in those areas for which you do have data just because there are other areas for which you have insufficient data.

Here are some examples of how you might solve part, but not all, of a staffing problem. In most organizations, there are really two kinds of jobs: core or foundation jobs (i.e., jobs that are probably needed regardless of the level of business volume or activity) and incremental jobs (those jobs where required staffing levels depend on business volume or activity). Usually, quite a lot is known (or can easily be determined) about the core/foundation jobs, including the staffing levels and capabilities that will be required. Because staffing for these jobs is more stable and is not volume-dependent, it is easier to forecast the number and types of individuals that will be needed to fill these jobs in the future. Thus, you can create specific staffing plans to ensure that the right talent is available for these critical positions at almost any point in the future. Even if no information is available for the incremental jobs (which is unlikely, by the way), it is still better create the strategies needed to fully address just the core positions than to do nothing at all until information on the incremental jobs becomes available.

In other cases, you may have very specific business plans for some parts of your organization, but not for others. If this happens, you should create specific staffing plans for those units for which information is available. Again, don't do *nothing* just because full information is not available for *all* units. Suppose you are sure of 20 percent of what your organization is going to accomplish. Create complete staffing strategies to support the implementation of that 20 percent. Don't think in terms of the missing 80 percent; instead, think that you will be better off if you fully address the 20 percent than if you do nothing for the 100 percent.

Conduct Scenario Planning

Some organizations incorporate various scenarios into their business plans. Each scenario probably has different staffing implications. One approach to creating a staffing strategy would be to try to determine which scenario will actually occur and then define staffing plans for that scenario. Not only is this difficult to do, but there could be significant problems if you choose incorrectly (i.e., staffing for one scenario and having another occur). Instead of choosing just one scenario, define the staffing requirements for each of the most likely scenarios and look for staffing requirements that are common to all (or at least most) of those scenarios.

Suppose that there are three possible scenarios for the expansion of a business unit. In case 1 (perhaps the least optimistic scenario), 40 new sales associates will be needed. In the second case (possibly your "most likely" scenario), 50 will be needed. The third case calls for "mega" growth; 100 new sales associates will be required. Rather than choosing one of these scenarios and defining the staffing requirements only for that scenario, create and implement a strategy for attracting the minimum number of associates. No matter which scenario occurs, you are likely to need at least 40 new sales associates, so create specific staffing strategies and plans to obtain and deploy those 40 sales associates. In addition to this, create separate contingency plans for hiring any associates that are needed above this number (or create more specific plans if and when more specific data become available). Think through what you might do to hire 10 additional sales associates (i.e., if scenario 2 occurs) or 60 more sales associates (to support scenario 3). You probably won't go out and hire those people, but you will have a better understanding of what you will do if that need for staff actually arises—and thus you will be better prepared to act. While obtaining the minimum number of required staff will not solve all your problems, you will certainly be better off having done that than if you try to scramble to hire exactly the right number on short notice once the actual scenario is determined.

Scenario planning can also be helpful when no business strategies exist. In such a case, it may be possible for you to develop a small number of likely business scenarios on which your staffing strategies and plans can be based. Remember to validate your business scenarios with line managers (and incorporate any changes that they think are necessary) before completing the staffing plans needed to support the implementation of those scenarios.

Here is an example of how scenario planning might be used to support staff planning. Two insurance companies were merging. Obviously, mergers can create a host of staffing issues, some more critical than others. One of the areas that was affected most significantly was claims administration. The company needed to create a staffing strategy that would allow it to combine the two claims functions as effectively and efficiently as possible. Prior to the merger, the claims functions of the two companies had been managed and staffed quite differently. One company was organized by (and staffing ratios were developed for) functions (e.g., verification and disbursement). The other was managed by (and staffing ratios were developed for) impairment category (e.g., long-term physical disabilities and psychological disabilities). A longer-term, succinct, focused staffing plan to integrate the two workforces was needed. Two separate scenarios were developed: one that assumed that the combined claims function would be managed by function and a second that assumed that the unit would be managed by impairment category. The staffing implications of both scenarios were defined, and a staffing plan was created to meet the minimum needs that would arise regardless of the approach chosen.

Prepare "What-If" Plans

Some plans are even less certain than the scenarios just described. With scenarios, specific options are defined; the uncertainty involves which scenario will actually occur. Some organizations have plans that are less well defined than scenarios. They may be debating among several general approaches or trying to better define alternatives. In these cases, the organization discusses potential business strategies and plans, but the implementation of these strategies and plans remains uncertain. Given the high level of uncertainty, it is not possible to select specific scenarios that may be implemented.

Even in these situations, strategic staffing is possible and can add value. True, it is not possible to select (and create staffing strategies and plans to support) just one business option. Neither does it make sense to staff up for each possibility so that all bets can be covered. However, despite the degree of uncertainty, some strategic staffing is possible.

It is usually possible to discuss, in this "what-if" sense, the staffing implications of the various business plan alternatives (e.g., "If we were to implement that strategy, we would need 200 additional network administrators"). These "what-if" discussions and analyses usually address such questions as:

- What skills would be required?
- How many people with those skills are out there?
- How many of these people could we attract?
- At what rate of pay?
- Where would we look?

In some cases, staffing trends or minimum staffing requirements emerge that are valid no matter which "what-if" scenario is studied. In these cases, it may be possible to define some specific staffing plans that are consistent with the trends or that support the minimum standards.

In other cases, it may be appropriate to use the "what-if" approach just to define contingency plans, but not specific staffing strategies and plans that could be implemented. With this technique, it is possible to identify possible scenarios, define the staffing implications of each, and identify the staffing strategies and plans that best address staffing needs. The difference is that these plans are not meant to be implemented per se. Instead, their value is in allowing you to "prethink" what you would do to meet staffing requirements if any of those scenarios were to actually occur. Since you have already identified issues and defined plans in advance of need, you will be better able to react to one of these scenarios if it really does occur. Sometimes it is even possible to take some preliminary steps based on contingency plans, such as identifying and having preliminary discussions with agencies that might later be called upon to provide specific talent in a very short time frame.

Here is an example of how "what-if" planning can work. A company had a large technical workforce with unique skills. The company estimated that most new hires needed eighteen months to two years to fully master their jobs. To account for this in its planning models, the organization defined a concept that it called "proficiency." Human resource staff adjusted their new hire data to reflect the learning curve of new employees. For example, a new hire was assumed to be only 50 percent productive in the first quarter on the job. Productivity was assumed to increase at a given rate until the individual was deemed fully proficient (e.g., after four full quarters on the job). This assumption had significant effects on required staffing levels. Conceptually, each time a fully proficient employee left the organization, that employee would have to be replaced by two new hires (since each was only 50 percent productive). To better understand the impact of these proficiency and productivity assumptions, the organization created a series of "what-if" plans, each one reflecting a given set of proficiency assumptions (e.g., what if we can accelerate learning through targeted development and get people to be proficient in one year, not two? What impact would that have on required staffing levels?). Though no changes in staffing or training practices were made right away, this analysis gave the organization a better idea of the specific actions that would be required later on.

There is another version of "what-if" planning that can also be quite helpful: sensitivity analysis. Organizations that use this technique try to define the impact that a known change in staffing drivers will have on required staffing. They then use the results of this analysis to help them choose from among the alternatives tested. The merging insurance companies used this technique when combining their claims functions. One claims group had a 40-hour workweek, the other a 37.5-hour workweek. The company used sensitivity analysis to define the losses in productivity that could be expected if all staff adopted the shorter workweek and the gains that could be expected if all staff worked a 40-hour week. The decision on which alternative to select was not based solely on this analysis (e.g., the impact on morale was also considered), but the information represented an important input to a critical management decision.

There is one more situation in which "what-if" staffing planning can be helpful. Suppose your organization has not yet finalized its business plans and strategies and is still considering three different alternatives. Create "what-if" scenarios that define the probable staffing requirements for each of the three alternatives and develop "what-if" staffing strategies that would best support the implementation of each of the alternatives. Once they are complete, share these scenarios (along with the staffing implications of each) with business and planning leaders. It is quite likely that the staffing implications and staffing strategies associated with each alternative might just influence the decision on which alternative will be pursued.

Creating Specific Plans in an Uncertain Environment: An Example

Here is an example of what one medical center did to create a staffing strategy for patient care staff in the face of great uncertainty. Note that the approach utilizes several of the techniques just described, not just one.

The medical center needed to define staffing requirements (and develop staffing strategies and plans) even though its patient load varied significantly from day to day. It was relatively easy for the center to calculate a staffing ratio that specified the number of patient care staff (e.g., registered nurses) required per patient in a given unit. That was not the problem (some states even mandate or regulate these ratios). The problem was that the center had very little idea of how many patients could be expected in any given unit at any given time. While the number of patients in each unit was not random, it fluctuated greatly on a daily basis. The center had attempted to predict the number of patients in each unit on given days (e.g., forecasting based on cyclicality and seasonality), but these efforts had proved fruitless. Consequently, staff planning seemed impossible. There was no clear way to determine a daily patient census to which the known staffing ratio could be applied. Schematically, the situation in one unit looked like the graph in Figure 8-1.

This graph indicates that the number of patients fluctuated significantly over the course of a year, following no particular pattern or cycle. At first, the daily patient census seems to be virtually random. However, the medical center realized that no matter how random the number of patients seemed, there were at least three pieces of critical information that were known for sure. First, historically the number of patients in this unit had never been less than 60. Similarly, the number had never exceeded 100. Finally, the overall actual mode (i.e., the number of patients most often observed) was 86 patients.

Figure 8-1.

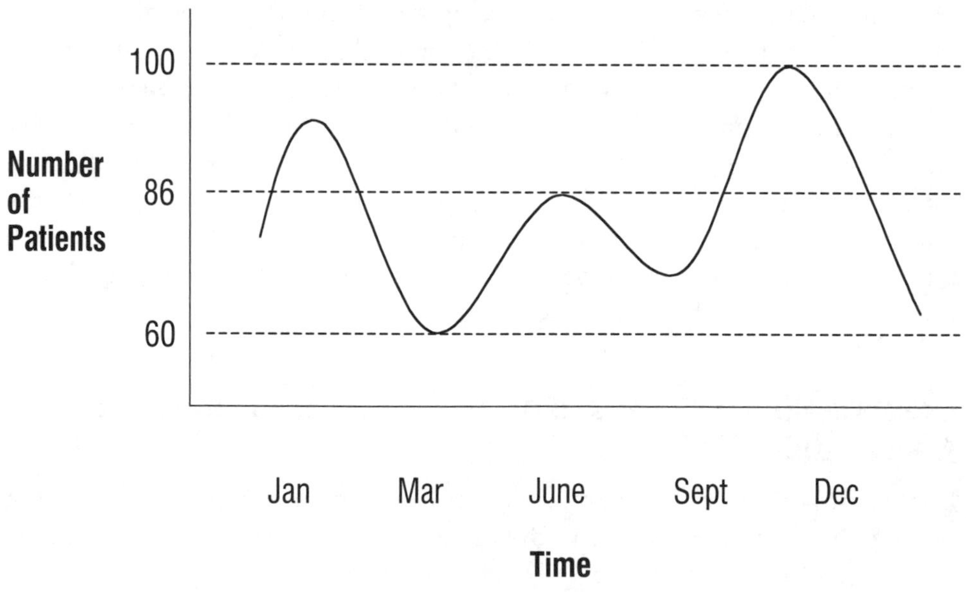

Suppose we were analyzing staffing requirements for nurses. As stated previously, the medical center had already established specific staffing ratios for each patient care staff position. If we assume (for example) a 2:1 patient/nurse ratio, we can determine that the minimum number of full-time equivalents (FTEs) required for this unit is 30 (i.e., 60 patients/2 patients per nurse), the maximum is 50 (i.e., 100/2), and the mode is 43 (i.e., 86/2). What staffing level was appropriate?

One alternative was to calculate and staff to the maximum, but this would be inefficient, and the cost would be prohibitive. Employing this alternative would create staffing surpluses (some of which would be significant) virtually every day. Another option would be to staff to an average number of patients, but this would mean that half the time the unit would be overstaffed (creating an expense that could not be tolerated) and half the time the unit would be understaffed (with dire impact on patient care and satisfaction). A third option would be to staff to the minimum, but then what would be done on those days (in fact, virtually every day) when there were more than a minimum number of patients?

The staffing strategy that the medical center actually devised had three parts. First, each unit would be staffed with the hospital's full-time staff up to the minimum required number (in this case, a base staffing of 30 FTEs). Second, whenever the number of patients exceeded the minimum but was less than the mode, the hospital's own part-time staff would be used. This was the level of uncertainty the hospital was willing to accept and deal with. For the unit in the example, that meant that up to 13 FTE nurses would be required from the center's part-time pool on any given day, where 13 equals the difference in staff needed to support the mode (43 FTEs) and the minimum (30 FTEs). Third, any staffing above the mode would be obtained from an external registry. In this case, required staffing levels could range from 0 to 7 FTEs, where 7 equals the difference in staff needed to support the maximum (50 FTEs) and the mode (43 FTEs). In effect, the hospital decided to outsource the greatest uncertainty regarding required staffing to its partner, the staffing agency.

This approach allowed the hospital to create some very specific staffing plans, even though there was great uncertainty regarding the number of patients that were expected on any given day. Because full-time staffing was based on a minimum that did not change, staffing plans for full-time staff could be developed completely, and in great detail. Given the approach that was taken, 30 FTEs were required every day, every shift—no matter how many patients there were.

There was some uncertainty regarding the number of part-time staff needed, but this approach allowed the hospital to define the size of the part-time pool that would be needed to implement this strategy. Once it knew the range for the number of part-time FTEs that would be needed (i.e., none when patient count was at the minimum up to a maximum of 13 FTEs when patient count was at the mode or above), the hospital could scope out the size of the part-time pool that would be needed to provide the required number of FTEs each day. In fact, the hospital realized further efficiencies (and reduced uncertainty even more) by creating common pools of part-time staff for units that had similar needs (e.g., one pool for medical-surgical units, another for the cardiac care unit and the intensive care unit, and a third for the emergency department). Because it was unlikely that all the units served by a given pool would require minimum (or maximum) staff at the same time, staffing requirements tended to balance each other and the number of staff in the pool could be modulated. In effect, there would always be a need for some staff, and there would never be a need for maximum staffing in all units.

There was even more uncertainty regarding the external pool (i.e., half the time none would be needed; the rest of the time as many as 7 FTEs might be needed), but this uncertainty was, in effect, absorbed by the agency. Because the hospital could provide the staffing agency with fairly specific parameters regarding its potential need (e.g., the maximum size of the pool, the skills required, and the turnaround time expected), the agency knew what was expected and could price the contract accordingly.

In the end, the hospital was able to develop and implement a very specific staffing plan even though it had no idea how many patients to expect on any given day.

Reducing Uncertainty: A Second Example

A state agency assumed that it could not do any strategic staffing because it perceived that the services it provided were subject to the whim of the legislature and could change at any time. In fact, however, only a portion of the agency's services was really in that category. Other services were well defined and regular in timing, and still others were at least predictable if not certain. In fact, staffing plans could be prepared for a large part of the agency. The agency created staffing strategies for each of these three categories of services.

The agency provided basic services to a segment of the state's population. These services were to be provided (and were not subject to legislative control) for the foreseeable future. Thus, very specific staffing plans could be prepared to ensure that these services would be delivered on an ongoing basis. A second set of services was to be transferred from federal control to the state level. This transfer was communicated well in advance, so the agency was able to define the staffing impacts of this increased activity and plan accordingly. Only a small portion of what the agency did was truly at the whim of the legislature; no staffing plans were developed for these services.

While the agency did not develop complete staffing plans for all services, it was certainly better off having created plans that supported the services that it could define.

Considering Project Probabilities

In some cases, it may be helpful to consider probabilities when determining staffing requirements in a project-based environment. In such an environment, it is usually possible to determine the staffing requirements for any given project. That's not the problem. What is unknown is which of the projects will actually be implemented.

On the one hand, it is not feasible to staff up to meet the requirements of all the possible projects. That would lead to significant overstaffing if any of the projects that were being considered were not implemented. On the other hand, it may not be realistic or possible to wait until project plans are certain, because that might leave insufficient time to identify, recruit, and deploy the number of qualified employees needed to implement those projects successfully. Applying a Monte Carlo approach can give the organization a head start on meeting its staffing needs while minimizing the probability of its taking on too many staff.

In order to apply this technique, you need to know two things: the staffing that would be required to implement each project fully, and the probability that each project will actually be implemented. Conceptually, the technique includes just three steps:

1. For each project, define the number of staff of each type that would be required if that project were to proceed.

2. Determine the probability that each project will occur and multiply this probability times the number of staff required in each category for that project.

3. Sum these results across all projects to define the required staff in each category.

The result of this analysis will be the number of staff that "should" be available prior to project initiation, across all projects. The analysis will not tell you how many staff are needed for each project (as you still don't know which projects will be implemented), but it will tell you the most likely staffing levels that you can use as a foundation (across all projects).

Here are two examples of how this technique might be applied.

Example 1: Staffing Strategies for an Oil Company

An oil company needed to prepare staffing strategies and plans to recruit the geologists and geophysicists that were required in order to support the company's exploration and production business. Staffing plans were needed on a quarterly basis. Defining the staffing needs of each exploration project was fairly easy; thus, straightforward staffing plans could be prepared for each producing project that was underway. The problem was that it was not possible to determine in advance exactly which of the exploration projects would become producing projects. If the go-ahead was given and an exploration project became a producing project, work would continue and staffing would be required. If an exploration project did not prove commercially viable (and thus did not become a producing project), work would stop and no staff would be needed.

Given the uncertainty of these project transitions, it might seem that it would be difficult for the company to create meaningful staffing plans and strategies. Waiting for plans to become more definite (so that more accurate staffing plans could be developed), however, was not an option. Competition for the geologists and geophysicists that were needed was intense. In order to identify and attract a sufficient number of qualified staff, commitments from recent graduates had to be received well in advance of need. Clearly, some kind of staffing plans and strategies was required.

Remember that earlier in this chapter I suggested that you should "do the most you can with what you have." At a minimum, the company could determine its staffing needs for all exploration projects and all producing projects in each quarter, because these needs were well defined. It did not "do nothing" just because it could not create definite plans for all jobs. Even if the company had stopped here, it would have been better off than if it had done no staff planning at all. But the company did not stop here.

The final component of the staffing plan addressed the staffing needs of those projects that would make the transition from exploration projects to producing projects during the planning period in question. As mentioned previously, the company could accurately forecast what its staffing needs for each such project would be, but it did not know which specific exploration projects would become producing projects (and thus would require staff) and which would not (and thus would have no staffing needs). Given all the data that were gathered during the exploration phase, it was possible to define the probability that any given exploration project would become a producing project. This probability was called P_s (pronounced "P sub S")—shorthand for "probability of success." Each project had its own unique P_s. To complete this component of the plan, the company applied the Monte Carlo method. First, for each exploration project that might become a fully operational producing project during the quarter, the company defined the staffing needs should that project make the transition. Next, it multiplied the staffing requirements for each such project by the P_s for that particular project. Finally, it summed the results across all projects to define its "best guess" regarding the number of staff that would be needed for the projects that made this transition. Figure 8-2 is a simplified example of what that analysis might look like.

Given these data, the company should recruit 22 geologists and 15 geophysicists to support the projects that would make the transition from exploration to producing during the quarter—whichever projects those were. Each of these numbers was significantly smaller than the total number of geologists and geophysicists that would be required for all four projects, but the probability of all four projects becoming viable was quite small (actually, it was just 0.0003!). At worst, hiring the 22 geologists and 15 geophysicists created a foundation; if additional staff were needed, they could be found and recruited later on.

Example 2: Staffing Strategies for a Technical Consulting Firm

A technical consulting firm had five large proposals outstanding. Each project required data "miners" and senior data analysts. Unfortunately, the firm did not know which of these proposals (if any) would be accepted. Still, the firm needed to recruit a pool of qualified staff in advance, because work on each project would have to begin as soon as the proposal was accepted by the client. Given the short time between proposal acceptance and project initiation, it was not possible to wait until plans became fixed to recruit the required staff.

Like the oil company in the previous example, the consulting firm defined the probability that each proposal would be accepted. Next, it defined the number of data miners and senior data analysts that would be

Figure 8-2. The Monte Carlo Method: An Oil Company.

Project	P_s	Geologists Required (if Project Proceeds)	Geologists $\times$ P_s	Geophysicists Required (if Project Proceeds)	Geophysicists $\times$ P_s
1	0.20	40	8	30	6
2	0.10	20	2	10	1
3	0.10	30	3	20	2
4	0.15	60	9	40	6
Total		150	22	100	15

needed for each project if that project were to be initiated. Finally, the firm multiplied the staffing requirements for each project by the probability that the proposal would be accepted and summed the results across all proposals. The result showed the firm how large the staff pool needed to be. Figure 8-3 shows an example of what that analysis might have looked like.

The consulting firm's staffing pool ought to include 47 data miners and 70 data analysts. As with the oil company, this should be considered a "best guess" or the "most likely outcome." Note that the number needed is much closer to the overall total for each job category (i.e., 77 versus 47 and 120 versus 70) than it was for the oil company example. This is because the probabilities of getting these assignments are much higher than the P_s for the oil exploration projects. In fact, the probability of the consulting firm's getting all five projects is 0.06075—not high, but much higher than the 0.0003 probability that all of the oil company's exploration projects will become viable.

Summary

When you create a staffing strategy, you don't need to have perfect data. Do the most you can with the data you do have. Plan fully for those parts of the organization where you have a good idea of future plans. Create scenarios when you have some idea of future plans but are not certain of them. Prepare "what-if" plans when you are unsure so that you will be better prepared to act when actual plans and strategies emerge. You will always be better off doing something about the part that you can define— and ignoring the part that you can't define—than you will be if you wait for those missing data to be developed. You may be waiting a long time!

Figure 8-3. The Monte Carlo Method: A Consulting Firm.

Project	Probability of Proposal Acceptance	Data Miners Required (if Proposal Is Accepted)	Data Miners Required × Probability of Acceptance	Senior Data Analysts Required (if Proposal Is Accepted)	Senior Data Analysts Required × Probability of Acceptance
1	0.50	10	5	20	10
2	0.30	20	6	30	9
3	0.75	12	9	20	15
4	0.60	15	9	30	18
5	0.90	20	18	20	18
Total		77	47	120	70

A Staffing Model Example

As described earlier, strategic staffing/workforce planning is, at its simplest, a form of gap analysis that defines the required skills and staffing levels, forecasts staff availability, calculates staffing gaps and surpluses, and defines the specific staffing actions that are needed in order to close gaps and eliminate (or at least reduce) surpluses.

This chapter provides a specific example of a process for creating staffing plans. The process described here is fully consistent with the context and approaches described in detail throughout this book. It focuses on the mechanics of the process.

The first seven steps describe how to define staffing gaps and surpluses; the next six steps walk you through the process of defining the staffing actions that will be needed to eliminate these gaps and surpluses. Figure 9-1 provides an overview of the process that is used in this example. To make it easier to follow, this example is also included among the files that you can download from the web site (www.amacombooks.org/go/StrategicStaff2E). Steps 1 through 7 are already filled in on the files you download; you can complete the remaining steps yourself as you go through the example.

You may wish to use this model as a template for your own process. Of course, remember that this is just an example. The process will need to be tailored to reflect the staffing issues that you are facing and the job categories that you are including.

Part 1: Defining Staffing Gaps and Surpluses

First, identify the issue to be addressed or the job categories on which your model will focus. For this example, let's assume that we are going to define our specific needs for software engineers and object-oriented pro-

Figure 9-1. The Strategic Staffing Process As It Appears in the Example.

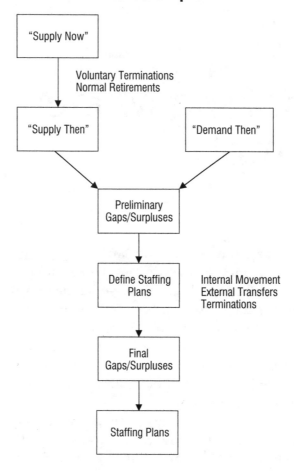

grammers because the demand for individuals with these "hot skills" far exceeds the supply. Our model will focus on and include only the positions that require these particular skills. If other positions are also critical, they would be defined in a separate model.

Step 1: Define the Model Parameters

Define the three planning parameters that you will use to structure your model: population to be included, planning horizon, and matrix structure.

Population. Define the existing positions in your unit that fall into the two job categories we are focusing on. We will include incumbents of these positions in our model. In an actual model, we would want to also include in the model any other positions that might require these critical skills and any positions that might be able to use these skills. To keep this example simple, however, we will assume that there are no other jobs that might be sources of or uses for these skills.

Planning Horizon. Now define your planning horizon. It will have two components:

1. **"How long": Define the end point.** If you are creating a one-year model, this will probably be the end of that year. If you are creating a staffing plan to support a five-year strategy, it would be a point five years into the future. In an area that is growing and changing rapidly, the planning horizon might be six months. Because technology is changing so rapidly, we will assume for this example that our long-term planning horizon is one year.

2. **"How often": Define the period of your model.** Your strategic staffing/workforce planning process might have a five-year end point, but it is probably helpful to define needs throughout that period, not just at the end. For a five-year horizon, the model would probably define staffing needs for each of those five years separately. If the model is supporting an annual budget, it may be sufficient to consider just one period (i.e., one year). If an objective is a quarterly staffing plan, however, that one year would need to be broken into quarters (with the model updated each quarter to define needs for the ensuing four quarters). In this example, our period will, in fact, be one quarter.

In our example, we would probably run a model for each of the four quarters of our one-year planning horizon (although the plan for only one of those quarters is shown here). This would allow us to create and update staffing plans on a quarterly basis—a time frame that is appropriate for the kind of staffing decisions we will be using the model to support. A longer time frame (e.g., one year) would not allow us to define the different points during the year when staffing actions will need to be taken; it would also prevent us from addressing seasonal staffing issues. Building a model around a shorter time frame (e.g., one month) would require a great deal of time and effort while providing a level of detail that just isn't needed.

Model Structure. Next, we need to define what row and column headings to use to structure our model. Figure 9-2 shows the suggested structure for this example. Columns usually denote areas of expertise, organization units, or locations (depending on the issue you are addressing). There is a

Figure 9-2.

	Software Engineers	Object-Oriented Programmers	Total
Project Manager			
Lead			
Individual Contributor			
Entry Level			
Total			

balance that has to be struck here between the need to differentiate adequately and the need to keep the model simple. A single column for "programmers" would create a simple model, but would eliminate the possibility of differentiating among various areas of programming expertise (and we will probably need to consider those differences when we create recruiting and staffing plans for this unit). In our example, we will have two columns, one for software engineers and a second for object-oriented programmers.

Next, define the row headings. In almost every case, rows depict increasing levels of capability or responsibility (i.e., entry level is at the bottom and lead practitioners or more senior managers are at the top). In our example, we have four levels, entry level, individual contributor, lead, and project manager. Since we are focusing on "hot" technical skills, there is no need to include any positions above project manager in our example, as this is the highest-level position for which some technical skills are still required. This matrix design will be used to capture data and organize results.

Step 2: Define Staffing Requirements ("Demand Then")

This version of the matrix contains staffing requirements (both capabilities and staffing levels). These demand estimates may come from plans, budgets, or interviews with managers. Document the required capabilities that you have assumed for each job category, either on a separate sheet or as a comment attached to each cell of the matrix. Here are some hints to keep in mind:

- **Identify a small number of really important capabilities.** Don't try to define all the capabilities for each job category. Instead, focus on those that are most critical. You should ideally identify less than ten, and you may find it possible to define as few as five. Try to identify those few capabilities that are needed to win the game, not just play it.

- **Identify capabilities that differentiate one job category from another.** When you build your model, you will probably assume that there are significant differences between cells in different rows of a given column or different columns of a given row. Try to define these differences in specific terms. For example, if the difference between one level/row and another is the addition of management skills, define just those additional skills. Similarly, if the difference between one column and another is a different technical discipline, define only the skills that are different.

- **Define capabilities in behavioral terms.** It is often helpful to define capabilities in terms of behaviors that can be observed. Instead of defining a particular skill, knowledge, or understanding, define what happens when that skill, knowledge, or understanding is applied to accomplish something particular. Select capabilities from a competency model if your organization has one.

Once the required capabilities have been identified, the required staffing levels can be defined. There are many common methods that can be used to define demand (several of these are described in Chapter 7). In this example, we have assumed that demand for staff in each category will simply increase by 15 percent. This means, for example, that for software engineers/lead, 25 would be needed (i.e., 22 $\times$ 1.15 = 25.3). Once you have determined the number of people that will be required, enter that number in the appropriate cell. For our example, assume that a detailed analysis produced the "demand then" matrix shown in Figure 9-3.

Step 3: Determine Existing Staff Level ("Supply Now")

Enter the number of people you currently have in each category into the appropriate cell of the "supply now" component of your model (e.g., enter

Figure 9-3. "Demand Then."

	Software Engineers	Object-Oriented Programmers	Total
Project Manager	12	9	21
Lead	25	21	46
Individual Contributor	62	52	114
Entry Level	83	77	160
Total	182	159	341

the number of entry-level software engineers currently on staff in the software engineers/entry level cell). Enter only the number of people that are actually in place. Usually these numbers can be extracted from a human resource information system. Alternatively, it is sometimes possible to actually count the number of individuals in each category and enter those numbers.

On a separate sheet (or in a comment field on the spreadsheet itself), document the critical skills that the employees in each of these cells now have. Remember to focus on a small number of really important capabilities.

For our example, we will assume the starting population shown in Figure 9-4.

Step 4: Define Voluntary Turnover

Voluntary turnover between "now" and "then" will reduce the number of people available to you. Estimate the voluntary turnover rate for each category and enter it in the appropriate cell. If you have historical data, consider what the turnover for this group has been, but make sure that you project what you think it will be. Will it be at that historical level in the coming period? Will changing economic conditions make it higher? Will they make it lower? Enter in the model the turnover rate that you think will apply in the period you are modeling. Remember to adjust the rate so that it is consistent with your model period. For example, if your annual turnover rate is expected to be 4 percent, enter 0.04 if your period is one year and 0.01 (i.e., 0.04 divided by 4) if your period is one quarter.

Your model should allow for a different turnover rate for each category, but this level of differentiation may not be necessary. Here are some simplifying assumptions:

- Turnover usually varies by length of service. People who have been with your company for a longer time are less likely to leave than those with less tenure. Consequently, the turnover rate may vary by

Figure 9-4. Existing Staff Level/"Supply Now."

	Software Engineers	Object-Oriented Programmers	Total
Project Manager	10	17	27
Lead	22	18	40
Individual Contributor	54	45	99
Entry Level	72	67	139
Total	158	147	305

row, with the lower rows having a higher rate than the higher rows. Estimate a rate for each row and use it for all columns.

- Turnover varies by area of expertise. In areas where there are hot skills, turnover will be particularly high. In these cases, use a rate for those columns that is different from the one used for all the other columns.
- Turnover varies by organization. If you are unsure of how turnover might vary, use the same rate for each cell.

Once turnover rates have been entered, calculate the expected number of voluntary quits for each category. Multiply the voluntary turnover rate for each cell times the number of people in that cell at the beginning of the period (as defined in the existing staff level/"supply now" matrix) and enter that number in the voluntary turnover matrix. In step 6 you will deduct this number from the corresponding number in the existing staff level/"supply now" matrix.

If the number of staff in any cell is small, using turnover rates might not forecast any turnover (e.g., a 15 percent rate applied to a cell that includes 2 staff would forecast turnover of 0.30 of a person). If this occurs, you may wish to change your turnover assumptions for those cells (e.g., assume that one person will leave that cell in the third quarter). To do this, simply overwrite the formula in the turnover matrix with the number you wish to use for that period.

For our example, we have assumed a voluntary turnover rate of 15 percent for software engineers and 11 percent for object-oriented programmers (Figure 9-5).

For each cell, multiply these rates times the starting headcounts (i.e., "supply now") to estimate the number of people in each category that will leave voluntarily. The losses that would be expected (rounded to the nearest person) are shown in Figure 9-6.

These numbers will be deducted from the corresponding numbers in the existing staff level/"supply now" matrix in step 6.

Figure 9-5. Voluntary Turnover Rate.

	Software Engineers	Object-Oriented Programmers
Project Manager	0.15	0.11
Lead	0.15	0.11
Individual Contributor	0.15	0.11
Entry Level	0.15	0.11

Figure 9-6. Voluntary Turnover.

	Software Engineers	Object-Oriented Programmers	Total
Project Manager	2	2	4
Lead	3	2	5
Individual Contributor	8	5	13
Entry Level	11	7	18
Total	24	16	40

Step 5: Estimate Retirements

Retirements should also be factored into your analysis. Review your work-force and identify those employees that will become eligible for retirement during your planning period, based on whatever assumptions you think are appropriate (e.g., those that will reach an average retirement age or meet standard retirement criteria). If, based on your assumptions, you are expecting retirements from any of the jobs included in the model, simply enter the number of retirements in the appropriate cell(s). Again, you will need to subtract these retirements from your existing staff level/"supply now" matrix in step 6. Figure 9-7 shows the retirements we assumed.

Note that your model may need to factor in other uncontrollable staffing actions at this point. This might include adding staff to reflect hiring commitments already made or adding or deleting staff to take into account the effects of planned leaves of absence. You should *not* include in this part of the model any controllable staffing moves that you plan to make. Chapter 5 includes a more detailed discussion regarding uncontrol-lable staffing actions. For simplicity, we have not included any of these types of actions in our example.

Figure 9-7. Retirements.

	Software Engineers	Object-Oriented Programmers	Total
Project Manager	1	2	3
Lead	1	0	1
Individual Contributor	0	0	0
Entry Level	0	0	0
Total	2	2	4

Step 6: Forecast Available Resources ("Supply Then")

This section of the model displays the number of people in each category that will remain at the end of your planning period, taking into account the losses that you have assumed.

Let's look at the software engineers/lead cell in our example. The calculation for that cell would be as follows:

Starting headcount	22
Less voluntary turnover	− 3
Less retirement	− 1
Available resources	18

Applying this logic to all the cells included in the example produces the available resources matrix depicted in Figure 9-8.

This is the population that you expect to have at the end of the period if all of your turnover and retirement assumptions are correct (and actually occur).

Step 7: Calculate Preliminary Gaps and Surpluses

Next, compare the "supply then" that you have calculated with the "demand then" that you have entered on a cell-by-cell basis. The results of this comparison (i.e., staffing gaps and surpluses) are displayed in a separate matrix (sometimes referred to as a net needs matrix). Subtracting demand from supply gives us a negative result when demand exceeds supply; therefore, negative numbers represent deficits or gaps, and positive numbers represent surpluses. This is the convention we will use.

In our example, in the software engineers/lead category, our net need is a deficit of 7 people (i.e., 18 people will be available and 25 will be

Figure 9-8. Available Resources/"Supply Then."

	Software Engineers	Object-Oriented Programmers	Total
Project Manager	7	13	20
Lead	18	16	34
Individual Contributor	46	40	86
Entry Level	61	60	121
Total	132	129	261

needed). Applying this logic to all the cells in our example yields the matrix shown in Figure 9-9.

Note that we don't calculate totals. That's because totals really don't make sense, and may actually be misleading. For example, there is a deficit of five project managers in software engineering and a surplus of four in object-oriented programming. Therefore, a total for that row would show an overall deficit of one project manager. This number, however, really isn't helpful. We created separate columns for software engineering and object-oriented programming in the first place because the capabilities required for those two areas are significantly different. From a staffing perspective, we probably would not be able to redeploy the project managers from object-oriented programming to software engineering because of these capability differences. Consequently, we have to define one set of actions to reduce the deficit of five project managers in software engineering and another set to alleviate the surplus of four project managers in object-oriented programming. If we simply looked at the row total, we might have been led to believe that all we needed to do was to hire one project manager, but clearly this would not be sufficient.

In an actual example, we would need to define staffing gaps and surpluses for all our planning periods before we defined staffing strategies and plans for any period. However, since this example includes only one planning period, we can move ahead to action planning.

Part 2: Defining Required Staffing Actions

Since this is a simple one-period model, the next step is to define the staffing actions that you should take to eliminate gaps and surpluses. If this were a real model, however, you would at this point "carry forward" the results of period 1 into period 2 and calculate gaps and surpluses for that period (assuming at this point, of course, that only *uncontrollable* staffing actions occur). Once gaps and surpluses for period 2 were defined, you would carry your results forward into period 3 (again, considering only uncontrollable staffing actions), then repeat this process until prelimi-

Figure 9-9. Preliminary Gaps/Surpluses.

	Software Engineers	Object-Oriented Programmers
Project Manager	−5	+4
Lead	−7	−5
Individual Contributor	−16	−12
Entry Level	−22	−17

nary gaps and surpluses had been calculated for every period. Next, you would review gaps and surpluses in each category across all periods and develop the longer-term staffing strategies that provide the context for the shorter-term staffing actions you are about to define. Again, this step is not necessary for our simple one-period model.

Once preliminary gaps and surpluses have been calculated, it is possible to define the specific staffing actions that are needed to eliminate those gaps and surpluses. Usually, your staffing strategies define a kind of pecking order: Certain kinds of staffing actions are preferred and take precedence over others. For example, in this example, we will assume that our staffing strategy dictates that we fill as many jobs as possible internally (e.g., through promotion or redeployment) before we hire from the outside. The order in which you define the required staffing actions should reflect the staffing strategies and preferences of your organization.

In this example, we have defined the required staffing actions only for software engineers. A similar process would be used to define the staffing plans for object-oriented programmers. You may wish to access (from the web site www.amacombooks.org/go/StrategicStaff2E) the computer file containing this example and define your own staffing actions for that column.

Remember that this section of the model should include all the controllable staffing actions that you will take. These actions will, of course, include internal transfers, external transfers, and new hires, but they should also include the use of part-time staff, overtime, external contractors, outsourcing of work, and any other controllable staffing action you are considering. Again, Chapter 5 includes a detailed description of these controllable actions. Our example includes only internal transfers, external transfers, and new hires.

Step 8: Define Internal Movement

The next two sections of the model (internal transfers out and internal transfers in) are illustrated in Figures 9-10 and 9-11. They allow you to define the internal transfers (including lateral moves, redeployments, and promotions) that you think are necessary to address the gaps and surpluses that you have identified. Note that for the purposes of this model, *internal movement* is defined as someone moving from one job in your model to another job in your model. Here is how these matrices should be used.

Assume that you wish to eliminate a gap of five in one job category by promoting qualified individuals from the category just beneath it. This action should be recorded by placing a 5 in the cell from which the people will be coming on the internal transfers *out* matrix and making a corresponding entry of 5 in the cell on the internal transfers *in* matrix that

Figure 9-10.

Internal Transfers Out

	Software Engineers	Object-Oriented Programmers	Total
Project Manager			
Lead	5		5
Individual Contributor			
Entry Level			
Total	5		5

Internal Transfers In

	Software Engineers	Object-Oriented Programmers	Total
Project Manager	5		5
Lead			
Individual Contributor			
Entry Level			
Total	5		5

corresponds to the job these people are being promoted to. Remember that each move you want to include must be documented on both of the internal movement in and internal movement out matrices (it's almost like double-entry bookkeeping).

There may be cases in which the people leaving one cell are going to two or more other cells. In this case, the internal transfers out matrix should show the sum of all the people that are leaving that cell, regardless of the cell that they are going to. Of course, the internal transfers in matrix will include those people in whatever cell they are going to. Similarly, there may be cases in which people are moving into a cell on the internal transfers in matrix from two or more other cells. In this case, the internal transfers in matrix should show the sum of all the people that are moving to that cell, regardless of the cell that they are coming from. The internal transfers out matrix will include those people in whatever cell they are leaving.

When you are done, verify that the overall totals of the internal movement in and internal movement out matrices are the same. If they are not the same, you have not included corresponding entries in both matrices for each of the moves you entered.

In some cases, internal transfers (whether lateral or promotional) are

Figure 9-11.

Internal Transfers Out

	Software Engineers	Object-Oriented Programmers	Total
Project Manager			
Lead	5		5
Individual Contributor	12		12
Entry Level	16		16
Total	33		33

Internal Transfers In

	Software Engineers	Object-Oriented Programmers	Total
Project Manager	5		5
Lead	12		12
Individual Contributor	16		16
Entry Level			
Total	33		33

feasible only if additional training is provided. If this is the case, make a note of the skills that will need to be strengthened and include a reference to this required training in your staffing plan.

In our example, we are going to address a gap of 5 at the software engineers/project manager level by promoting 5 individuals from the lead category of that group. Figure 9-10 shows how that particular staffing action would be recorded.

Of course, promoting these 5 people will increase the deficit at the lead level from the original 7 to 12. This deficit will probably be dealt with by promoting 12 individual contributors, but this action will increase the deficit at that level from 16 to 28. In our example, we have determined that only 16 of those slots can be filled by promoting staff from the entry level. The remaining openings will be filled through outside hires. By definition, none of the openings at entry level can be filled by promotions.

Our final internal transfer matrices for software engineers would look like the ones in Figure 9-11.

Step 9: Define External Transfers

The next two sections of the model (external transfers out and external transfers in) address movements of people from jobs in your model to other units in your company or into jobs in your model from other units in your company. Remember that in this case, *external* is defined as jobs that are not included in your model; they are not external to the company. Because in these cases you are interested only in movement into and out of your model, no double entries are required. For example, if you plan to eliminate a surplus by redeploying 10 individuals to another unit (i.e., one that is not covered by your model), simply enter a 10 in the cell on the external transfers out matrix from which the individuals will come. Similarly, if you want to address a gap in a job category by accepting 15 people from another unit, simply enter 15 in the appropriate cell of the external transfers in matrix. Of course, corresponding entries would be made in models that are being developed for those other units (if such models are indeed being prepared separately).

We have assumed no external transfers in our example.

Step 10: Determine New Hires

Enter the number of new hires you expect to make in each category. Just to be clear, the model assumes that these people are being hired from outside the company—a "new hire" from another unit of your company should be considered an external transfer, not a new hire.

In our example, we assumed that 16 of the 28 openings at the individual contributor level in software engineering will be filled through promotion. The remaining 12 will be filled by new hires. At the entry level, we now have 38 openings (the original deficit of 22 plus the deficit of 16 that we created by promoting these individuals to the individual contributor level). All of these openings will be filled through new hires. These staffing actions would be recorded in the new hires matrix as shown in Figure 9-12.

Step 11: Define Involuntary Terminations (If Any)

If you plan on reducing surpluses through early retirement, reductions in force, or any other method beyond normal retirement and attrition, that

Figure 9-12. New Hires.

	Software Engineers	Object-Oriented Programmers	Total
Project Manager			
Lead			
Individual Contributor	12		12
Entry Level	38		38
Total	50		50

information should be entered in this section of the model. Simply create another matrix with the same format, and remember to subtract these numbers from your supply when calculating gaps and surpluses. If no voluntary terminations are needed, no entries should be made in this section.

I sometimes label this matrix "opportunities for deployment" instead of referring to losses in any way. The data included in the matrix remain the same, but the message the matrix sends tends to have a more positive spin.

Step 12: Calculate Final Gaps and Surpluses

This section of the model should display the gaps and surpluses that still exist after all the staffing actions you have included in your model (i.e., those from steps 8 through 11) have been taken into account. In most cases, your objective is to define the staffing actions that will make this matrix contain nothing but zeros. If you still have gaps or surpluses, you should go back to steps 8 through 11 and make additional (or different) assumptions regarding staffing actions (e.g., increase hiring if gaps still exist; institute reductions in force if there are still surpluses).

In some cases, gaps and surpluses might be acceptable. For example, you may choose to carry a gap forward if it is unrealistic to assume that you could fill all the expected openings in a given planning period. Similarly, you might carry a surplus forward if you know that people with those skills will be required in the subsequent planning period (rather than laying people off in one period and trying to hire replacements in the next).

Step 13: Create Staffing Plans

Once you are satisfied with the results of your model (i.e., when all cells of the final gap matrix include zeros or some other acceptable numbers), you will need to create staffing plans. This entails documenting the staffing assumptions you have made along the way, including each kind of move that you have assumed will take place. You should also document any supporting actions that you assumed (e.g., training needed to support the internal transfers you need).

Figure 9-13 provides a very simplified structure; Figure 9-14 depicts what a final staffing plan for our model for software engineering might look like.

Don't forget that in a real case, you would also need to define the staffing actions required to address issues for object-oriented programmers (e.g., identifying the specific individuals who will be promoted as part of the staffing plan).

Follow-on actions should also be documented (e.g., any training that

Figure 9-13.

Step/Type of Action	Information to Be Documented
Voluntary turnover	Rates that were assumed
Retirements	Number of retirements for each cell
Internal transfers (both in and out)	For each type of transfer, document the number of people moving, the job category they are coming from, and the job category they are moving to (noting any training or development needed to support the move)
External transfers in	For each type of transfer, document the number of people moving, the unit they are coming from, and the job category they are moving into
External transfers out	For each type of transfer, document the number of people moving, the job category they are coming from, and the unit they are moving to
New hires	Number of hires for each job category
Involuntary terminations (all types)	Number of terminations per job category by type

Figure 9-14.

Type	Staffing Action(s)
Promotions	5 from software engineers/lead to software engineers/project manager
	12 from software engineers/individual contributor to software engineers/lead
	16 from software engineers/entry level to software engineers/individual contributor
New hires	12 into software engineers/individual contributor
	38 into software engineers/entry level

may be needed to support the assumed promotions). You should also specify the individual(s) responsible for implementing the plan and the start and end dates for that implementation. I have also used the plan to estimate the resources (e.g., staff time and costs) that will be required to implement the plan. You may also choose to document any staffing gaps and surpluses that you have not addressed, including your rationale for not addressing those differences.

The computer files on the web site, www.amacombooks.org/go/ StrategicStaff2E, include an example of a more detailed (and more realistic) example of a staffing plan. This file provides a template that you may wish to use to support your actual planning efforts.

10

Effective Strategic Staffing/Workforce Planning: Case Studies and Examples

This chapter describes three specific case studies in which strategic staffing had a major impact on the organization implementing the process. It also includes several shorter, less detailed summaries of successful strategic staffing projects. In each case, the company specifically used some version of the strategic staffing/workforce planning process described in this book.

Case 1: A Pharmaceutical Company

Introduction

This case study describes a project that was completed for a large pharmaceutical company. The organization chose not to follow the traditional one-size-fits-all process (i.e., expecting every unit of the organization to create staffing plans at the same time, at the same level of detail, with the same planning horizons, using the same templates). Instead, this company developed a targeted staffing strategy that focused on a particular unit within the information technology (IT) organization that was about to undergo significant growth. This case study identifies the issues that had to be faced and describes the planning approach that was taken. It also highlights the results of the project—both longer-term, broad staffing strategies and shorter-term, specific staffing plans and actions.

The Strategic Context

The staffing strategy described here was developed for the technical support group within the IT function. The technical support group provides critical services to the business units of the firm, such as local and/or wide area network (LAN/WAN) setup, cabling, server configuration, operating system installation, and telecommunications support. In the near future, the company as a whole was expected to grow significantly; consequently, demand for the services that the technical support group provided was expected to grow significantly as well. At the start of the project, full-time employees of the technical support group were handling the majority of the work, but it had become clear that the existing staff would be unable to support all the projects that would result from the planned growth. The technical support group manager wanted to develop a staffing strategy that would ensure that his unit had a sufficient number of qualified staff available to provide these services when they were needed.

The Strategic Staffing Model

As a first step, staffing needs were defined. A strategic staffing model was developed to support this analysis. The basic format of that model is described here.

Model Structure. The core of the model was a two-dimensional matrix. Each row of the matrix combined two concepts: the particular technical area of expertise (e.g., WAN, LAN, voice, desktop, or messaging) and the role that was to be played. There were two roles defined for each technical area:

1. Oversight, which included defining the work to be done, setting objectives, preparing work plans, providing technical guidance, and supervising the work of others

2. Staff, which included those actually doing the work in the hands-on sense

Each row of the model described a pairing of technical expertise and role (e.g., Wide Area Network (WAN) oversight, WAN staff, voice oversight, voice staff). Each of the three columns of the model denoted a particular level of expertise:

1. Senior: Individuals who had a deep knowledge or understanding of a particular technical area (e.g., a platform or set of software) as it was applied within the company's business context

2. Individual contributor: Individuals who had the technical skills, experience, and understanding of the company's technology, systems, platforms, and business practices needed to contribute to projects without constant supervision

3. Foundation: Individuals with basic capabilities and aptitudes but no in-depth understanding of the company's technology, systems, platforms, or business practices

Conceptually, each job (i.e., each cell of the matrix) could be described as a particular combination of technical area, role, and level of expertise (e.g., WAN oversight at the senior level, voice staff at the individual contributor level). Figure 10-1 shows a portion of the model framework.

Time Frame. The overall planning horizon for the model was one year; staffing plans were developed for each of the four quarters within that year. The plan was to be updated on a rolling basis (i.e., each of the four quarters included in the plan would be updated on a quarterly basis).

The Modeling Process. The model itself was a fairly traditional, spreadsheet-based supply/demand model.

Overall staffing requirements were calculated by defining the staffing requirements of each project to be supported and then summing the staffing requirements across all projects on a job-by-job, quarter-by-quarter basis. The initial supply was defined to be the existing pool of full-time technical support group employees (i.e., those who were already employed full time at the beginning of the planning period). For each period, the model compared demand to supply and calculated gaps and surpluses for each job category (i.e., each cell of the matrix).

Managers in the technical support group first reviewed staffing gaps and surpluses for the first quarter and determined the staffing actions that would best eliminate those gaps and surpluses for that quarter (e.g., reallocating the time of existing employees among projects, contracting work out, or hiring). Once these staffing actions were entered in the spreadsheets, the model then determined the numbers and types of employees and contractors that would be available at the start of the second quarter

Figure 10-1. Case Study Model Framework— Technical Support Staffing Model.

Job Category	Senior	Individual Contributor	Foundation
LAN oversight			
LAN staff			
WAN oversight			
WAN staff			
Voice oversight			
Voice staff			
Etc.			

(assuming that all the first-quarter staffing actions were implemented as planned). It also compared that supply to the requirements for the second quarter, and recalculated the gaps and surpluses. Again, the technical support group managers determined how best to eliminate the staffing gaps and surpluses for that quarter and entered those data into the spreadsheets. This process was repeated for all four quarters of the one-year planning period.

The Staffing Strategies and Plans That Emerged

Once specific staffing needs had been defined, the overall staffing strategies that would meet those needs most effectively were developed. The first strategies that were developed clearly defined what the oversight and staff roles would be in the future and (ideally) how openings in each of these roles should be filled. When the managers looked at technical areas and roles (i.e., the rows of the model), they reached the following general conclusions:

- **Oversight roles would primarily be filled by full-time technical support group employees.** Oversight roles were especially critical to the mission of the technical support group. The individuals who served in these roles should bring a depth of technical expertise and an overall understanding of the company's business context that was especially valuable. These roles were thought of as core in that they directly supported the implementation of company strategies and provided a distinct competitive advantage. Because of the strategic value of these roles, it was determined that they should be staffed by the company's own full-time employees.

- **Staff roles should be filled by contractors on a short-term, as-needed basis.** The individuals in staff roles provided critical services, but those services were not unique to the company and provided no particular competitive advantage. In most cases they involved skills that could be learned outside the company's business context. The services could be thought of as commodities that were readily available outside the organization. As a result, it was decided that contractors should be used to staff these roles.

When they looked at the various levels of expertise (as denoted by the columns of the model), the managers drew the following conclusions:

- In addition to all of the oversight roles, some senior- and individual contributor–level staff jobs were also considered core. This was especially the case in technical areas that were deemed critical or proprietary in nature (e.g., systems development and architecture).

- None of the roles included in the foundation column of the model were considered core.

Once core roles had been identified, the company decided (at a strategic level) to focus its recruiting, training, and development efforts on providing and strengthening core roles and capabilities. Few resources, if any, would be spent on recruiting and training in noncore areas. This strengthening would be focused on two areas in particular:

1. **The oversight capabilities of technical support group employees.** For current employees, development efforts would be aimed at enhancing oversight capabilities (e.g., planning, supervising, and managing performance), not technical skills.

2. **Capabilities relating to and supporting the development and implementation of proprietary technologies.** Where necessary, specific individuals would be developed in technical areas that were also identified as core.

It was also decided that changes in core roles had to be implemented over time, not all at once. Initially, oversight capabilities (such as planning and supervising) would be positioned as additions to the technical capabilities that were already developed and demonstrated by individuals at these levels. Over time, however, the development and utilization of oversight capabilities would be emphasized and the development of new technical skills would be deemphasized.

Additional Short-Term Actions

Within the context of these staffing strategies, several more specific, short-term staffing actions were also defined.

A Logic for Eliminating the Staffing Gaps and Surpluses Defined by the Model Was Developed. Managers created a rationale or set of priorities that could be used to eliminate staffing gaps and surpluses in each quarter. If a need for a core role was defined, managers would first try to meet that need by reallocating surplus time from a current technical support group employee. If that was not possible, a new employee would be hired (if the need was ongoing) or a contractor would be retained and developed (if the need was short-term). If a need for a noncore role was identified, managers would still try to reallocate surplus time from a current technical support group employee. If that was not possible, a contractor would be retained.

Specific Training Plans Were Developed. If the staffing plans that emerged from the strategic staffing model were implemented as designed, the work being done by several full-time technical support group employees would change significantly. For example, one individual would move from having no responsibilities in the messaging area in the first quarter to working solely in that area in the fourth quarter. The individuals whose responsibilities would change so significantly would probably require additional (concentrated) training in order to perform satisfactorily in these new technical areas. Targeted development plans were developed for these individuals so that during the second and third quarters they could acquire the skills that they would need in the fourth quarter.

Plans for Increasing the Effectiveness of Contractor Relationships Were Developed. The staffing strategy clearly identified the areas in which contractors would be needed over the coming year. In some cases, actions had to be taken in advance of need to ensure that a reliable source of qualified contractors would be available when needed. These actions might include:

- Reviewing staffing needs with those companies that are already providing talent to ensure that those companies will continue to provide contractors with the needed skills and capabilities.

- Identifying new sources of talent if current suppliers are unable to provide sufficient numbers of properly skilled talent.

- Identifying new sources of qualified talent in areas where contractors have not been used previously. This might include identifying suppliers, discussing staffing requirements with those suppliers in advance of need, and gathering information regarding what would have to be done if a particular supplier were to be called upon to provide talent (e.g., what the lead times and contract terms/provisions might be)

Other Key Findings

In addition to the strategic and short-term staffing initiatives just described, there were two additional findings:

- Deferring projects would not alleviate any staffing issues. Prior to the analysis, managers had assumed that since many projects were front-loaded into the early quarters of the planning period, there would be staffing shortages in those quarters and staffing surpluses in later quarters (when fewer projects were planned). If this were true, staffing gaps and surpluses might be balanced by simply deferring some projects to later quarters. The results of the analysis did not support this conclusion.

- It had been thought that there might be some cases in which it would be less expensive to add individuals with noncore skills as full-time staff (as opposed to using contractors) if those skills were needed on an ongoing basis. The staffing strategy showed that this was not the case within the technical support group. There was no set of noncore skills that was needed throughout the planning period; consequently, there was no need to add full-time employees to provide noncore skills.

Conclusions

Taking a more strategic approach to staffing had a significant impact on this organization's staffing actions. By developing a longer-term staffing strategy and using that strategy as a context for near-term decision making, the company was able to define the staffing actions that would allow it to best meet its needs for talent in both the long and the short term. Without that strategy, it is likely that the technical support group would have implemented staffing actions that were less effective and more costly than those that were implemented as a result of using this process.

Case 2: An International Bank
Introduction

In this case, a staffing strategy was to be developed for a development unit of an international bank. Each of the bank's development units supports lending operations by providing borrowers (primarily developing countries) with the technical and functional expertise they need if they are to implement the projects for which bank funds were being loaned. Initially, strategies and plans had been developed to revitalize this particular development unit, and the bank's board of directors had approved a sizable budget increase to support these efforts. Work had begun on a staffing strategy that would support these revitalization efforts. Then, rather unexpectedly, the political climate both inside and outside the bank changed, and the expertise offered by this development unit was suddenly on everyone's agenda. The revitalization effort took on new importance, and staffing that effort became even more important.

The Strategic Context

Traditionally, this development unit of the bank had directly supported education-related lending. It provided both technical and operations support. Developing countries turned to the bank for the capital, expertise (both economic and educational), and project management needed to build schools, conduct teacher training, obtain and create textbooks, develop curricula, and provide other infrastructure. The unit's efforts (both lending and development) focused on all aspects of learning, from pre-school through adult education.

As the bank's business environment changed, so did the role of this development unit. In many cases, education efforts became a part of larger projects (e.g., a program to reduce a significant health risk) rather than stand-alone efforts (as had been the case previously). In addition, the bank began to move toward program-based lending. Instead of providing capital and expertise that focused on particular projects (as it had traditionally done), it provided capital to countries in need as long as they achieved certain policy goals and milestones (e.g., improving literacy rates). The sudden emphasis on education also meant that this development unit would have to provide additional services and support both to its traditional lending and to emerging programmatic loans. The board of directors also called on the unit to define specific progress measures (including one addressing staffing) and to report progress against those measures on a quarterly basis.

The bank was organized by region. Within each region, there were individuals with expertise in education. There also was a centralized unit that provided staff, some level of expertise, and administrative support to the education professionals located in the regions. Some staff were functional experts; however, most spent a large part of their time managing projects and tasks.

It was in this environment of growth and change that a strategic staffing process was to be implemented. Initially, the bank began to implement the approaches described in this book. As the project progressed, however, some significant differences emerged.

Critical Business Issues

As described earlier in this book, the strategic staffing process normally begins with the definition of the staffing implications of business strategies and plans. In this case, however, as the strategic staffing project began, several larger business issues were identified. Among the senior managers, there was some difference of opinion regarding what this development unit was to accomplish during the planning period. First, there was a lack of consensus regarding the overall mission of the bank in general and of the education unit in particular. Some managers felt that the bank's main role was to have a significant positive impact on the countries being served (e.g., to maximize the impact that the bank's capital would have on learning). Others felt that the bank should concentrate more on lending operations and less on development. Some felt that the new program-based lending was appropriate in most cases; others felt that it should be implemented only on a selected basis. Complicating this situation was the fact that the performance evaluation of most country managers was based largely on the size and performance of their lending portfolios. The impact of their development efforts carried much less weight. Obviously, all these differences in business objectives, strategies, and approaches were significant. The staffing needed to implement some of these alternatives varied widely.

Initiating the Strategic Staffing Process

Once the basic parameters of the model had been defined (e.g., population, planning horizon, and model structure), efforts to define the staffing requirements began.

The bulk of the staff within the development unit fell into three job categories: economics, education, and operations. Each of these streams included three levels of jobs: individual contributor, senior level, and lead level. In addition, there were research analysts and operations analysts. Traditionally, the bank hired younger professionals (including many Ph.D.s) who had a particular expertise in educational economics or in some education specialty.

A staffing model was built to support the development of staffing strategies and plans. The model included all staff that directly supported the lending activities of the development unit. It focused on staff within the existing three job streams (i.e., economics, education, and operations) both in the regions and in the corporate unit. It also included the operations and research analysts; it excluded the small number of managers.

The columns of the model denoted the organization unit (e.g., region or corporate, headquarters or field locations). Jobs in each region were divided into three categories on the basis of location (i.e., corporate headquarters, corporate positions in the field, and local office positions). The rows of the model denoted job stream and level. While the qualitative portion of the project looked ahead three years, the quantitative model focused on the coming fiscal year. The model structure is shown in Figure 10-2.

The actual model included all regions, not just the two shown in the example. It captured current staff levels, forecast future staff availability, defined staffing requirements, and calculated staffing gaps and surpluses.

Strategic Staffing Issues

Even given the uncertainty surrounding the business, several well-defined staffing issues were identified. One staffing issue emerged early in the project. The three job streams (i.e., economist, education specialist, and operations officer) had been designed to be quite different. However, a

Figure 10-2.

Job	Region 1 HQ	Region 1 HQ–Field	Region 1 Local	Region 2 HQ	Region 2 HQ–Field	Region 2 Local	Corporate
Lead economist							
Senior economist							
Economist							
Lead education specialist							
Senior education specialist							
Education specialist							
Lead operations officer							
Senior operations officer							
Operations officer							
Operations analyst							
Research analyst							

review of existing job profiles, internal postings, external ads, and other documents showed that staff in all three streams were primarily playing the same role—that of project manager, not that of technical expert. The capabilities required in the three streams were more alike than different. Although many of the individuals in the sector had been hired because of their technical expertise, most of this specific expertise was not being applied; instead, they were working as generic task managers. The more these individuals focused on project management, the more rusty and outdated their technical expertise became. Moreover, many of these people had become disheartened and disillusioned—they had been hired by the bank to apply their expertise, but they were unable to do so. This lack of differentiation would be less of a problem if the bank were to focus on lending, but it was a critical problem if the bank were to focus on development.

A second staffing issue was related to organization structure. While each region required some education expertise, not all of the regions were large enough to afford full-time education staff. Since the smaller regions could not afford individual experts, many of them had created positions that spanned or combined functional areas (e.g., education, health, and social programs). These regions then chose to employ staff with some expertise in these multiple functions rather than take on experts in each area. While most of the people playing these combined roles met the minimum qualifications for each functional area, few of them were experts in all the areas in which they worked. As a result, there was a general lowering of the bar regarding technical expertise. This was a particular problem in countries and situations where extremely deep expertise was required. This lack of deep expertise would only get worse where the bank was called on to provide development assistance in addition to capital.

A third staffing issue was related to the move to program-based lending. To support this approach, the bank would need staff that was experienced in creating and developing the high-level policies and strategic objectives that served as the standards by which country performance was measured. Program-based lending required staff with experience in meeting with high-level government officials and conducting meaningful policy-level dialogue. The bank did not have a large enough pool of staff with this expertise to support a significant number of program-based loans.

A fourth staffing issue involved the inappropriate use of consultants. In a move designed to reduce fixed costs and provide additional flexibility, the bank had mandated that most staffing needs in all units (including the education unit) should be met by a blend of full-time, "core" staff and short-term consultants. In fact, it set a specific ratio of core staff to consultants that could not be exceeded. For many units, this mandate reduced the number of "core" staff and increased the number of short-term consultants that were working. However, in many cases, there was more "value-adding" work required than could be handled by the core staff that remained. As a result, core staff tended to be "overprogrammed," and less experienced contingent staff and short-term consultants were doing much of the "real" work that might be completed more effectively by core staff. This approach was inefficient in the near term and also created significant problems in the longer term. Critical expertise that the development unit would need in the future was being developed in short-term consultants, not core staff. Consequently, this needed expertise could be lost as contracts expired and these short-term consultants left the bank.

The final staffing issue related to management depth. There was an insufficient number of qualified managers available to fill the vacancies that were expected in the near future. This lack of qualified candidates would probably force the development unit to replace those that retired with external hires. Given that the bank's prior experience with placing external candidates in senior-level positions was tenuous at best, an overreliance on external hires could create significant performance and staffing problems in the next few years.

There were also several issues regarding the bank's staffing processes and practices. Most staffing programs were reactive in nature; staffing efforts began only after specific openings were identified. Other programs were not specifically needs-based. In many cases, "promotions" were position upgrades based on performance and credentials, not staffing actions that were implemented to meet particular needs. A batch hiring process brought skilled individuals to the bank, but these individuals were normally not recruited or selected to fill particular openings.

Finally, the bank tended to have a one-size-fits-all approach to staffing processes. New processes tended to be implemented across the board. Relatively few targeted solutions were developed and implemented to address specific staffing issues.

The Staffing Strategies and Plans That Emerged

As a result of this project, several staffing strategies were proposed to address the staffing issues that were identified:

- **Differentiate job streams to support needed specialization.** Job profiles, accountabilities, and definitions of required skills would be changed to allow technical specialists to develop and apply the deep expertise needed to support the bank's mission. Education economists would focus on economics, education specialists would focus on their particular area of expertise, and operations officers would focus on project and task management.

- **Position and develop the corporate unit as a "center of excellence."** Rather than being purely administrative, the corporate unit would now provide the regions with the specific expertise that they currently could not afford. Individuals with deep economic and education expertise would be part of the corporate unit, but would be allocated to the regions on an as-needed basis. This would allow a region that had a need for a third of a full-time equivalent in education to apply the needed expertise. The region would no longer have to compromise by using a less experienced generalist who happened to be available.

- **Recruit and develop high-level policy development expertise.** Since the bank lacked individuals with this expertise, it would actively recruit from the outside to fill the positions needed to support the move to program-based lending. These recruits would be provided with accelerated development so that they could get up to speed on the bank's procedures and operations.

- **Redefine the role of short-term consultants.** The unit would identify and designate as "core" those jobs that were absolutely critical to implementing plans and strategies, required specific technical or functional expertise on an ongoing basis, provided a significant competitive advantage, and required a full, in-depth knowledge of bank or development unit policies, procedures, and systems. Wherever feasible, these core positions would be filled by full-time staff. Further, all of the unit's recruiting and development efforts would focus on these core positions. All positions that did not meet one of these four criteria would be filled using consultants. Short-term consultants should also provide any expertise that was needed for a short period at a particular point in time.

- **Develop management candidates in advance of need.** The development unit would work to develop a "pool" of candidates for critical senior management positions in advance of need. This would ensure that there were qualified internal candidates that could be considered and selected to fill senior management openings that might arise (whether as a result of retirements, transfers, or voluntary turnover). Effective management succession and development processes are quite proactive. They usually include the definition of specific management requirements and the identification and development of candidates (in advance of need). The objective of such a process should not be to identify the specific individual who will be placed in a particular position when the incumbent leaves.

Needless to say, these staffing strategies could not be finalized or implemented until the significant business issues (as described previously) were addressed. The managers in the development unit were not in a position to dictate this resolution. Instead, they needed to develop contingency plans and compromises that would allow the sector to move forward with its revitalization as solutions to the business issues were developed.

The Role of Quantitative Analysis in This Project

In most strategic staffing projects, a staffing model is developed and used to define specific staffing plans and actions that are needed to eliminate (or at least reduce) critical staffing gaps and shortages that are expected in each planning period. While gaps and surpluses were defined as part of this project, specific staffing plans and actions were not. Managers were willing to talk about qualitative staffing issues and strategies, but they were reluctant to discuss those staffing issues in quantitative terms. Some did not see the value of being so specific. Others had participated in quantitative workforce planning efforts in the past that had proved to be primarily "number-crunching exercises" that were of little value. Still others had done some quantitative staffing analyses of their own areas and saw little benefit in doing a similar thing for the unit as a whole. Most managers seemed to think that implementing the specific, quantitative staff planning approach that had been proposed would be very difficult, given some of the bank's current practices regarding headcount planning and control. Some of these impediments included:

- **Inflexible budgeting processes.** Staff planning was part of the annual budgeting cycle. This made it difficult to adjust staffing requirements and staffing plans as changes occurred during the year. Further, since managers had to rejustify staffing needs before even previously approved positions could be filled, proactive staff planning and action was difficult at best.

- **Fixed staff cost ratios.** The fixed/variable staffing ratios that had been set limited management flexibility regarding staffing decisions. The ratios were not fully based on need and were set at somewhat arbitrary levels. In some units, effective staffing might require a higher percentage of "core" staff than the ratio allowed. In other units, it might be possible to perform the work adequately with a higher percentage of consultants. The fixed nature of the ratios eliminated the possibility of this needed variation.

- **Unclear accountability for staffing decisions.** Within the bank's matrix structure, accountability for staffing was not well defined. Managers preferred to have staff report directly to them and were not comfortable with using staff (no matter how highly skilled) that reported to another manager. In concept, functional managers were to play critical roles in staffing regional positions, but in reality, the regional managers were the ones making the "final" staffing decisions. Because staffing accountability was not fully defined, some managers were able to "work around" the system (e.g., not communicating openings until preferred candidates were identified and hiring talented individuals who did not necessarily meet predefined position requirements). Many of these work-around practices were contrary to the open, proactive nature of strategic staffing.

- **Strict policies and procedures regarding staff reduction, made it difficult to add appropriately skilled staff.** The bank's policies and procedures regarding staff reductions were quite strict. Because of this high standard, managers were unwilling to take the difficult steps necessary to remove or redeploy staff—even those whose performance was inadequate or whose skills had become obsolete.

Given that headcounts and budgets were strictly limited, new recruits who had newly required skills could be hired only if other employees left to make room for them. Yet the bank's strict staff reduction policies made it hard for managers to remove poor performers in order to make room for these needed recruits. Again, these practices made it difficult to be proactive regarding staffing and to implement staffing practices that would meet the unit's needs.

In order to implement strategic staffing effectively, including its quantitative components, the bank needed to change some of these practices. To the extent that the impediments remained, the bank would be unable to plan strategically to meet its staffing needs and would be forced instead to react on a tactical, short-term basis.

Because of these concerns, the quantitative staffing analysis and planning proceeded no further. While the lack of a well-developed quantitative staffing model may not prove to be an issue in the near term, the lack of quantitative staffing information may become more of a problem in the future because:

- **Staff losses were not considered.** Even in its preliminary format, the model indicated that the numbers of staff that should be added during the planning horizon were higher than management estimates for that same period. The primary cause of these differences was staff losses. In some cases, managers were thinking incrementally (i.e., determining how many more than the current headcount would be needed) and were not considering the fact that staff would be leaving (e.g., as a result of contracts with individuals expiring, voluntary turnover, and probable retirements). For example, a manager might estimate that three staff should be hired to support planned growth (thinking in terms of a net increase). In fact, six staff might be required (the increase of three plus three more to replace other staff who will be leaving the bank during the planning period). The more detailed, quantitative analysis would have identified the actual number of openings that could be expected more precisely. Staffing plans that do not consider the need to replace individuals who leave are ineffective and incomplete.

- **Progress measures could not be created and applied.** As stated earlier, the bank's board not only charged the education unit with meeting its business and staffing objectives, but also asked for regular progress reports that addressed staffing needs. The lack of quantitative data would make it difficult for the unit to report what its needs were, the particular staffing actions that were taken, the impact these actions had, and what needs remained.

- **Plans would be difficult to implement.** It is always extremely difficult to implement qualitative plans effectively and efficiently. By definition, qualitative plans can only be directional in nature; they cannot and do not describe scope measures in any way. Such plans may be able to determine that "more" staff with policy-making expertise will be needed, for example, but they cannot describe how many more such staff will be needed and when those people should be placed. If the organization hires 10 more people, is that the right number? Might there be a need for more than just those 10? Might fewer be needed? Staffing plans just can't be developed or implemented effectively unless they contain some quantitative measures.

Conclusions and Recommendations

This project did a good job of raising and crystallizing critical staffing issues. The strategic staffing process provided a good forum for discussing these issues and proposing and evaluating staffing strategies. For the most part, the strategies that were proposed were a direct result of these discussions and had not been considered before. However, the reluctance to analyze the quantitative data in detail proved problematic later on; managers found it increasingly difficult to implement purely "directional" plans and measure progress against generic objectives.

Even though bank policies and procedures may have inhibited the effectiveness of the strategic staffing process, they in no way prevented its implementation. Based on the findings drawn and the conclusions that were reached during this project, it was recommended that the education unit take the following steps:

- Complete the quantitative staff planning work that was suspended, developing staffing plans for all regions and increasing the planning horizon from one year to three years.
- Implement each of the staffing strategies described previously.
- Analyze each of the impediments to effective strategic staffing that were described, identify those that might be modified or eliminated, then create plans for making those modifications and working within those that cannot change.

Case 3: A Utility
Introduction

As discussed earlier in this book, strategic staffing/workforce planning efforts are often limited by a lack of required data. I have included this case because it exemplified exactly the opposite—this project was a showcase for how powerful (and accurate) the strategic staffing/workforce planning process can be when rich data sets are available and can be applied.

The Strategic Context

The utility in this example is headquartered in a southern state but has operations in eight separate geographic areas spread across several states throughout the southeastern United States. Service and repair positions are among the most critical jobs in any utility. These people are critical to the smooth running of the company (e.g., maintaining maximum "up time" for the system) and are often also the "face" of the company when dealing with customers. This utility was specifically looking to create some kind of staffing model that would accurately forecast the demand for service personnel and define the staffing actions needed to maintain these staffing levels on an ongoing basis. Staffing actions to be considered included internal movement, use of job pools/job sharing, overtime, use of regular part-time staff, transfers to and from other service jobs in the company, callbacks of retirees, use of external contractors, and recruiting. Of particular interest was the impact that retirements were going to have on this segment of the workforce.

The strategic staffing/workforce planning process focused on the two largest (and arguably most critical) positions, Field Service Representative and Utility Technician, across all eight service areas of the company.

The Strategic Staffing Model

Given the focus of this project, a fairly simple staffing model was required. The model would include only two positions, field service rep and utility tech. These would be the rows of the model. Columns would be used to capture the eight geographic areas. Given the nature of the decisions to be made, the utility chose to create a rolling four-quarter model. The model would be updated each quarter, looking out at the next four quarters. Finally, the model would be constructed to provide results at both the individual (i.e., "whole body") and FTE level.

One of the most interesting components of the model was a module that was created to calculate staffing requirements for each job in each area. As mentioned earlier, the utility was a veritable gold mine of work and activity data for each of the two positions that were included in the analysis. Each service vehicle had been equipped with a computer and a GPS system. All scheduling was computerized, with schedules and updates transmitted to each individual service vehicle throughout the day. Service personnel logged the time they started and ended each call and activity. These data were very detailed, completely accurate, and gathered on a regular, ongoing basis. They were also fully segmented by job type, geographic area, and month. Using spreadsheets, the data were combined in a unique way to define required staffing levels. The following data were used:

- **Time standards by order type.** Based on a wealth of actual, historical information that was updated monthly, the utility calculated the standard amount of time that was required to complete every type of order (e.g., specific tasks like turning service on or off at a customer location) that Field Service Reps and Utility Techs were called upon to perform. There were approximately 125 different order types for each of the two positions. Separate standards were set for orders that were completed (i.e., where service was performed and problems were resolved) and those that could not be completed (e.g., where a repair could not be made because a customer was not home). All service personnel logged actual time spent on each service call (by type); these data were used to update the standards to keep them current and realistic.

- **Order volumes.** The company tracked on its computer system the number of orders that were filled for each order type for each month of the year. This included both completed orders (where a service was provided) and uncompleted orders (where a service call could not be fulfilled).

- **"Paper order" volumes.** Occasionally, service orders were created using a paper system. These "paper orders" represented actual work, but they were not part of the computerized scheduling system. They were, however, recorded in a separate database.

- **"Windshield time."** By comparing the time one job ended and the time that the next job started, average transit times between jobs could be determined for each area (e.g., allowing for differences in transit times between rural and urban areas).

All these data were gathered, segmented by job type and service area, and placed in spreadsheets. The demand component of the model was calculated as follows (on an area-by-area basis):

- Assumptions were made about the order volume that was expected in the coming year. Based on changes in the number of customers to be served, current order volumes were adjusted up or down as required. These estimates also accounted for seasonality. Separate adjustments were made for each service area.

- Order volumes were totaled for each order type (simply summing the number of computer-based orders and the number of paper-based orders).

- Time allocated to orders was calculated by multiplying the total number of orders of each type that were expected by the time standard for that order.

- Total windshield time was calculated by multiplying the windshield time standard by the total number of orders of each type.

- Total time spent on service calls was calculated by adding total time spent on orders and total windshield time.

- Staffing requirements were calculated by dividing this total number by the number of hours available per FTE (assumed to be 2,080 hours/year/FTE).

The results of these calculations were automatically fed into the demand component of the staffing model that was described earlier. Supply-side data were entered directly into the model. The forecasted supply of staff ("supply then") included a special adjustment for productivity that is described in detail later in the case study.

Adjusting for "Downtime". Another interesting aspect of this project was the concept of "downtime." Most strategic staffing/workforce planning processes tend to assume that each individual counts as one full FTE. This organization knew that a certain amount of downtime was actually scheduled for all service personnel and additional, unplanned downtime could be expected. As a result, the strategic staffing/workforce planning process had to incorporate an adjustment that took into account the fact that the actual availability or productivity of each person was something less than one full FTE.

Once again, the organization had a wealth of good data that could be used to create this adjustment. In fact, a specific, different adjustment was created for each separate service area, based on data for the individuals actually working in that area. For example, the vacation time component was calculated based on the actual vacation entitlement of each person working in that area. The reductions in productive time considered included the following:

- **Vacation time.** As stated earlier, the actual entitlements of the service personnel in each area were used. Historically, these workers took all the vacation time that they were entitled to.

- **Sick days.** Eight days of sick time per year per individual was assumed.

- **Displaced time.** This was time that was spent on company business, but not on service calls. On average, this amounted to 16 hours/year/employee.

- **Training time.** The corporate standard of 54 hours of training/year/ employee was used.

- **Holiday time.** The corporate standard of 10 days/year/employee was used.

- **Paid breaks.** Each service employee was entitled to two 15-minute breaks per day.

- **Start time.** Each service employee was allowed 10 minutes at the start of each day to prepare for work (e.g., to review the day's schedule and inventory the tools on the truck).

- **Bereavement leave.** While it did not have a major impact, an assumption of 1 day per individual every four years was made.

- **Meetings.** Time spent in meetings amounted to 47 hours/year/employee. This assumption was based on actual historical data.

Time lost to all these categories amounted to approximately 0.30 FTE (of course, the actual value varied by service area). Consequently, each full-time worker was actually "productive" only about 70 percent of the time. This number was used to reduce the FTEs that were actually available. For example, if a job category in a given area included 10 staff currently, "supply then" would be 7 FTEs (i.e., 70 percent of the 10 staff), not the full 10. On the other hand, given the algorithms that were used, demand was defined in terms of full FTEs. Consequently, for the sample job category just mentioned, the model would show a deficit of 3 FTEs even if "supply now" and "demand then" were both 10 FTEs (assuming that there would be no uncontrollable staffing actions):

"Supply now":	10 FTEs
"Supply then":	0.70(10 FTEs)
	= 7 FTEs
"Demand then":	10 FTEs
Staffing gap:	7 FTEs – 10 FTEs
	= −3 FTEs

Thus, staffing plans had to account for this downtime in addition to addressing any normal staffing gaps and surpluses that arose.

The Staffing Strategies and Plans That Emerged

For this organization, the real value of strategic staffing/workforce planning was in the detailed staffing plans that emerged. Never before had the company had such comprehensive, detailed information regarding its staffing needs. The strategic staffing/workforce planning process provided managers with an opportunity to apply all the staffing-related data that they had been gathering in a way that yielded realistic, implementable results. Area managers could now define specific plans for both full-time and contract/part-time staff.

One significant staffing strategy also emerged. Because needs were defined in a consistent way across all service areas, they could be compared directly for the first time. This allowed the organization to develop some preliminary methods for sharing staff among geographic areas in ways that balanced surpluses and deficits at the same time—thus benefiting both the "lender" and the "borrower" of that staff.

Finally, the implementation of staffing plans was given a boost by the credibility of the process itself. The most senior staff in each area (line managers, remember, not just HR) developed the process and incorporated realistic assumptions that the organization as a whole could support. They also deemed that the results of the staffing requirements analysis were realistic and usable. These managers also controlled the resources that were needed to implement the staffing plans that were created.

Additional Examples

Here are several more examples of companies that have successfully implemented strategic staffing/workforce planning processes. For each example, I have summarized the strategic context in which the strategy was developed, described the components of the strategic staffing process that was used, and highlighted the outcomes and benefits that were realized.

Telecommunications Company

Strategic Context. This company was about to implement a new, radically different technology for voice transmission. The change was to be installed nationwide, on an office-by-office basis, over a four-year period. The company anticipated that the change in technology would affect required capabilities and staffing levels in both technical (e.g., local facility troubleshooting and repair) and "soft" (e.g., customer service) skills areas. Complicating this situation, many individuals in the current workforce were nearing retirement.

Strategic Staffing Approach. Initially, staff planning efforts focused on technical jobs (separate models for customer service positions were completed later on). For planning purposes, the company created the new role of central office technician, a category that encompassed several existing jobs and titles. First, the company defined the skills and capabilities that would be required in this new position to fully support the implementation of the new technology. Next, it defined how many such technicians would be required, in which locations, during which planning periods (following the rollout plan that had been prepared). Several staffing models and supply/demand scenarios were developed, including some that analyzed the impact of several different retirement scenarios.

Outcomes/Benefits. After a review of the various scenarios, the company decided that most of its needs could, in fact, be met through redeployment of its current employees. It created specific redeployment plans for each planning period and defined the specific training and development that would be needed to support those moves. The company also developed plans for selective hiring and targeted staff reductions (e.g., eliminating staff with obsolete skills who were unwilling or unable to develop new skills) in cases where needs could not be met through redeployment.

Insurance Company

Strategic Context. As a result of a strong economy, this company expected to grow the consumer component of its business quite rapidly over the coming five-year period. Unfortunately, the strong economy also meant that opportunities abounded; thus, an increased number of managers were expected to leave the company to take jobs elsewhere. This combination of business growth and increased turnover would create a large number of openings for branch managers that would need to be filled in the coming years. The traditional career path for branch managers (through underwriting) would be unable to provide a sufficient number of qualified branch manager candidates, so alternative sources of talent had to be identified.

Strategic Staffing Approach. The company created a staffing model that focused on branch manager positions and the career paths that fed these positions. The model defined how many candidates could reasonably be expected to move along the traditional career path through underwriting into branch manager slots and how many additional openings would have to be filled through external hiring and increased internal placements. Two scenarios were generated. The first assumed that the development and promotion of candidates would proceed normally and that all additional openings would be filled through external recruitment. The second assumed that accelerated development and movement would be used to increase the number of internal candidates that would be available during the planning horizon, with recruitment used only as a last resort.

Outcomes/Benefits. By analyzing the two scenarios simultaneously, the company was able to determine the optimum blend of accelerated promotions and external recruiting that was needed to fill the branch manager openings that were anticipated. The model allowed the company to plan for the development effort that would be needed in terms of scope (how many individuals needed to be trained), objectives (what capabilities needed to be developed), and timing (when training needed to begin). The model also let the company determine how many external candidates would be needed, and when.

Aerospace Company

Strategic Context. This government contractor always worked on several major projects simultaneously. To facilitate its accounting, the company chose to create a separate organization unit for each project, with each such unit operating relatively autonomously. Given the nature of the work that was being done, there was a great need for engineering talent in all project units. In the past, each project and organization had created its own staffing plan to meet the needs of that particular project, hiring engineers as the project geared up and laying them off when the project geared down (or was cancelled). Because the projects were run separately (and there was no real coordination of staffing among projects), it was not unusual for one unit to be laying off engineers while another was looking for external candidates with those very same skills. Needless to say, this uncoordinated approach was costly, created much confusion, and had a negative impact on continuity and morale.

Strategic Staffing Approach. The company decided that it needed to coordinate engineering staffing among projects. It created a single staffing model that analyzed engineering requirements and availability by discipline, across projects. This allowed the company to manage its critical engineering talent as a pool, allocating engineers to and from projects as required.

Outcomes/Benefits. Obviously, there was an immediate and significant reduction in simultaneous hiring and firing, and a major reduction in related staffing transaction costs. The change in staffing practices also brought about improved utilization of engineering talent and experience and more efficient placement of engineering staff.

Medical Center

Strategic Context. A major chain of hospitals decided to open a new medical center in a geographic area that it did not currently serve. The size and scope of the facility was determined after a rigorous analysis of the demographics of that new area.

Staffing the facility with the right talent was critical. Some positions would be filled using local talent; experienced staff that was transferred from existing facilities would fill other jobs. A key question that emerged was: How could the company staff the new facility with the experienced talent that it needed while minimizing the talent drain on the existing medical centers?

Strategic Staffing Approach. The company created a series of staffing models that included the new medical center and all other existing facilities from which talent might be drawn. The models were segmented by unit (e.g., Medical/Surgical, Intensive Care, Emergency Medicine). Separate models were necessary because different assumptions had to be made regarding the likelihood that individuals with these skills would be willing to commute to the new center. For example, intensive care unit staff might be willing to commute long distances (e.g., because job opportunities for individuals with these specialized skills were limited), but medical/surgical staff would not (e.g., because they had many opportunities to work at other medical facilities that were close to their homes). In each case, the staffing model defined specific needs for both the new and the existing medical centers. Where needs in the new center were met by transferring staff from existing facilities, the models and plans defined the staffing actions to be taken to fill the openings that the transfers created.

As part of the strategic staffing process, the company also conducted an economic analysis of the area to be served (to better define the mix of patient care services that would be needed) and a demographic analysis (to identify what skills would be available in the area surrounding the new facility).

Outcomes/Benefits. Several important conclusions were reached. The company discovered that there was a critical shortage of skilled medical technicians in the geographic area surrounding the new medical center. To meet this need in the near term, the company was forced to relocate many more individuals from existing facilities than it had originally thought. The staffing model allowed the company to identify (and develop plans to address) the "back fill" issues that the large number of relocations created. Many of those who were replacing the relocating staff needed specific training so that they could perform in their new assignments.

The company determined that future, longer-term staffing needs for medical technicians in the new facility had to be met locally; additional relocation from existing medical centers was not feasible. To this end, the company actively funded external education (e.g., trade schools), built alliances with nearby teaching hospitals, established community college license programs, and implemented a co-op program at local high schools. It also convened a task force to address recruiting issues on an ongoing basis.

3

Implementing and Supporting Your Strategic Staffing/ Workforce Planning Process

11

Implementing Your Process Effectively

Implementing any new methodology, process, or tool can be a daunting task. No matter how well it is designed, a tool can fail miserably if it is not rolled out effectively. Strategic staffing/workforce planning is no exception. This section describes an approach for implementing the strategic staffing/workforce planning process that I have found to be particularly useful. (By the way, while this approach is specifically appropriate for the strategic staffing process, it also applies equally well whenever a new process or tool is being introduced.) The section also summarizes implementation roles and responsibilities and highlights some obstacles that may hinder the effective implementation of your strategic staffing process.

An Effective Implementation Framework

Here is a model that you can use to help you create an effective plan for implementing the strategic staffing/workforce planning process in your organization (see Figure 11-1). Whenever an organization is implementing a new process, it must balance two separate parameters: scope and impact.

- **Scope.** Think of scope as the size of the group to be included in the process. It might be defined in terms of the number of jobs, job levels, locations, functions, or organization units. Usually, scope is not defined in terms of the number of individuals. Simply defined, you could implement this process for "a few" jobs or units, for "many," or for something in between. In Figure 11-1, scope is shown on the x (horizontal) axis.

- **Impact.** Think of impact as the extent to which the new process is positively affecting the organization. A new process could have an

Figure 11-1.

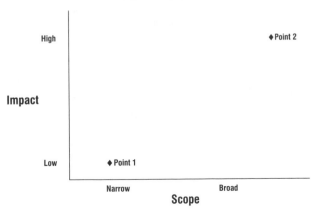

impact that ranges from low to high. In Figure 11-1, impact is shown on the *y* (vertical) axis.

If this is truly a new process, you are probably starting out at point 1 at the bottom left-hand side of Figure 11-1 (i.e., there is no process currently or the existing process is having little impact over a narrow organization scope). Normally, your objective would be to get to point 2 on the upper right-hand side of Figure 11-1, where your new process will be having a high impact over a broad scope. But how do you get to point 2 from point 1?

Clearly, it would be possible to get to point 2 from point 1 in a single step only if massive resources were available to support implementation. Because staff time, money, and other critical resources are almost always limited, it is generally not possible to have a high impact over that broad scope all at once. Some kind of step-by-step approach to implementation is more feasible. There are two basic approaches to consider.

Approach A

Figure 11-2 depicts a horizontal approach—approach A. Your objective is still to have high impact over the whole organization, using a step-by-step approach. The "given" with approach A is that you must initially include a broad scope of the organization in your implementation. With approach A, you complete *each* implementation step (thus having some impact) for a *wide scope* (perhaps even all) of the organization for which the new process is being developed. Once a step is complete for that broad scope, the next step can be taken (again including all the units that are included in this implementation). Following this step-by-step approach will allow you to implement the new process over the entire scope of the organization.

Figure 11-2. Approach A.

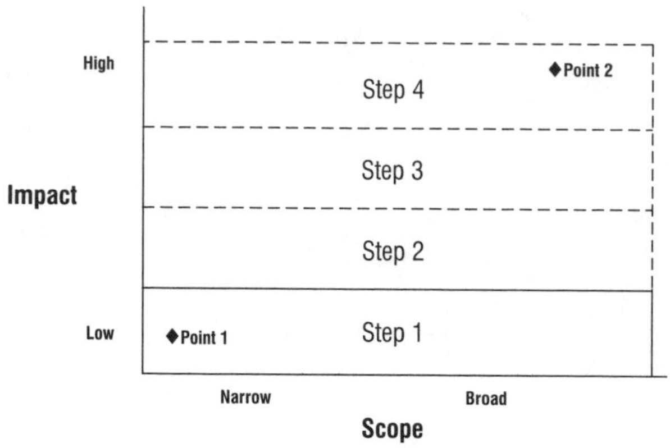

Here is an example of approach A. Suppose that your staffing process included these four basic steps:

Step 1: Understand the longer-term business context.

Step 2: Define staffing requirements and availability.

Step 3: Define required staffing strategies and plans.

Step 4: Implement staffing plans.

Suppose further that your objective was to implement this process simultaneously in four organization units. If you were using approach A, you would first develop an understanding of the long-term business context of each of the four units. Once that understanding was developed, you would define staffing requirements and availability for all four units (step 2). Once step 2 was complete, you would create staffing strategies and plans for all four units (step 3). Once these staffing strategies and plans were complete, you could begin step 4 (implementing those plans) for all units. Once step 4 was complete, you would have met your objective of creating and implementing a staffing strategy for each of the four units.

Approach B

Figure 11-3 depicts a vertical approach—approach B. Your overall objective is still to have high impact over a broad scope of the organization, and you must still use a step-by-step approach. The "given" this time is that you must have a high impact right away (as opposed to having some impact over a broad scope, as you did with approach A). With approach B, you complete *all* the implementation steps (thus having high impact) for *one* piece of the organization, thus applying the entire process over a narrow scope of the organization. Once all steps have been taken for a given piece of the organization, the process can be implemented in a second piece.

The entire process is implemented on a piece-by-piece basis until it

Figure 11-3. Approach B.

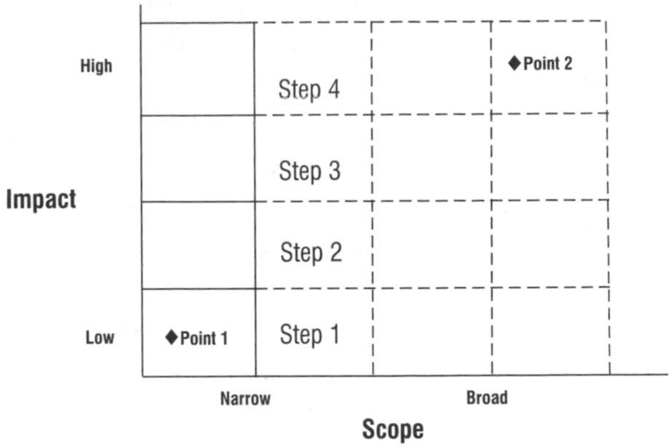

has been fully implemented across that broad scope. Like approach A, approach B also allows you to eventually implement the new process over the entire scope of the organization.

Here is an example of approach B. Suppose that your strategic staffing process included the same four basic steps described in the example for approach A. Suppose further that your overall objective was to implement this process eventually in four organization units. If you were using approach B, you would first develop an understanding of the long-term business context of unit 1, then define the staffing requirements and availability for unit 1, then define staffing strategies and plans for unit 1, and finally begin implementing the staffing strategies and plans for unit 1. Once the implementation of the unit 1 plans had been initiated, you could begin the process for unit 2. Similarly, once plans for unit 2 were under way, you could begin the process for unit 3, and then for unit 4. This would meet your objective of creating and implementing a staffing strategy for each of the four units.

Which Approach to Use

Which approach is more appropriate? Would you choose approach A or approach B? At first glance, it seems that the correct answer would be "sometimes A and sometimes B." In reality, when you are implementing a strategic staffing process (especially for the first time), I fervently believe that approach B is always the preferred approach. And just in case you think that I have left some wiggle room in that conclusion, let me say that approach A never works. Here are some reasons why I feel so strongly that this is the case.

The Impact Argument. Part of the reasoning for choosing Approach B is rooted in a very particular definition of impact. For this model, I always define "high impact" as "fixing a problem," "resolving an issue," or "answering a question." In these cases, there just is no benefit to having "some" impact. All these definitions all make "impact" a binary concept. Either you fix a problem or you don't. Either you resolve an issue or you don't. Either you answer a question or you don't. Consequently, given my definition, either you have high impact or you have no impact at all. With approach B, when you set out to implement a new process, your objective is to have high impact in the near term, which means that by definition you must narrow the scope of your efforts to ensure that you can solve, address, or answer fully the problem, issue, or question for that piece of the organization. In fact, each of the vertical bars shown in Figure 11-3 is not really a "piece" of the organization at all—it is really one of the most critical staffing issues that you have identified in your strategic staffing/ workforce planning process.

Contrast this approach with approach A. Remember that I have defined "impact" in terms of solving problems or addressing critical staffing issues. How much of any staffing issue can you address by taking just step 1 (e.g., understanding the unit's business plans), as you would if you were following approach A? None! That step is necessary, but taking it does not in itself address the issue at all. What about defining staffing requirements and availability? Does that in itself solve any problems? No, it doesn't. What about the creation of staffing strategies and plans? Again, this is a necessary step, but it adds no value by itself. Only when the staffing strategies and plans are implemented is there any value seen. With approach B, you begin to add value very quickly, once all steps are taken and the first issue is addressed.

The Elapsed Time Argument. In Chapters 2 and 4 of this book, I suggest that instead of creating staffing strategies for business units, you create staffing strategies that address specific, critical issues. Approach B is particularly effective in these cases. You should narrow the scope of your initial efforts by focusing on one *issue* at a time, not one *unit* at a time. In this way, you will have the high impact you are looking for when you create and implement the staffing strategies that best address that critical issue.

If you were to use approach A, how long would it take for you to understand the long-term business context of all four units in the example? Probably several months—if not longer. How long would it then take to define staffing requirements and availability for all those units? Probably several more months. What about developing staffing strategies and defining specific staffing plans for each unit? Yet more time. By the time you got around to implementing the strategies and plans, you would be "fixing" the problems that you thought would occur when you began the process a year or more ago—which are not necessarily the issues that managers now consider critical.

The Credibility Argument. By actually resolving critical issues sequentially, you will be building credibility for your process and your expertise. You will be building a reputation as a business-oriented problem solver, not just an implementer of processes that may or may not have significant impact. The more problems you solve, the more managers will think positively of you, and the more opportunities you will have to solve critical problems. These satisfied managers will become your best marketers, telling their colleagues of the value that you added.

What impact will an implementation using approach A have on your credibility? How long will managers be willing to wait for you to address their staffing issues? Probably not as long as a full implementation of approach A will require. What will happen if, after much time has passed and little value has been realized (while you conduct the first three steps of your process), you finally begin to implement strategies that address the wrong issues? Is that going to improve your credibility? I doubt it.

The Education Argument. Many organizations that are implementing strategic staffing/workforce planning processes are just not sure what an effective process entails or what form it should take. They do not know what data are required or what outcomes can be expected. By fully implementing the process for a given issue, you will be creating a realistic example that you can use to educate your audience regarding what an effective process includes and entails. Effective process examples, created as you address critical issues, can be used to train others in the strategic staffing/ workforce planning process and applications.

The Leverage Argument. One possible drawback to approach B is that it appears that only one issue can be addressed at a time. That is not necessarily the case. Most companies create a task force or work team that is charged with developing and implementing the strategic staffing process for the first time. Suppose that there are six members on such a team. The entire team, working together, can develop a staffing strategy that addresses the first issue, perhaps completing its work in a month or two. In so doing, each member of the team learns what strategic staffing entails and how effective strategies are developed. Once the first issue has been addressed, each of the six team members can lead a team (with each team including five new team members), permitting six simultaneous efforts to develop staffing strategies for six more issues. Thus, at the end of a three-month period, seven strategies will have been developed. If the process continues (theoretically speaking, of course), thirty-six more issues can be addressed in the third wave. Needless to say, while this strict geometric progression may not continue, this approach certainly will allow a large number of staffing issues to be addressed in a relatively short period of time.

Are you still not convinced that approach B is usually the better way to proceed? Here is one more example. Suppose that you have been called in to develop a plan to fight a massive wildfire. This huge fire is threatening a thousand square miles of territory that includes populated areas, industrial zones, parks, and wilderness. Suppose further that you have a limited supply of water, flame-retarding chemicals, and firefighters at your disposal. What would you do? I seriously doubt that you would spread the water and chemicals evenly over the entire thousand square miles. In fact, that might be the least effective use of your scarce firefighting resources. There might be some initial benefit, but soon the fires would flare up, and you would then have no resources left to fight them. Instead, you should probably allocate the water and chemicals wisely, in ways that would maximize the effectiveness of their use. It is likely that you would first begin to fight the parts of the fire that were directly threatening the lives and safety of people. Only after those parts of the fire had been put out (or at least substantially brought under control) would you move to fight the parts that were threatening property but not lives. In the meantime, the parts of the fire that are burning in the unpopulated wilderness may just have to keep burning. If, after controlling the parts of the fire that were threatening lives and property, you still have some resources left, you might then move on to fight the fire in wilderness areas. By fighting the fire sequentially, and in order of priority, you would maximize the impact of your limited supply of water and chemicals.

Your organization may be analogous to this wildfire. There may be dozens of fires that seem to require your attention. Many managers will be asking you to help them address their staffing issues. However, your resources (i.e., your time and your budget), just like the water and chemicals, are limited and must be used wisely. Clearly, the least effective approach is to spread your limited resources evenly across all the issues to be addressed (i.e., doing something for everyone). This may bring some initial relief, but no manager's staffing issues will be fully addressed if you do this. Like burning embers that were not fully extinguished, the issues will just flare up later—but by then you will have exhausted your resources and will be in no position to fight further. Just as you need to set priorities in fighting the wildfire, you must set priorities when addressing staffing issues. Just as you did not move on to the parts of the fire that were threatening only property until you had brought those that were threatening people under control, you must address one staffing issue before trying to move on to the next. And just as you left the parts of the fire in the wilderness burning, you may find it necessary to leave some less critical staffing issues unaddressed.

In summary, approach B (i.e., narrow scope/high impact) is far superior and should be implemented each time a staffing strategy is to be developed. When you are launching strategic staffing for the first time, select a critical issue and work to create and implement a staffing plan that fully addresses that issue. By so doing, you will have a positive impact on the organization in the near term (a quick win), you will build your own credibility, and you will clearly demonstrate the value of the process to your organization.

Implementation Roles and Responsibilities

Now that we have set the stage for effective implementation, it's time to define roles and accountabilities. Ongoing roles and accountabilities are described in detail in Chapter 15; these paragraphs focus on the roles and accountabilities associated with the initial implementation of your strategic staffing/workforce planning process.

The responsibility for developing and implementing staffing strategies and plans lies with those who define the amount and type of resources that will be needed to implement business strategies and then allocate those resources once they become available. In most companies, line managers play this role.

There is no question but that line managers are expected to manage financial and material resources. I think this also applies to human resources. I strongly believe that, in the long run at least, the primary responsibility for developing and implementing staffing strategies and plans lies with line managers, not human resource (HR) staff. Are you unconvinced? Compare staff planning to the budgeting process.

Budgeting is a clearly defined management responsibility. Managers fully understand this and work accordingly; most organizations even provide training opportunities so that managers can better understand the budgeting process and build their skills in this area. The finance function usually supports the process by providing structure and assistance, but it does not prepare budgets for line managers. Why should staff planning be any different? In some ways, the staff planning process and the budgeting process are really quite similar. Both require planning, definition of required resources, allocation of those resources, measurement of results, and adjustments to allocations if the objectives are not met. Are not people just another resource that line managers should manage?

Clearly, then, strategic staffing/workforce planning is not the legacy of HR or the key to long-term job security among HR staff! It is the job of

HR to ensure that line managers are doing this well. HR staff must play critical supporting roles if managers are to create and implement effective staffing plans and strategies. In the near term, these managers may not even be aware of this responsibility and may very well lack the skills and experience they need in order to develop and apply the strategic staffing process effectively. HR staff can play key internal consulting roles here, supporting the managers who are preparing the staffing plans. Specifically, HR staff should:

- Define why strategic staffing is needed and the value it provides.
- Create and support the strategic staffing process.
- Ensure that managers have the tools and resources that they need in order to define staffing needs and develop realistic staffing plans.
- Act in partnership with managers to identify critical issues and develop effective strategies.
- Train managers in the use of the process.
- Work with managers to resolve difficult staffing issues.
- Serve as conduits for transferring and processing critical staffing information.

Needless to say, it will be necessary to build this line management accountability over time. It won't (and shouldn't) happen overnight. Instead, the approach should be phased in. As an external consultant, I am often called in to "transfer" my strategic staffing/workforce planning understanding and knowledge to company staff. To do this, I often suggest to clients that when implementing the strategic staffing process for the first time, I should do it and they should watch. The second time, we do it together. The third time, they do it and I watch, providing insight and guidance where necessary. The fourth time, they complete the process on their own; I remain available to answer questions, but I do not participate in the process directly. That approach will probably work well for you as well, with you serving as an internal consultant and your manager being the client.

In addition to serving as internal consultants, HR staff can identify common needs and integrate staffing strategies and plans across units. They can identify when similar issues are identified in different organizations. Their cross-unit perspective greatly facilitates this role; managers who operate primarily within a given unit cannot be expected to do this.

Obstacles to Effective Implementation

Some organizations may have to overcome significant obstacles in order to develop and implement the strategic staffing process. In some cases, line managers, especially those who do not fully understand strategic staffing, impede the implementation process. In an equal number of cases, however, it is HR staff that hinder effective implementation.

Line Managers

Line managers will never fully embrace a process that they do not understand. Typically, many line managers have a short-term results orientation that seems inconsistent with the longer-term perspective of staffing strategy. Other managers are sometimes unaware of (or unconvinced of) the benefits and value of strategic staffing, especially when those benefits are not measured in specific terms. Still others resist the strategic staffing process itself, viewing it as added work that brings them little reward.

When you implement your process, make sure that managers really understand what will be done. Show them that the process will be tailored to meet their needs—that it is not the one-size-fits-all approach that they may think it is. If they have a short-term perspective, emphasize that the process can help them right now. Explain that one of the main benefits of strategic staffing is that it provides a longer-term context within which they can make better decisions in the near term. Chapter 13 describes in detail what you should do to both engage and involve line managers in the strategic staffing/workforce planning process on an ongoing basis. As for measuring the impact and benefits of the process, show them that you are indeed measuring and tracking both the effectiveness and the efficiency of the process (more on measurement is included in Chapter 22).

HR Staff

In some cases, one of the most significant obstacles to the effective implementation of the strategic staffing process is HR staff themselves. As I sometimes say in my presentations, "We have met the enemy and it is us." One of the most difficult biases that HR staff need to overcome is the one that assumes that staffing is by its very nature reactive and tactical. HR staff that believe this find it hard to think of staffing in any strategic way. Other HR staff have an egalitarian perspective that is more consistent with organization-wide, one-size-fits-all approaches than it is with the targeted, issue-focused approach that I suggest. Some assume that in order to be fair and meet business needs, the process must be applied to all jobs in a consistent way. Still other staff lack the in-depth understanding of their business plans that is necessary to define critical HR issues. Finally, some HR professionals still think and act primarily within functional silos, where every problem can be fixed by applying processes, practices, and tools from one given function (like training or recruiting).

As a human resources professional, ensure that your strategic staffing process is implemented effectively and really brings value to your organization by making sure that you:

- Understand that staffing should be proactive. Learn that forward-looking staff planning is not only valuable but absolutely required if business strategies are to be implemented as planned. Your staffing processes will never be fully effective as long as they remain reactive.

- Understand that staffing can often be strategic in nature, and that long-term staffing strategies may be required if significant, critical staffing issues are to be addressed. Make short-term staffing decisions only within the context of long-term staffing strategies.

- Develop a full understanding of your business, including its mission, objectives, strategies, and tactics. This understanding is needed if you are to function as a business partner in general, but it is absolutely critical when developing and implementing the strategic staffing process.

- Create and support processes that are tailored to meet the needs of your managers. Don't expect or force them to use a common process and identical planning parameters where that just isn't necessary.

- Develop staffing strategies and plans that integrate aspects of various traditional HR functions. If the staffing issues that you have identified are truly strategic, it is unlikely that they will be fully addressed by applying processes and tools from just one HR functional area. Pull together teams that utilize staff from all those HR functions that will contribute to the solution to each issue.

Above all, position yourself with your line managers as a helpful, realistic business problem solver with a particular expertise in staffing. If you do this, you will surely be successful. Chapter 15 provides a more detailed description of what your role should be and the skills that you will probably need if you are to play that role effectively.

Summary

No matter how well defined it is, the strategic staffing process is helpful only when it is implemented effectively. Always follow the focused approach B. Carefully define the roles and responsibilities of line managers and HR staff, both for the initial implementation and on an ongoing basis. Work and communicate with line managers to avoid implementation obstacles. And finally, make sure that you don't end up impeding your own implementation by approaching strategic staffing from the wrong perspective.

12

Placing Strategic Staffing/Workforce Planning Within Your Business Context

By now you know that strategic staffing/workforce planning is the process of identifying and addressing the staffing implications of business strategies and plans. Clearly, then, any strategic staffing process must be fully consistent with the organization's overall business planning processes. What separates truly effective planning processes from those that are not very effective is the nature of the relationship between strategic staffing and business planning.

This chapter describes how the two processes can be related. It also includes a simple diagnostic that you can use to evaluate your own planning context and identify ways to improve the effectiveness of your planning processes.

Integrate, Don't Align

It is not sufficient to simply align or link the business planning process and the strategic staffing process—after all, two components can be aligned or linked only if they are in fact separate to begin with. To be fully effective, strategic staffing must be seamlessly integrated into the fabric of business planning on an ongoing basis.

To gain the maximum benefit from strategic staffing, you must ensure that:

- **Your business planning and staffing processes include the right components to begin with.** For example, a well-developed planning process includes both long-term business strategies and shorter-term operating plans. Similarly, you should be developing both long-term staffing strategies and short-term staffing plans. It is unlikely that your planning processes can be effective if any of these major components are missing.

- **The major components of your planning processes mesh fully.** All the components of your planning process need to fit together like the proverbial well-oiled machine. Even if each component is developed masterfully, the planning processes will fail if the linkages between the components are not strong and dynamic. For example, there need to be strong relationships (and information flows) between long-term business planning and long-term staffing strategies. If the relationships between components are weak (or, worse yet, nonexistent), the planning process will be incomplete and ineffective.

- **All of the various pieces and processes within each component of your planning process are fully integrated.** Each major component of the planning process includes various pieces that must fit together and build on one another. For example, strategic objectives usually define what is to be accomplished during the planning horizon. Strategies then define specifically what is to be done to achieve those objectives. When these two pieces are well integrated, all the objectives will be achieved if the stated strategy is implemented as designed. When they are not well integrated, strategy implementation may leave some key objectives unmet.

Those well-managed companies that we all hear about typically have well-defined business strategies and plans that cover both the long and the short term. Similarly, these companies often produce and implement both longer-term staffing strategies and shorter-term staffing plans that fully support the implementation of their business plans. In your organization, however, it is possible that some of these planning processes need to be improved, better integrated, or created from scratch. In fact, you may be using this book specifically to create a strategic staffing/workforce planning process in an organization where one does not currently exist. How can you quickly assess your business planning situation and determine where strategic staffing fits in best?

A Simple Diagnostic

In some organizations, there are many different planning processes and components that are used to varying degrees to guide actions and resource allocations. Understanding the objectives of these components, and how they fit together, is an important precursor to implementing any strategic staffing process. The diagnostic in Figure 12-1 can be used as a framework to help you identify and evaluate the components of your planning proc-

Figure 12-1. The Basic Framework.

	Business Planning	Staff Planning
Long Term		
Short Term		

esses and assess the relationships among those various components. The diagnostic should be used in two ways:

- It can help you to develop the components of the strategic staffing/ workforce planning process and integrate them into ongoing planning efforts *as they apply to your company specifically*. This analysis will allow you to define the context in which your strategic staffing/ workforce planning process will be implemented. It will help you to identify what you have to work with and define the business and staff planning components that you can build on. You will be able to identify missing pieces, "bad fits," and other impediments to effective business planning and strategic staffing. Armed with the results of your analysis, you can then focus and prioritize your strategic staffing/workforce planning efforts, adding those needed components and processes.

- The diagnostic may also help you to identify specific opportunities for improving the effectiveness of your current business and staff planning processes. By using this diagnostic, you can identify key elements of the planning process that may be missing, opportunities to better integrate the pieces within various components of the planning process, and ways of better meshing the components themselves.

This tool should be applied at the organizational level for which staffing strategies are being developed. For example, apply the diagnostic at an overall corporate level (e.g., defining corporate business strategy) if a corporate staffing strategy is to be developed. Similarly, apply it at a business unit level (e.g., defining business unit strategy) if the staffing strategy to be developed is for a business unit. Avoid mixing levels, though (e.g., defining business planning at a corporate level and staff planning at a business unit level). If you are trying to define a unit staffing strategy, but there is no specific unit business strategy, try to define what the unit will need to do to accomplish its part of the overall corporate strategy. On the other hand, if corporate values apply at the business unit level as well, feel free to include them.

Each of the four steps of the diagnostic process is described in detail. To help you further, there is a diagnostic worksheet at the end of this chapter that you can use to document your analysis, findings, and recommendations. A blank copy of the worksheet is also included in the files that you can download from www.amacombooks.org/go/StrategicStaff 2E. You can then print and use a copy of that form if you don't want to write in the book itself.

The simple two-by-two grid shown in Figure 12-1 forms the basis of the diagnostic. The columns address the two major elements of your planning process:

- **Business planning.** The business planning column will be used to capture any or all aspects or components that can help your business to define and allocate required resources other than people. Typically, this includes all aspects of your strategic planning, budgeting, and operations planning processes.
- **Staff planning.** Include in the staff planning column any processes or components that can help you to define your needs for and allocate staffing resources in particular. This will include all aspects of your staff planning and staffing processes. (Remember how broad my definition of "staffing" is.)

The rows of the diagnostic address your particular planning horizon:

- **Long term.** The top row includes all long-term planning, however you define "long term" for your particular organization or unit. In many cases, "long term" is defined by the planning horizon of your strategic planning process (e.g., three to five years). For some units, however (such as information technology), "long term" may be defined as a much shorter period—perhaps just 12 to 18 months.
- **Short term.** The bottom row addresses the short term, again as you define it. For many companies, this is often defined as the time frame for the annual budget or operating plan. In other cases, it may be defined as a single quarter.

Thus, the diagnostic defines the four major components of your business planning process: long-term business planning, long-term staff planning, short-term business planning, and short-term staff planning.

Step 1: Take an Inventory of Your Current Processes

Next, identify what your company is actually doing in each of the four cells and document that in the matrix itself. Include only those things that you currently have; do not include things that you "should" have or things that you plan to implement. Specifically document each process in the appropriate cell. Don't just think about the elements; actually write the name of each component in the appropriate cell of your matrix. If you are simply using this tool to analyze the effectiveness of your current processes, it is probably sufficient to simply identify each component. If you are using this tool as a guide for creating a strategic staffing/workforce planning process, however, a more in-depth understanding of each component may be required. If this is the case, actually gather, document, and study each component (e.g., actually obtain and read a copy of the business strategy). If there are multiple versions of the same components (e.g., if there are different vision statements for the business unit you are analyzing and for the company as a whole), obtain copies of all versions.

Here are some examples of what you might find and document in each cell/component of your planning process:

- **Long term/business planning.** List in this cell any efforts that help your organization to identify requirements for or allocate resources over the long term. This might include your company's mission statement, vision statement, values, strategic objectives, and business strategy.

- **Short term/business planning.** List in this cell any efforts that help your organization to identify requirements for or allocate resources over the short term. This usually includes your operational plan, budget, and headcount control modules.

- **Long term/staff planning.** List in this cell any efforts that help your organization to identify requirements for or allocate staff over the long term. This would include your human resource (HR) and staffing strategies (if they exist). Be discriminating here. Include only those pieces that are truly long term. Exclude those pieces that appear to have some long-term context, but are really implemented on a short-term basis. For example, include your succession planning and development process here if it is truly viewed and applied as a strategic tool, but place it in the short term/staff planning cell if it is primarily an annual process that drives short-term decisions regarding selection, placement, and/or development.

- **Short term/staff planning.** List in this cell any efforts that help your organization to identify requirements for or allocate staff over the short term. This includes staffing and staffing-related processes implemented within your organization that support short-term decisions (e.g., all recruiting and staffing decisions that are made to meet immediate needs). In many organizations, the vast majority of staff planning and actions occurs in the short term and thus should be included in this cell. You may also wish to include processes that directly support the staffing processes (such as training and development). Again, remember how encompassing my definition of "staffing" is.

When conducting your inventory, be as complete and thorough as you can be, but keep your analysis at a big-picture level. It is not necessary to capture every variance and nuance. Figure 12-2 shows what a typical diagnostic looks like once all processes and components have been identified and recorded in the appropriate cell.

Step 2: Review Each Cell

Once you have completed your inventory, the real diagnosis can begin. Begin your analysis by reviewing the content of each of the four cells, answering the following questions.

Figure 12-2. A Typical Result.

	Business Planning	Staff Planning
Long Term	Mission Vision Values Objectives Strategies	HR strategies Staffing strategies
Short Term	Operating plans Budgets	Recruiting Movement Career planning Succession planning Development Training

Is There Anything That Is Missing?

Are there any key pieces that you think are missing from any of the components? For example, in the long term/business planning cell, there might be a well-defined business strategy, but no clear objectives. Does a business strategy exist? In some cases, the long term/staff planning cell may be empty—for example, when neither a comprehensive HR strategy nor long-term staffing strategies currently exist.

If you do identify missing pieces, determine whether they are absolutely necessary or simply "nice to have." If they are absolutely necessary, develop plans for communicating these needs to those who should be developing those pieces (e.g., line managers, planners, or HR business partners). You may wish to take on the work of developing these missing pieces, but you probably would not do that under the umbrella of strategic staffing.

Are Any of the Pieces Ineffective?

It may be that a component includes all the right pieces, but the pieces are not as effective as they should be. Does your business strategy really describe *how* business objectives are to be met, or does it just restate those objectives (e.g., it states that you are to become a low-cost producer or a "top five" player in your market, but it does not say what will be done to accomplish this)? Are your short-term staffing practices adequately proactive or primarily reactive?

If you identify opportunities to improve the effectiveness of any of the pieces within a business planning component, separate those pieces that you can fix (i.e., those for which you have the accountability and the necessary resources) from those that you cannot. Where improvements are outside your area of accountability, make sure that you document the improvements that are possible and pass that information on to those who can implement the needed changes.

Is There Anything That Is Redundant or Unnecessary?

Are there any pieces of the planning process that exist, but that should be ignored? In some cases, there may be components that exist, but that really have no impact on the business. Does each piece directly support decision making? Are any of the pieces redundant? If the pieces are in fact critical to the business planning process, consider them when you create your staffing strategy, but if they are not critical, ignore them. Here are some common examples of pieces that might be ignored:

- Many organizations have mission statements. For some, these statements are a valuable component of the business planning process, perhaps even defining why the organization is in business. For others, however, while the statement exists, it does not affect decision making in any appreciable way. One organization that I'm familiar with has a mission statement that was created by a team of senior managers (probably during a facilitated, off-site session). It incorporates glowing language and all the right buzzwords. The problem is that this mission statement does not really affect decisions or resource allocations at all.

If your mission statement is valuable (and used), then factor it into your strategic staffing efforts. If it isn't, then don't.

• Company values are often defined but not integrated into the business. I know of an organization that developed, documented, and disseminated a set of corporate values. As a way of communicating these values, the organization printed posters that were hung in every conference room and elevator lobby. In addition, the values were printed on laminated cards that could be included in every employee's day planner or affixed to the back of everyone's employee ID. The problem was, however, that in this organization, those value statements didn't influence individual behavior in any significant way. The words never got beyond the slogan stage. There was no component of the performance management process that allowed managers to assess the extent to which subordinates put these values into practice on a day-to-day basis.

If company values exist and drive decision making in your company, incorporate them into your strategic staffing process. If they don't, consider ignoring them.

Are the Components Well Integrated?

Look at the processes and pieces *within* each cell of the diagnostic and assess the extent to which they are working together as that well-oiled machine to implement your plans and achieve your objectives. Are they pieces of a puzzle that fit together well, or are they somewhat separate, disjointed initiatives that compete for management time, attention, and resources? Pay particular attention to the long term/business planning and short term/staff planning cells.

Long Term/Business Planning. Each piece should be fully consistent with the piece before and the piece after. For example, consider "mission" to be your reason for being in business. "Vision" should be a description of what you want your organization to look like—the place your company wants to get to over time. "Objectives" are the signposts you pass along the way on your journey from where you are to the place described in your vision. "Strategies" should be the plans that describe how you will move from signpost to signpost (i.e., from objective to objective).

When these pieces are not well integrated, each of them tends to stand alone. For example, as described earlier, there may be a mission statement that is disconnected from the other pieces of the resource allocation process. In some cases, organizations have created vision statements that are virtually indistinguishable from their mission statements. Some organizations have several unintegrated vision statements that were created by separate groups at separate times. Perhaps worst of all, some organizations have developed strategies that, when implemented, will not allow them to achieve their stated objectives.

If the efforts in your long term/business planning cell are well integrated, make sure that your strategic staffing efforts are consistent with that integrated approach. If the pieces do not fit so well with one another, determine which efforts are actually driving decision making and ensure that staffing strategies are consistent with those efforts in particular.

Short Term/Staff Planning. To what extent are your short-term staffing processes integrated? Have you developed cross-functional plans that, when taken together, will ensure that you have the right people in the right place at the right time? Indeed, staffing efforts should be integrated with one another. Yet this integration may not need to occur at an overall, functional level. If you are taking the issue approach, you may want to integrate recruiting, staffing, internal movement, and development in ways that most effectively address a particular issue. As an example, you might bring together particular individuals (with particular expertise) from these functions and charge that team with addressing an issue of insufficient management depth. Don't assume that you need to bring together the entire recruiting, staffing, and development functions to create an integrated solution.

Do you think the various functional components of your short-term staffing processes are well integrated? Here are three tests to see if they are:

- Are representatives of each function present, and are they active participants when staffing decisions are being made? If they are, it is likely that your processes are integrated. If they are not all present, if they develop separate functional plans, and/or if integration is left to communication outside such a session, then integration is unlikely.

- Do you have separate plans for each function in HR? For example, do you have separate strategies for recruiting and development? Many companies do create separate strategies for different HR functions. This approach, while common, is difficult to implement well. In some cases, it creates competition for resources among functions that actually impedes the required action.

- Think about your development planning processes. Some organizations create separate development plans as part of their performance appraisal, career planning, succession/development, and high-potential programs. If these plans are created at different times, using different criteria and standards, and result in different/separate plans, it is unlikely that your HR/staffing functions are sufficiently integrated.

Step 3: Examine the Relationships Between Cells

Once you have completed your analysis of each cell, look at the relationships between cells. Draw arrows to show the direction(s) in which information flows. If there is dialogue and two-way communication, show an arrow in each direction. Use the thickness of the arrow to show the quality of that information flow (e.g., solid for good flow, dotted for partial flow). Remember that there probably cannot be any relationship at all between a well-developed component and a poorly developed one (e.g., an empty box on the diagnostic).

Here are four examples of what your analysis might include:

1. **Long term/business planning and short term/business planning.** This is the relationship between business strategy and budgets/operating plans. When this relationship is effective, the short-term budget is fully consistent with the longer-term strategy. For example, the budget or operating plan may actually be the first year of a three-year business plan that is updated annually. If this is the case, draw a dark arrow from the upper left cell to the lower left cell. When this relationship is ineffective, the budgeting process is not really linked to strategy at all. The binder (or deck of slides) that describes the business strategy may exist, but the business strategy has little or no impact on how the business is managed or how resources are actually allocated; it is the short-term budget that really drives decision making. I sometimes refer to this situation as SPOTS, or strategic plan on top shelf. If this is the case, draw a very light arrow from the upper left to the lower left—or perhaps no arrow at all.

2. **Long term/business planning and long term/staff planning.** Are staffing issues raised when your business strategies are first proposed and

developed? Or are staffing strategies created only after business objectives and strategies have been defined? Might there be staffing strategies that really are not directly related to business plan implementation? If staffing strategies are prepared primarily in response to business plans, then draw a dark arrow from the upper left to the upper right. If the number and type of available staff affect the strategies that are proposed (e.g., if you decide to enter a market because of the talent that is available internally), then draw an arrow from the upper right to the upper left. If staffing issues are identified and discussed as part of the business strategy process (and strategies for addressing those issues are developed as part of that process), then perhaps arrows should be drawn in both directions.

3. **Long term/staff planning and short term/staff planning.** When the strategic staffing process is implemented effectively, this relationship is usually quite clear. As stated earlier, long-term staffing strategies form the context for short-term staffing decisions. If short-term staffing decisions are made in this longer-term context, draw a dark arrow from the upper right to the lower right. If short-term staffing decisions are not made in this long-term context, then draw a light arrow (or no arrow at all).

4. **Short term/business planning and short term/staff planning.** What is the relationship between budget and staffing actions? Does the budget process really define the amount of resources that are available? Do you then simply translate these available resources into the number of people to be hired, promoted, and trained? Does the finance function define the maximum number of staff allowable in each unit based on financial criteria? If so, draw a thick arrow from the lower left to the lower right. Do you sometimes define the numbers and types of staff that will be required (and the plans needed to ensure that this talent will exist) and then build a coherent business case for securing the resources to do this? Do you define the resources that will be needed to implement the staffing plans you define? Are you able to describe specifically what won't get done if the organization is unable to secure the staffing you have determined is required? If so, draw a dark arrow from the lower right to the lower left.

Note that there are no diagonal relationships or lines of communication defined here. For example, it is impossible to directly link long-term business planning and short-term staff planning. Such relationships are not feasible.

When you have completed this step, look at the direction and relative thickness of the arrows you drew. When your company is operating effectively, you will have dark arrows in both directions in two places: between long term/business planning and long term/staff planning and between short term/business planning and short term/staff planning. You will also have dark arrows (probably pointing down) between long term/business planning and short term/business planning and between long term/staff planning and short term/staff planning.

You may end up with two sets of arrows, pointing in both directions: between long term/business planning and long term/staff planning and between short term/business planning and short term/staff planning. This implies that there is meaningful dialogue between business and staff planning in both the long and the short term. This dialogue is essential to developing meaningful, realistic staffing strategies and plans. However, creating arrows between these two rows that point in both directions is actually not your ultimate objective (although, at a minimum, it is the place to start). In the final analysis, you want to remove the line on your model that separates the business planning cells and the staff planning cells. This indicates that business planning and staff planning are fully integrated, not just separate processes that are linked well or aligned effectively.

Opportunities to improve the effectiveness of this part of your processes are usually characterized as adding an arrow that does not exist (i.e., creating a relationship or line of communication) or making a light arrow darker (i.e., strengthening a relationship that already exists). Adding an arrow usually entails the creation of a new mechanism or process that facilitates discussion and data exchange. Darkening an arrow usually means that the effectiveness of an existing mechanism needs to be improved. Here are two examples:

- If you need to add an arrow between long term/business planning and short term/business planning, define the process by which short-term plans should be made within the context of the long-term business strategies that exist.

- If you need to darken the arrow between long term/business planning and long term/staff planning, consider making discussions of staffing implications a regular part of the development of business strategies.

Figure 12-3 shows what a completed diagnostic for a well-developed process might look like. When complete, the strategic staffing/workforce planning process will include all four of the horizontal arrows as well as the vertical arrows linking long-term staffing and short-term staffing.

Creating or strengthening the relationships between the boxes of this model should be one of your major areas of focus. This book is filled with ideas and suggestions for what you can and should do to develop (or

Figure 12-3. A Well-Developed Planning Process.

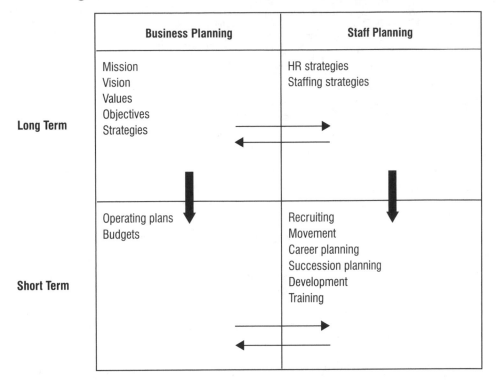

thicken) the arrows that relate to staffing. Table 12-1 lists some ideas for what you might do to create or strengthen each arrow. A chapter reference is provided for each idea.

Some Final Thoughts

Needless to say, the strategic planning process varies widely from company to company; indeed, it may vary among units of the same company. Consequently, there can be no set way of creating the necessary relationships between your business strategy and strategic staffing processes. You should use this diagnostic as a framework to guide your thoughts and actions, not as a cookbook to be followed line by line.

This diagnostic is meant to facilitate action, not prevent it. Consistent with a theme that was raised in Chapter 8, do the most you can with what you have. Even if you find that some pieces or some points of integration don't exist, you can still begin to develop your strategic staffing process. Take full advantage of the processes and information that do exist, and create first-generation staffing strategies and plans. Simultaneously, work with others to improve the overall business and staff planning processes, perhaps even using this diagnostic as your framework for discussion.

Table 12-1. Strengthening the Arrows.

Relationship	Supporting Idea	Chapter
Long term/business planning → long term/staff planning	• Define and focus on critical staffing issues • Identify and apply staffing drivers	Chapter 4 Chapter 5
Long term/staff planning → long term/business planning	• Identify opportunities for available talent to influence business strategies • Define staffing issues that are not directly related to business change (e.g., retirement)	Chapter 4
Long term/staff planning → short term/staff planning	• Apply the "upside-down T" • Create long-term staffing strategies that provide the context for short-term staffing decisions • Create and run staffing models for multiple planning periods	Chapter 2 Chapter 4
Short term/staff planning → short term/business planning	• Define staffing-related costs • Calculate long-term savings • Define what won't get done if staffing resources are not available	Chapter 23

Here is an example: A multinational oil company wanted to develop a series of staffing strategies for positions that were difficult to fill. Since the company had never developed these strategies before, it used this diagnostic to assess where it was. During the inventory phase, the company determined that a business strategy existed, but during the integration phase, it discovered that this strategy consisted primarily of restated business objectives. It lacked the "how" part—it did not describe what was going to be done to achieve those objectives. As stated in Chapter 2, it is not possible to develop a staffing strategy that is based on objectives. Rather than do nothing, the team decided to build its first strategy around a well-crafted vision statement that did in fact provide some of that missing direction. As work on the staffing strategies continued, the team leader worked with the business planning group to create a business strategy that was more descriptive of what would be done, not just what was to be accomplished. During the next planning cycle, this second version of the strategy formed an excellent foundation that was used to create the second-generation staffing strategy.

Engaging and Involving Managers in Strategic Staffing

For any workforce planning efforts to be successful, line managers must fully embrace, support, and participate willingly in the process. Yet many organizations try to implement workforce planning processes in which managers participate reluctantly, or perhaps even not at all. What can an organization do to ensure that managers will be active players in workforce planning? How can we get managers to value the process and enthusiastically implement the staffing strategies and plans that result?

Clearly, the active involvement of line managers is critical to the success of any workforce planning process. But before managers will become actively involved in workforce planning, they must be fully engaged in the process. This chapter describes how you can gain that engagement and, building on that engagement, ensure the active involvement of your line managers.

Engaging Line Managers in Workforce Planning

Managers will always support processes that they find valuable—those whose results outweigh the time and effort that the process requires. Usually, many of the managers who are not engaged in the workforce planning process just don't feel that it helps them to manage more effectively or to meet their day-to-day objectives. These managers may recognize that workforce planning yields some "greater good" or macro-level benefit for the organization as a whole, but they often feel that there is nothing in it for them as individuals. If workforce planning really did help these people to manage more effectively, they would participate in the process willingly. However, traditional workforce planning processes often waste managers' time by asking them do things and provide data that are simply not valuable or required. Here are just a few examples:

- Workforce planning processes routinely require managers to "forecast" staffing requirements too far into the future—beyond any time frame where those estimates can be realistic or useful. This forces managers to provide forecasts that at best are guesses, just to fill in the blanks on a form. Ask an IT manager (or any manager in a unit where technology is changing rapidly) how confident she is about estimates of staffing requirements three to five years in the future, and just how valuable staffing plans based on those estimates might be. The answer you will get will probably be "not very." Yet these long-term estimates are often included in many workforce planning processes. The time that managers spend on these meaningless forecasts is simply wasted, and any workforce or staffing plans based on those forecasts cannot be valuable.

- When implementing workforce planning, HR often asks managers to analyze all positions in the process, including those for which longer-term staffing strategies and workforce plans are just not warranted or valuable. Creating long-term staffing strategies for positions where simple short-term staffing plans are more than adequate represents time lost and effort wasted—more reason for managers to shun the process.

- HR sometimes tries to "sell" managers on workforce planning by telling them that the process will be helpful to the organization as a whole in the long term. Yet organizations usually hold managers primarily accountable for achieving shorter-term objectives for their specific units. This causes at least some managers to see workforce planning as a corporate responsibility that does not affect their ability to manage their units effectively in any appreciable way. They feel that they are not rewarded at all for doing what they are asked to do in this area; in fact, the time needed to do it must be taken from some other activity that they do value. Consequently, they see no direct, personal benefit or value in participating in the workforce planning process. For some of these managers, workforce planning becomes a task that they just want to get off their desks as quickly as possible with as little effort as possible.

You must convince managers that the workforce planning process is indeed valuable—that each of them will benefit from the process in ways that exceed the time and effort they must expend to participate in it. But you won't be able to gain their cooperation and support by making an inappropriate workforce planning process more efficient. It is not a matter of reducing the work or the time needed to complete forms or baseless forecasts, nor of finding a system or software that will greatly facilitate the gathering of meaningless data. Instead, you must greatly increase the effectiveness of the workforce planning processes that you implement, so that managers see and realize tangible benefits. What changes must you make to develop and implement workforce planning processes that are truly effective?

The answer to these questions is, at least in part, "workforce planning at 30,000 feet"—the hybrid approach to workforce planning that is described in Chapter 6. With this approach, companies mandate workforce planning processes that have common approaches and parameters up to a point (i.e., the 30,000-foot level), but allow managers flexibility in how they develop, implement, and apply workforce planning below that level. This approach ensures that workforce plans are developed in a consistent way across the organization, yet allows managers to tailor the process so that the workforce plans they create address what they perceive to be their most critical staffing needs.

Implementing the following four solutions within the context of the 30,000-foot approach will ensure that workforce planning is effective and that managers will value the process and its output.

Solution 1: Explain to managers that the new approach to workforce planning (including the redefined objective) will help them manage more effectively right now. If we define the objective of workforce planning to be "avoiding future staffing problems," we are in effect asking managers to expend time and resources now to help their future successors—something that they may be less willing to do. On the other hand, if we define the objective of the process to be allowing the organization to make effective decisions right now, managers themselves will realize some direct, immediate benefits from participating in the workforce planning process. Managers will obviously be more willing to support a process that they perceive as helping them to meet their own performance objectives (as opposed to those of their successors).

When done effectively, the workforce planning process provides both longer-term staffing strategies (describing how staff needs are best met across planning periods) and staffing plans (defining specifically what should be done to meet staffing needs in any given planning period). Explain to managers that by taking these two components together, they will be able to define the most effective, efficient near-term staffing plans possible (within the context of longer-term staffing strategies).

Solution 2: Define an overall direction for workforce planning, but do not force managers to use a particular approach. While a common direction is usually helpful, not all components of the workforce planning process need to be exactly the same and applied consistently across an organization unit. Provide managers with some high-level commonality, but allow them the flexibility they need to tailor a particular approach beneath that 30,000-foot level.

Your common, overall direction for strategic staffing/workforce planning should include:

- **A clear understanding that workforce planning is a management accountability.** Before you worry about the process, make sure that all managers understand that they will be held accountable for identifying and addressing the staffing implications of their strategies and plans (in both the long and the short term) on an ongoing basis. Also, make sure that managers have the skills and understanding needed to do this effectively.

- **A consistent definition of the process.** Define for managers (from an overall/overview perspective) what the workforce planning process is (e.g., defining and addressing the staffing implications of business plans and strategies) and what its expected results are (e.g., both long-term staffing strategies and short-term staffing plans). However, do not define the process in detail or specify exactly how managers must implement it. Of course, you may wish to provide and support a suggested process that managers may choose to use if they have no alternative method of their own.

- **Mandated output, but not process.** Hold managers accountable for identifying critical staffing issues and for developing and defining the staffing strategies and plans that will address those critical issues most effectively. However, don't force them to use a particular "one-size-fits-all" process to accomplish that. If managers can achieve the expected results using a workforce planning process that is different from the one developed corporately, let them. On the other hand, be prepared to help them implement the suggested approach to workforce planning should they want to use that method.

- **Developing corporate staffing strategies only where absolutely necessary.** Strategic approaches to staffing are absolutely required for some staffing issues—but not all staffing issues. Don't waste managers' time and resources by forcing them to spend time creating corporatewide staffing plans where such plans really are not required. Workforce planning addresses critical staffing issues; don't assume that there needs to be one coordinated, integrated "plan" that addresses all the staffing issues a company is facing.

Solution 3: Allow managers to tailor the process to better meet their needs. While the organization's direction and objectives must be common among units, process need not be. At the detail level, don't implement a single approach to workforce planning or force consistency for consistency's sake. Instead, allow managers the flexibility that they need to develop and implement the staffing strategies and plans that they think address their most critical staffing issues most effectively. This might include:

- **Developing "issue-oriented," not "unit-oriented," staffing strategies and plans.** Make sure that managers develop the staffing strategies and plans that they need in order to address critical issues, but do not ask them to develop strategies and plans for their organization unit as a whole.

- **Allowing managers to identify the staffing issues that they think are most critical.** Let managers choose which staffing issues warrant the time and effort required to apply the workforce planning process. Don't force them to apply the process everywhere or to address staffing issues that they just don't think require a strategic perspective.

- **Letting managers identify the jobs to be included in the process address each issue.** Not all jobs are so critical that they should be included in a truly strategic workforce planning process. Because workforce planning requires a lot of time and effort on the part of managers, maximize the effectiveness of that time and effort by allowing managers to focus solely on those positions that require such a high level of scrutiny that comprehensive workforce planning is, in their minds, warranted.

- **Allowing managers to define critical planning parameters.** Different units will be facing staffing issues that have different rates of change and levels of detail. While mandating a long-term view, don't define what the length of that view needs to be. For some units that are facing rapidly changing conditions, "long term" might be 18 months; in other areas facing less change, "long term" might be three to five years. Also, don't try to set one level of detail to be used by all units. In an IT area, for example, a small number of particular technical skills may adequately define staffing requirements, while a longer list of more generic management competencies might be appropriate at senior levels in another part of the organization.

Solution 4: Provide resources, tools, and support that managers find helpful. Don't just tell managers what to do. Instead, provide them with whatever tools and resources might help them to understand workforce planning better and implement the process most effectively. Here are some specific suggestions:

- **Clearly show what you think the workforce planning process should look like.** While not holding them to a particular approach, provide managers with a fully developed version of a workforce planning process that they can choose to implement if they wish to identify critical staffing issues and develop the staffing strategies and plans that best address those issues.

- **Provide tools and support that are consistent with the approach you are suggesting.** Develop and widely distribute the tools, templates, forms, and other resources that managers might need to support their workforce planning efforts. This might include process outlines and diagrams, spreadsheets that can be used to define staffing gaps and surpluses, completed examples of staffing strategies and plans, workbooks and resource guides, and easy access to workforce planning web sites. However, don't mandate that managers use these resources (e.g., that they have to fill out a particular form). Let managers use any resources that they feel are necessary and helpful. Do provide ongoing, tailored internal consulting help that directly supports workforce planning, regardless of the specific process that a manager is using.

- **Involve managers in staffing strategy development.** Don't expect that HR should be solely accountable for developing staffing strategies and plans across an organization. Instead, have managers work with HR business partners or functional staff to develop staffing strategies and define staffing plans. Involving managers in this aspect of the process ensures that the solutions that are developed are appropriate for each unit and increases the chances that those managers will actually support and implement those solutions.

- **Provide customized support.** Where feasible, work with individual managers to provide the specific support that they need. Some may need help identifying critical issues, but no help at all in developing staffing strategies and plans for addressing those issues. Others will be able to identify the issues, but may need help in implementing workforce planning to address those issues. Still others might need assistance in the more quantitative aspects of workforce planning, such as calculating staffing gaps and surpluses. Whatever assistance is needed, keep the focus on addressing critical staffing issues, not on following a given process by rote. HR business partners, functional leads, and workforce planning staff can all help provide this service.

In summary, never ask managers to participate in an ineffective workforce planning process. Garner their support by implementing workforce planning processes that address the staffing issues that they find most critical. Strike the right balance between "common" and "tailored." By implementing the four solutions given here, an organization will develop workforce plans that are adequately consistent in approach and output to address those staffing issues whose solutions span units. Yet by allowing for tailoring of the process—and thus ensuring that the value of managers' time and effort is maximized—you will produce workforce plans that are effective and realistic. This will ensure that you will engage managers willingly and directly in the process, instead of dragging them along kicking and screaming!

Involving Line Managers in the Process

Once managers are engaged in and support workforce planning, it is time to define the role that they will play in the initial and ongoing implementation of the process. Line managers must play an active role in the strategic staffing process—after all, it is their staffing needs that the process is designed to meet. Managers also provide critical information at key points along the way, such as estimating staffing requirements and evaluating the feasibility of proposed staffing actions.

Before attempting to involve line managers in workforce planning, you will need to ensure that they fully understand the workforce planning process and are willing to buy into its results. They will need to know what is being done (e.g., the steps of the process), agree with the information and assumptions you use, understand the expected output, and feel comfortable with the staffing strategies, plans, and actions that the process suggests. As you work with line managers to develop and implement your strategic staffing process, make sure that they:

1. **Understand what is in it for them.** As described in the first half of this chapter, managers must be engaged in the workforce planning process and understand how implementation of the process will help them to be better managers right now. The development and implementation of the strategic staffing process will ensure that managers have the talent they need in order to implement their business plans and meet their near-term performance objectives and bonus targets. In practical, day-to-day terms, this means that their needs for talent will be quickly identified and met (e.g., the time needed to fill openings with well-qualified talent will be reduced significantly).

2. **Understand the objectives and outcomes of the process.** Verify that managers fully understand the objectives of the process and the expected

level of detail of the output. This is especially important when you are implementing the more focused approaches to workforce planning that are suggested in this book. Some managers will have participated in the past in processes that were burdensome or that produced lackluster results. Make sure that these managers understand how this process will be different from what they have done before. Explain that the process will not use a one-size-fits-all approach and that planning parameters (such as the overall time horizon) will be tailored to reflect their particular needs. Make sure they understand that the analysis will be applied only where necessary (e.g., for critical jobs) and need not be applied to all jobs. Show them that the output (i.e., staffing issues, staffing strategies, and staffing plans and actions) is realistic, specific, and implementable.

3. Are familiar with the process itself. Managers need to understand how the strategic staffing process will be implemented (especially for the first time). They need to understand the various components of the process and how these components fit together. They need to feel confident that the process is robust, yet is flexible enough to reflect changes, emerging priorities, and other contingencies. However, there may be some managers who will not be interested in the details of the process. These managers need to know just enough about the process to allow it to proceed. If there are managers who do want to see and understand the detail, then provide them with as much information as is necessary to secure their support. Don't give all managers all the detail just because some of them want or need it.

4. Understand the role that they will play. Managers want to know what their role in the process will be. They want to know the extent of their involvement, particularly how much of their time will be required. Therefore, you need to clearly describe what their role will be. Initially, managers must identify and discuss the staffing issues and implications that they think are most important. Usually, they also provide at least some of the information that the process requires (e.g., defining the capabilities and staffing levels that will be required in the future). Often, they help to develop various planning scenarios and staffing assumptions. Finally, they need to provide input regarding the feasibility of the staffing actions that are the result of the process.

Remember to clearly differentiate the level of effort and management participation that will be needed during the initial implementation of the process from the level that will be needed to maintain the process on an ongoing basis. There is quite a lot of information that managers will need to provide the first time you implement the strategic staffing process. However, when it comes time to update the process, managers can simply modify or revise the information that they provided initially. Clearly, this updating will require far less time and fewer resources than were needed to develop this information from scratch.

Make sure that you strike a proper balance here. Identify the information that managers must provide, and make those requirements known. Identify areas in which management input is welcome but is not required, and provide ample opportunity for managers to provide this input as they see fit.

Much of this communication and dialogue with managers can be facilitated if you have a prior example of the process that you can share. Nothing makes some of these points better than seeing what a good example of the process looks like. Rather than describing the benefits in conceptual terms, share the actual benefits that were realized in a prior implementation of the process (e.g., one from another unit or one that addressed a different staffing issue from the one being faced now). Better yet, get a manager who has seen the value of the strategic staffing process to share his perspective with the managers with whom the process is to be implemented. Instead of showing managers conceptual models, show actual spreadsheets and results. Don't describe what their role could be; share what the actual level of involvement of a prior group of managers was.

When launching a strategic staffing/workforce planning process, it is usually most effective to present the process (at an overall, overview level) to a group of managers, then follow up with each manager individually. Included in the computer files that you can access from the book's web site at www.amacombooks.org/go/StrategicStaff2E is a set of slides that can be used for this type of group presentation. In its current form, it highlights the process at an appropriate level of detail, providing a big-picture overview of the process and its implementation. The presentation can be edited if you need to tailor it to meet your own particular needs. Above all, remember to be open to questions at all times and to be readily available for management discussions on an ongoing basis.

Defining Staffing Implications: An Interview Guide

There are times when business plans or strategies simply don't contain the clearly defined, detailed information that is needed to identify staffing issues and implications. Staffing profiles don't exist, and there is no obvious information regarding staffing requirements. In such cases, the needed information can often be gathered quickly and efficiently by interviewing the line managers and planners who were responsible for creating the plans.

This section contains some hints that you can use in preparing for and conducting such interviews. In general terms, you will need to prepare by identifying current staff availability (both skills and staffing levels) for the manager's unit. During the interview, discuss the manager's business plans and objectives for the coming period, and then discuss the impact on required capabilities and staffing levels that implementing those plans will have. These discussions are also good opportunities to identify staffing issues, propose staffing strategies, and test the viability of staffing plans and actions.

Preparing for the Interview

Prepare for such an interview by learning about the manager's business (if you don't already know). Make sure that you are familiar with:

- Services and products currently offered
- Business objectives, strategies, plans, and unit performance measures (if any)
- Longer-term changes in strategies and objectives

Once you are fully familiar with the nature of the unit's business itself, define current staffing levels for the unit (in broad categories such as job family or management/nonmanagement) and the broad capabilities of each job category. Next, review the business plans for the unit in detail and identify and highlight any changes or aspects of the plan that you think might have staffing implications. You may even want to create a staffing issue crib list (or maybe even a little table) that identifies key business changes and suggests staffing implications for each change. You can also use this list during the interview to make sure that all issues are addressed. Staffing issues/implications might include the following:

- Significant changes in business activity may affect staffing levels (e.g., through growth or contraction).
- Major changes in products offered may imply changes in required capabilities (e.g., new technology may create a need in one area and a surplus of individuals with obsolete skills in another).
- New services that may require skills that are currently unknown or undefined.
- Plans may require you to recruit for skills that the company has not needed previously (e.g., it will take time to identify new sources or develop new selection criteria).
- Implementation may require skills that are scarce or for which there is high competition among employers.

- There may be instances in which the obvious or traditional solutions are no longer feasible (e.g., where training and development might normally be used, but would now take too long).

- There may be instances in which the indirect impacts are as critical as any of the direct staffing needs that you define (e.g., changes in one job category may affect the number and type of staff needed in another category).

Identify and write down the staffing issues that you think are the most critical. Test each of these with the manager you are interviewing. Don't just focus on these, however. Be prepared to supplement this list with issues that you did not identify prior to the session itself. If you have already identified possible solutions for some of these issues, document your suggestions clearly so that you can discuss them with the manager.

Finally, schedule the interview. Ideally, try to reserve an hour and a half with the manager. Realistically, make full use of whatever time you are offered.

Conducting the Session

During the interview itself, set your sights on identifying critical staffing issues (i.e., gaps or surpluses) and their implications. Initially, focus on problems, not possible solutions. Work to define the right question when you are presented with answers (e.g., when an interviewee says, "What we need to do is . . . ," get that manager to define the problem for which that approach is the solution). Try to stay focused on future issues and implications, not on the problems that the unit is currently facing (unless, of course, these are critical and can be expected to continue). Where necessary, ask follow-up questions to ensure that you fully understand the issues that are raised. Finally, get at least some input regarding priorities (e.g., by asking if the issue just discussed is more or less important than the one that was discussed previously).

It is often helpful to focus on change—how the business is changing. Change nearly always has staffing implications. Refer to the staffing drivers that are defined in Chapter 6 of this book. Remember that your objective is to define significant changes in required staffing levels, required capabilities, or both. Discuss possible solutions only after you have obtained some level of agreement regarding the issues that are to be faced.

In most cases, it is most effective to conduct these interviews with individual managers following a more general session in which the basic concepts regarding strategic staffing have been presented to a group of managers. In these situations, use the interview to obtain feedback on the process that is being proposed. If, however, no such general session is conducted, make sure during the interview that the manager fully understands the process that is being suggested.

Possible Interview Guide

Here is an outline of a guide that you can use to structure the interview itself.

Introduction/Stage Setting

- Thank the person for taking the time to meet with you.
- Give the person an overview of your project/objective (or ensure that the perspective of it that the person already has is accurate).
  - —Human Resources (HR) has a need for a high-level corporate staffing plan that identifies staffing issues that span business units.
  - —The plan will help ensure that the company has the staff it needs in order to implement its overall corporate strategies.
  - —This plan will provide a context for creating specific, shorter-term staffing plans.
  - —Consider reinforcing this point by showing the person the "upside-down T" diagram (Figure 2-1).
  - —Clarify that you are there to talk about staffing issues, gaps, and problems, not answers or solutions.
- Discuss with the manager what the overall process for creating a staffing strategy will look like (or obtain the manager's perceptions of the process if it has already been presented).
- Tell the manager how the information you gather will be used or shared.

Discuss Business Plans/Changes

- Provide a quick overview of your understanding of the unit's current business.
  - —Potentially, you could take the lead here, summarizing the business and getting the manager to supplement or clarify your description.
  - —"It seems to me that currently your business does this/provides this. . . ."
  - —Get the manager to confirm or expand your understanding.
- Review and verify current staffing levels (from a face validity or "looks pretty close" perspective only).

- Get the manager to describe future changes.
  - —Ask the manager to talk about what is to be accomplished during the planning period and the ways in which that represents a significant change from the current situation.
  - —Provide prods or hints and ask clarifying questions (e.g., "It seems to me that . . .") based on your knowledge of the business plans (from your homework) to make sure that you really do understand what the business is going to accomplish.

Discuss Staffing Issues/Implications of Future Plans

- Ask the person what staffing issues are foreseen.
- Identify the areas or job families that will be affected:
  - —First
  - —Most
- Remember to address both skills and staffing levels.
- Identify any major changes in organization or structure (e.g., a change from a product focus to a customer/market orientation, not at the level of who will report to whom).
- If discussion lags, use your potential staffing issue crib list and your definition of current staffing levels to encourage it:
  - —"It seems to me that this expansion will mean an increase in staffing levels."
  - —"It seems that this proposed change in technology will have a real impact on required skills in your technical workforce, but not much impact on Customer Service."
  - —"Right now you have about 100 people in this job family/category—will that go up or down significantly when you implement this change?"
- Clarify any broad statements that the manager makes, but don't be too detailed.
  - —If the manager says "more," get her to differentiate between "a lot more" and "a few more," but don't worry about whether the number is 67 or 72.
  - —If the manager generalizes, get him to identify specific job families.
- Address all the potential issues on your crib sheet.
- Ask the manager if she thinks that any of these issues are being faced by other business units (and thus might be addressed from an integrated perspective).
- Try to assess criticality (i.e., identify the most critical issues).

Obtain Feedback Regarding Proposed Solutions

- Ask the manager for feedback regarding staffing strategies (e.g., "One way of addressing this issue would be to do X. What do you think of that? Would that work here?").
- Ask the manager for feedback regarding staffing plans.

Close the Interview

- "If you could address only one of these issues, which would it be?"
- "What questions didn't I ask that you thought I would?"
- Tell the manager what he can expect from you, if anything.
- Thank the manager for her time and input.

Summary

When implementing strategic staffing, appropriate line management engagement and involvement is crucial. Make sure that the line managers fully understand the process and its value. Ensure that they are actively engaged in the process and prepared to implement (or at least consider implementing) its results. Above all, make sure that they understand how the implementation of strategic staffing will make them better managers right now. Finally, when you talk with managers to obtain the information that you need (e.g., staffing requirement information), be prepared. Understand their business and define their current staffing availability (both staffing levels and capabilities). Discuss with those managers how their business will be changing, and then (and only then) discuss the impact that these changes will have on future staffing requirements.

14

Developing a Strategic Staffing/Workforce Planning Web Site

Clearly, strategic staffing/workforce planning is a powerful tool that can be used to identify and address staffing issues almost anywhere in an organization. Whether those implementing the process are managers or primarily human resource (HR) professionals, they need ready access to strategic staffing knowledge, experience, tools, examples, information, and other resources. Needless to say, it doesn't do much good to develop processes that managers don't know about or understand or to develop tools that no one has access to. Nor does it work to hoard the data and support within HR, doling it out carefully on a controlled, need-to-know basis. You should get your strategic staffing/workforce planning capability out there to all those who need it as efficiently as possible. A strategic staffing web site, running on your company's intranet, can meet these needs quickly and inexpensively.

Why Create a Web Site?

Strategic staffing is an ideal Web-based application. Whether it is on the Internet or on your own intranet, a strategic staffing web site can provide your users with exactly the help they are looking for, exactly when they are looking for it. In different situations, user needs can vary widely, but a Web-based application can offer the kind of flexibility required to meet varying needs effectively and efficiently. There are many good reasons for developing a Web site, but four of them are particularly important.

Expand the Reach of Your Expertise

It is likely that many managers in your organization will be participating in the strategic staffing/workforce planning process at some level. At some point, each of these individuals will need information or tools in order to develop staffing strategies and plans. Traditional communication channels may provide what is necessary, but these channels are probably going to be ineffective (e.g., they may provide all users with the same information, regardless of need). They may also be inefficient (defined in terms of cost and response time), which means that distribution of the information will be limited (e.g., in order to control process costs). Requests may stack up if they are coming in faster than they can be resolved.

A strategic staffing web site can provide users with immediate and constant access to the specific information and tools that they need in order to develop and implement their staffing strategies and plans. There will be no gatekeepers or bottlenecks that restrict the flow of needed information or limit access to helpful tools. Managers will not have to wait for HR staff to become available to answer their questions. Use of a web site will allow users to find what they need 24 hours a day/7 days a week—an especially critical requirement in a global company that is conducting business around the clock. An "ask the expert" section allows users to post, and receive customized answers to, their specific questions without having to track down individual HR staff.

Because all important strategic staffing/workforce planning information and tools are located in a single place, it will also be easier for you to maintain and update this information; this means that users will always be accessing the most current information and tools that are available.

Build Knowledge and Skills

Your users' level of strategic staffing expertise will vary widely. Some experienced users may simply need an answer to a particular question or help with a particular part of the process (e.g., defining staffing requirements). Less experienced managers (e.g., those who are doing it for the first time) may have to learn about strategic staffing from the ground up and may need to be taken by the hand and led through the process of developing, interpreting, and implementing staffing strategies.

A well-designed web site will meet the learning needs of both of these groups (and everyone in between). By navigating an efficient series of menus, those who understand the process will be able to move quickly to locate the answer they need (or to find someone they can ask). Information (such as process descriptions) can be provided at varying levels of detail, allowing users to click and "drill down" to the level that they require. The site can also contain a search capability that allows users to pinpoint the exact sections of the site that contain the help they need. Those who need a better understanding of the process can learn about strategic staffing/workforce planning at their own pace by reading the text, following examples, playing with the templates, and interacting with strategic staffing experts. It is also possible to integrate into the site various training modules that provide a more formal, structured approach to learning.

Increase Collaboration

A message board on a strategic staffing web site can provide users with a forum for discussing strategic staffing issues, identifying common problems and concerns, and sharing best practices (whether internal or external). It can also provide a place to go when a manager needs to ask another manager for guidance ("What should I do?"), advice ("How did you solve this problem in the past?"), or opinions ("What do you think of this proposed solution?"). The site can also be used to identify staffing issues that are common to several business units and solutions that have proved to be particularly effective.

Intranet web sites can also prove valuable in the data collection process. Through such a site, users can exchange information and send in pieces that need to be compiled into a whole (e.g., they can submit staffing requirements for individual projects so that an overall definition of requirements can be developed). The web site can also serve as a forum for facilitating staffing actions, allowing managers to talk to one another regarding staffing needs and opportunities.

While this kind of communication is obviously available face to face within a limited group, use of the message board will allow managers and other users to cast a wider net. They can initiate and develop contacts with a much larger group of people—many more than they could possibly talk with on a one-on-one basis.

Increase Implementation Efficiency

If you have a specific process in place (or if you are implementing a process for the first time), a strategic staffing web site can make that process more efficient. The site can be used to describe the context and structure of the process to be implemented. It can provide users with all the forms, instructions, and staffing information that they need in order to complete their staffing strategies and plans. Users can also submit implementation-related questions and obtain answers quickly. The site can also be used as a centralized point for gathering and compiling staffing information from decentralized units and participants.

Designing Your Site

First, create a web site (or add a series of pages to an existing site) that can be accessed easily and directly by all your proposed users. Make sure that the site is secure, but don't let password protection impede access unnecessarily. If in doubt, err on the side of providing access to more people. Provide hyperlinks to the site from other internal human resource and business planning web sites and pages.

There is now a wealth of information regarding how an effective web site should be formatted and structured and what an effective site includes. There are individuals (whether consultants or company employees) who know far more about this than you do. Take full advantage of their expertise; don't try to design and build the site yourself.

When designing your web site, consider the following hints:

- Keep the site as simple as possible (or at least have it appear to be simple). A well-designed site can provide a lot of information in a way that never overwhelms the users.

- Build the site with users and customers in mind. What they need and want may differ from what you think they should have.

- Organize your site so that the various sections clearly and logically map to the specific needs of your users. Design the menus so that it is easy for users to pinpoint the type of help they need and locate the module, section, or web page that contains just that help. Include each main point as a clickable option on your site's home page.

- Make sure that your opening/welcome screen is clean and inviting, not intimidating. Its design should encourage users to stay and dig deeper, not turn and flee.

- Use lots of pictures, diagrams, and other visuals. There are many figures in this book that explain and cement key concepts far better than my words do. Include diagrams and pictures such as those.

- Make it easy for users to print whatever information they think is helpful. Don't force them to print an entire section or page if what they need is contained in a single paragraph.

- Build the site so that it can be easily accessed and navigated, even if that makes it more difficult for you to maintain and update.

- Create ongoing processes for routine tests and site maintenance.

Finally, create and execute a plan to market your site to potential users. Do whatever is needed to create a "buzz" about the site and create a demand for its use, employing any and all media that you have access to. "Hype" the benefits that can be realized. Clearly describe how the site will help users to implement the strategic staffing/workforce planning process more effectively. Merely communicating the existence of the site will generate little or no interest among users.

Site Content and Objectives

Share Information

On this section of the site, post all the information that users need in order to understand your strategic staffing process and how it works.

- **Overall strategic staffing concepts.** Define the objectives of strategic staffing and describe the context in which it works best. Provide diagrams (like the "upside-down T" shown in Chapter 2) that visually reinforce the points you are trying to make. Where necessary, also say what strategic staffing is not (e.g., describe the less effective, traditional approaches and why they should be avoided).

- **Generic process descriptions.** Describe, in general terms, the processes for developing longer-term staffing strategies and shorter-term staffing plans. Discuss the relationship between the two (i.e., that staffing strategies provide a long-term context within which more effective short-term staffing decisions can be made). Describe the components of the process and how they should be integrated. Provide diagrams to reinforce your descriptions.

- **Company-specific process descriptions.** Describe your actual strategic staffing process. Provide an overview or road map of the process itself. Discuss the various components of your process and how they fit together. Include diagrams that show the relationships among components. Some organizations have included detailed process diagrams; clicking on a component of the diagram brings up a more detailed view of that part of the process. Provide specific instructions for completing each step of the process. Describe roles and accountabilities. Talk about timing and describe links to other existing processes (such as business planning, budgeting, succession planning, and job posting). Where possible, provide hyperlinks to other areas of your intranet where those processes are described and supported.

- **Specific examples.** Provide specific examples of the process. Use actual numbers when describing staffing plans. Provide examples of typical outputs and expected deliverables.

Share Tools

Provide users with direct access to the tools that they need in order to develop their own staffing strategies and plans. Specifically provide versions that practitioners can download, tailor, and use to meet their actual needs. This might include the following tools:

- **Spreadsheet templates.** Create generic versions of supply/demand staffing models that utilize existing, readily available spreadsheet software. Preload each model with all necessary calculation routines, formulas, and linkages so that users can simply adjust the number of rows and columns, load their data, and run their initial models. Don't forget to provide full instructions on how to use and update the spreadsheets.

- **Reusable examples.** Provide preformatted examples that users can easily edit (e.g., word processing tables containing draft staffing plans that completely describe required staffing actions). This will ensure that users' work is complete and well organized.

- **Your forms.** If your process requires the completion of forms or templates, provide them in a downloadable, ready-to-use format.

- **Data-gathering procedures.** If your process requires the submission of completed forms, provide users with the ability to submit their data directly through the site (eliminating paper transactions).

- **Suggested communications.** Provide samples of reports, analyses, presentations, and other communications that practitioners can tailor and use to describe the results of their processes to their constituencies.

- **Diagnostics and assessments.** Provide simple diagnostic tools and process assessments that allow your users to evaluate the effectiveness of their existing staffing strategies (including the processes they use to create those strategies) and identify opportunities to improve the effectiveness and efficiency of their strategies. Examples of diagnostics and assessment tools are described in Chapter 12 of this book.

Share Expertise

Provide ready access to the strategic staffing knowledge base that has been built within your company. Provide a wide array of options, from canned responses to common questions to real-time, online coaching and consulting. You might do the following:

- **Organize by problem and structure walk-throughs.** In some cases (especially with new users), it will be difficult for people to even know where to begin the strategic staffing process. Use a simple form of expert system to help these individuals, providing a structured approach to identifying and resolving their issues. Here is a suggested process:

—Provide a list of common strategic staffing problems that managers in your organization face (e.g., a shortage of a particular skill or the need to focus attention on a job category that is particularly critical). Have the user click on the problem that is most relevant.

—Have the site prompt the user to define key planning parameters for the selected issue (e.g., time frame, planning horizon, and population to be included).

—Present a series of pointed questions that helps users to define appropriate rows and columns for their staffing models.

—Based on the responses so far, have the site suggest to the user the data that will be needed to build the model that has been designed. Using a generic list, have the site suggest to the user where those needed data might be located.

—Link the user to the spreadsheet templates that are located elsewhere in the site. Describe how those sheets should be modified and loaded to support the analysis.

—Provide a list of possible outcomes (e.g., staffing gaps or staffing surpluses) and a list of staffing actions that might be relevant for each type of outcome.

—Provide a link to the templates (e.g., word processing tables) so users can document findings, conclusions, and proposed staffing plans.

- **Provide implementation guidance.** Provide specific advice that supports the effective implementation of the strategic staffing/workforce planning process. Describe what can be done to avoid pitfalls, work around obstacles, and minimize resistance to the implementation of the process. From a more positive perspective, describe what should be done to facilitate implementation. Many of these concepts are described in Chapters 11 and 12.

- **Provide access to an "e-coach."** Allow users to interact with strategic staffing experts, either on a real-time/online basis or through e-mail. Identify people with strategic staffing expertise and provide users with direct links to those people. If e-mail links are used, you might even want to create specific Web addresses that allow users to gain expedited access to the experts without having to negotiate normal e-mail channels. Make sure that you measure response time and quality.

- **Provide message boards.** Create a strategic staffing message board that allows users to post questions, ask for advice from other users, or have interactive discussions regarding strategic staffing topics and issues.

- **Address frequently asked questions.** Provide a list of frequently asked questions and the answers to those questions.

Share Resources

Provide direct links to other resources that support the development of staffing strategies.

- Often, there is a great deal of helpful information that already exists within the company. In your strategic staffing web site, provide direct access to such internal resources as:

  —**Company data.** Describe relevant company databases and their content. Provide hyperlinks to the search engine of each database.

  —**Related company systems.** Provide direct links to company systems that are related to, but different from, strategic staffing (e.g., job posting, succession planning).

  —**Internal experts.** Provide a list of internal staff that can provide help in specific areas or answer particular questions. List the areas of expertise of each individual so that the user can quickly identify the most probable source for the needed information.

  —**Available training and development.** Provide a list of internal training and development resources that a practitioner might use to gain a better understanding of strategic staffing (e.g., courses, computer/Web-based training).

- There is also a wealth of information available on the Web. Rather than try to provide such information in your own strategic staffing web site, simply provide hyperlinks to the sites where the needed information resides. That way, you won't need to maintain the information. Check your links frequently; Web addresses change often, and you don't want your users to become frustrated trying to access sites that have moved to new addresses. External resources might include:

  —External databases (e.g., federal and state demographic databases, Internet job posting boards)

  —Financial and economic forecasts

  —Professional societies, both human resource and industry-specific (e.g., Society for Human Resource Management, Human Resource Planning Society)

  —Providers of relevant workshops, seminars, and other training

(e.g., AMACOM, World at Work, various university executive education programs)

—Online bookstores (e.g., AMACOM, Amazon, Barnes & Noble)

—Web sites of known external experts

You should also provide a search capability so your users can quickly locate the specific information or assistance that they are looking for.

One last suggestion: Include a direct link to a person that users can contact if they cannot find what they need or still have questions.

A Final Note

As you read through this section, you may have noticed that the sections of the web site that I propose and the sections of this book match quite closely. That is no accident. The information that is provided to you in this book is the information that your users will need to support their strategic staffing efforts. Feel free to include some of the concepts and ideas described in this book as starting points for the various components of this site (although obviously you can't just copy this text!).

15

C H A P T E R

Supporting Strategic Staffing/Workforce Planning: HR Structure and Required Skills

By now you should have a good idea of what an effective strategic staffing/workforce planning process entails, as well as an understanding of the context within which that process should be implemented. But how should the HR function be structured to support strategic staffing/workforce planning? And what skills and capabilities should HR staff possess in order to play the roles that they are expected to play?

This chapter provides at least one structure for the HR function that is capable of supporting strategic staffing/workforce planning on an ongoing basis. Other structures may also be appropriate, but the one I present here has proved effective in several companies. Needless to say, I am not expecting you to implement this structure right away. However, this chapter might provide you with a vision of what your HR structure might be at some point in the near future.

Some of you may have adopted this structure (or something similar) already. For those that have, you might find opportunities to fine-tune the roles that your people are playing within that structure. Those of you that have a different structure for your HR function may wish to implement the structure just as it is described or try to "cherry-pick" the parts that you think might be needed in your situation.

With regard to skills and capabilities, there may be less flexibility in what is required. Regardless of how you choose to organize your HR function to support strategic staffing/workforce planning, the HR staff that are involved in the process must have certain capabilities and perspectives if the strategic staffing/workforce planning process is to be implemented successfully. I have tried to identify and describe the most critical of these required skills and capabilities for each staff role I have described.

Should Strategic Staffing/Workforce Planning Stand Alone?

In my work with companies, I have seen no one consistent "home" for strategic staffing/workforce planning within the HR function. In some cases, it is its own unit (even if it is a "unit" of one person!). In other cases, workforce planning is located within another, more traditional HR function (such as recruiting or staffing). I have also seen workforce planning included within Talent Management, Succession and Development, and even Diversity Planning.

From my perspective, strategic staffing/workforce planning is a discipline in and of itself. It has its own roles, accountabilities, and expectations, and it feeds nearly every other HR function (e.g., staffing, recruiting, training, development, and succession). As a result, it simply cannot be linked to just one of those functions. When strategic staffing/workforce planning is first implemented, it is possible that the workload it generates can be handled along with that of another function. However, as soon as the value of workforce planning is recognized, demand for the process will generate much work and require significant resources. At that point, it is unlikely that the staff of any unit that combines workforce planning and another function will be able to do a good job of either one. Further, strategic staffing/workforce planning requires a set of skills and capabilities that other HR functions don't. Consequently, strategic staffing/workforce planning warrants its own unit within the HR function. In the recommendations that follow, I have assumed that there will be a unit of some kind that is dedicated to workforce planning—but don't jump to any conclusions regarding what the role of that function will be!

The Overall Structure of HR

Before focusing on strategic staffing/workforce planning, I'd like to provide an overall model of what I think the organization of the HR function should be. While this proposal is completely consistent with my recommendations regarding workforce planning in particular, the overall structure could also be implemented in an organization that has no dedicated workforce planning capability at all. Figure 15-1 provides a schematic of what this structure looks like.

This HR structure has three major components that work together to meet the needs of line managers. At times, two components might be sufficient; at other times, all three are needed. In the case of workforce planning, I believe that there is a role for each of the three components on an ongoing basis. Here is a brief description of each component.

Figure 15-1. A Suggested Organization Structure for Human Resources.

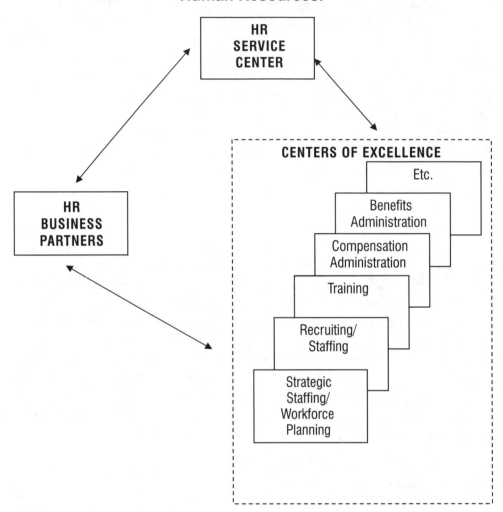

The HR Service Center

Let me start by saying that the following paragraphs apply equally well whether you have an in-house service center or one that has been out-sourced. A well-designed, efficiently run HR service center is the corner-stone of any HR function. While grouping like activities in a service center setting might reduce operating costs, that is not its major objective. The service center should be taking on all of the administrative and repetitive tasks so that managers and HR staff don't have to allocate any time or resources to these nonstrategic (though absolutely necessary) tasks. The more time managers and HR staff spend on short-term/tactical issues and administration, the less time they have to spend on longer-term, more strategic concerns. Once freed of these responsibilities, managers and HR staff can concentrate on things strategic—including workforce planning.

The normal role of the service center is to provide basic administrative support to the HR function. For many organizations, this includes benefits administration, salary administration, HRIS/data management, and governmental reporting. But in the organization structure I am proposing, the service center needs to play a much more extensive role than this. It should handle any and all HR tasks that are regular, repetitive, or not related to the needs of a specific business. This should include such activities as:

- Applicant tracking
- Basic applicant screening (e.g., conducting initial interviews)
- Ongoing recruiting to meet regular, nonstrategic needs (e.g., replacement of administrative staff), including identifying, evaluating, and presenting slates of qualified candidates
- All regular, recurring job posting activity
- All repetitive training (e.g., first-level management courses), including all orientations
- Basic career planning and development programs
- Day-to-day labor relations concerns
- Administration of any and all "employee self-service" activities

This list is by no means exhaustive. There could be many more activities in your organization that should be performed within a service center.

The service center will also play several key roles in supporting workforce planning:

- Since the service center is handling much of the day-to-day activity of recruiting and staffing, HR functional staff will have the time they need in order to focus on and address the most critical issues that they are facing. No longer will those staff need to put off addressing strategic staffing issues in order to fight the fires of the day.
- The service center will be the source of much of the data that are needed to create and run staffing models (e.g., past turnover data needed to develop future projections, accurate information on current employee headcounts, lists detailing retirement eligibility).
- It is also likely that the service center will host and maintain the workforce planning web site. This will allow the workforce planning unit to focus on value-added planning and staffing work instead of administration.

With regard to required skills, these HR service center functional leaders will need such skills as:

- A basic understanding of the business of each unit
- An in-depth understanding of the appropriate function (e.g., recruiting)
- Good communications skills (both giving and receiving information)
- A good understanding of the strategic staffing/workforce planning process (especially the expected outputs, such as staffing plans and actions)
- Good organizational skills
- The ability to evaluate and set priorities (e.g., which "fire" to fight first)
- An "efficiency" mindset (e.g., the ability to get a lot of good work done in a speedy, cost-efficient manner)

HR Business Partners

Many organizations have this position, but few of them define the role as it should be defined. When implemented effectively, the HR business partner is meant to be a very strategic role, focused on helping the business unit to meet its long-term objectives. As a valued member of the strategic inner circle of the business unit, the HR business partner is meant to help senior managers to identify and address critical, long-term HR issues such as:

- Identifying and addressing the HR implications of business plans and strategies
- Defining the implications of major organization changes
- Implementing and supporting executive succession and development activities
- Identifying high-level talent management gaps and developing appropriate strategies
- Using strategic staffing/workforce planning, working with managers on an ongoing basis to:
  —Identify critical staffing issues and implications
  —Define staffing requirements
  —Gather input regarding turnover and retirement scenarios
  —Review staffing model output and develop staffing strategies
  —Work with managers to define realistic staffing plans and actions

(e.g., identifying who will actually be promoted or redeployed, identifying which positions will be contracted out)

—Monitor unit staffing plans to ensure that they are being implemented as expected and that staffing needs are indeed being met

Take special notice of that last item—it is one of the most important roles that an HR business partner can play. Note that the business partner role includes nothing that is tactical or short term. To be effective, the business partner must focus on the big picture.

To play this role effectively, an HR business partner must have such skills and capabilities as:

- An in-depth knowledge of her business unit (i.e., an understanding that is on a par with that of the business leaders of that unit)
- An ability to think and act with a strategic perspective
- The confidence of and credibility with managers, from a peer-to-peer perspective
- The ability to communicate effectively with (and appropriately challenge) line managers
- A good understanding of the strategic staffing/workforce planning process and its objectives
- An in-depth understanding of staffing processes (remember my very broad definition of what staffing includes)
- Creative problem-solving skills

Many organizations that have the business partner role implement it in a most ineffective way. Somehow, the business partner has become a kind of "one-stop shop" for addressing any or all HR problems faced by the business unit. In most cases, this means that the partners are not supporting strategic decisions, but are instead focusing on tactical issues, short-term crises, and day-to-day firefighting. So much time is spent on these short-term problems that the partners have little or no time or resources to allocate to things strategic. This approach also tends to lead to a vicious downward spiral. The more HR business partners become involved in day-to-day problems, the deeper they fall into this abyss. When this happens, they have even less time to perform the strategic role that is the very focus of the position. But if HR business partners do not address these strategic issues, who will?

Clearly, the short-term issues of the business unit need to be addressed. If this is not the job of the HR business partner, how will those problems be solved? From my perspective, there are at least two things that need to happen:

- Many of the short-term issues can be dealt with by staff in the HR service center. Remember that I have suggested a role for the service center that includes responsibilities for compensation, recruiting, staffing, training, labor management, and other such areas. When managers are facing short-term problems in these areas, they should turn to the service center, not the HR business partner.

- Still other short-term problems can be addressed by employees themselves and thus require no input at all from the business partner. Employees are perfectly capable of participating in posting, signing up for training, and keeping their HRIS records and other profiles (e.g., internal career résumés and development profiles) up to date. Middle- and lower-level managers can work directly with the service center to fill approved positions, replace regular turnover, conduct employee orientations, and run basic training programs.

By eliminating the time spent on these day-to-day issues, HR business partners will suddenly have time and resources to allocate to strategic staffing/workforce planning. There might, however, be two obstacles to overcome (both of which are of our own making) if the partner is to be truly strategic:

1. Stop measuring HR business partners' performance in terms of how quickly they respond to short-term crises. Similarly, no longer gauge management satisfaction with business partners' service by measuring how well they address short-term, tactical problems. Instead, use those measures to evaluate the overall performance of the service center. Consider evaluating how well managers utilize service center support and capabilities. Finally, develop and apply more strategic measures to assess HR business partners' performance.

2. The second change is more sensitive. Many HR business partners gravitate to more tactical roles and choose to respond to short-term issues because they lack the skills, capabilities, or inclination to operate in the realm of strategy. These people prefer to fight fires rather than identify and address strategic issues. They address short-term problems not because managers are forcing them to do so, but rather because they are more comfortable operating in a near-term, reactive environment. Some of these HR business partners may be intimidated by senior managers (or lack the confidence of or credibility with those managers). Others lack strategic perspective. Still others may lack the in-depth understanding of

the business that is necessary (even though they may think that they may have that understanding). As you implement the strategic role of HR business partner, don't just define a new set of accountabilities. Make sure that you fill each HR business partner slot with an individual who has the experience, perspective, understanding, and capabilities to truly "partner" with line managers in a strategic arena. Finally, consider having the partner report directly to the head of the business unit, not to the head of HR. It is difficult to partner with a group that works together on a constant, day-to-day basis if you are viewed as an outsider or a visitor. Sometimes you just have to be "inside the tent" to be privy to what is really going on.

Strategic Staffing/Workforce Planning (SWFP) "Center of Excellence"

As you read these paragraphs, remember that at first this might be a "unit" of one individual. Also, bear in mind that some of what is described here is an organic role that develops and expands over time as demands for services and the availability of staff and resources all grow.

The SWFP unit is the organization's "expert" on strategic staffing/workforce planning. The staff of the unit work with all the HR business partners as internal consultants to help them to identify, and develop strategies to address, their most critical staffing issues, drawing support from the HR service center as required. Over time, a strategic staffing/workforce planning leader may head up a small unit that provides strategic staffing/workforce planning services to the organization.

On an ongoing basis, the unit is responsible for such things as:

- Creating, updating, and maintaining strategic staffing/workforce planning processes that meet the company's needs and are appropriate in terms of size and scope

- Working to support HR business partners and line managers as required so that they can implement the strategic staffing/workforce planning process effectively and efficiently

- Helping partners and managers to apply the process to "frame" and address particularly difficult or complex staffing issues

- Working with HR service center staff to create and implement the near-term staffing and development plans that are needed to implement long-term staffing strategies

- Identifying opportunities to manage staff across business units or implement coordinated staffing strategies that address common staffing issues

- Developing staffing cost analyses
- Developing and maintaining a strategic staffing/workforce planning infrastructure (including creating and updating the web site and developing and conducting workforce planning–related training)

Note that this role can be played only within the context of the organizational changes and accountabilities described earlier. The leader can support the business partners only if those partners understand and play the roles I have defined. The leader can define and implement coordinated staffing strategies and plans effectively only if the HR service center is providing the services that I have described.

Initially, the leader probably will need to be directly involved in workforce planning in order to demonstrate its value to the organization and train others (e.g., HR business partners) in the process itself. As this organizational capability is developed, the role can gradually "morph" into the long-term role that is described here.

In order to play this role, the strategic staffing/workforce planning leader should possess such skills and capabilities as:

- An in-depth understanding of strategic staffing, including its objectives, the process itself, the application of process results, and a mastery of the tools and techniques to be employed
- An in-depth understanding of the business of each unit
- A strategic, big-picture perspective—thinking both long term (e.g., five to ten years in the future) and broadly (e.g., identifying opportunities to implement solutions that span units)
- The confidence of and credibility with managers, from a peer-to-peer perspective
- The ability to communicate effectively with (and appropriately challenge) line managers
- The ability to identify, frame, and describe potentially complex staffing issues and implications
- The ability to describe complex staffing issues, implications, and solutions to line managers in terms that they can understand
- A good understanding of all the staffing processes that are used by the organization and the staffing options that are available (again, remember how inclusive my definition of staffing is)
- A cross-HR functional perspective (e.g., recognizing that the solution to many staffing issues will require input from several HR functions)
- A results orientation (e.g., focusing on solving staffing-related problems, not just creating workforce planning processes)

- Creative problem-solving skills
- Good organizational skills and a penchant for detail
- Basic financial analysis skills (e.g., the ability to define the financial implications/cost savings of staffing strategies or determine the costs of implementing specific staffing plans)
- An intermediate mastery of spreadsheet technology
- A basic understanding of web site design
- Basic supervisory skills (for when the unit becomes more than a unit of one)

Note that some skills that are traditionally associated with the position are not included on this list:

- An in-depth knowledge of spreadsheet technology is not needed because the staffing models that are built and applied are just not that complex.
- An in-depth understanding of the capabilities and content of your HRIS is not needed because the detailed interaction with the HRIS will be handled by the HR service center, not this position. The service center will also provide any data mining that is required.
- A mastery of external demographic data and analysis is not required because external demographics play a limited role in this version of workforce planning. If such analysis is needed, it can be better provided on an as-needed, cost-effective manner by external consultants.
- An in-depth understanding of web site design and maintenance is not needed. Such web site administration and support will be provided by the service center.
- Research skills are not required. If your workforce planning leader is doing in-depth data research, then he is moving down the wrong path. Such research rarely helps an organization to identify and address the critical, company-specific staffing issues that it is facing.

Suppose for a minute that you do not have someone in your organization that meets all these criteria. Is it better to take a staffing professional and develop in that person the understanding of the business and strategic perspective that the position requires, or is it more effective to take an effective business leader (who presumably already understands the business and can think strategically) and teach that person workforce planning and staffing? In this situation, most organizations would reach out to the HR or staffing professional and try to develop the missing business and strategy-related skills. I suggest that you do the exact opposite. An under-standing of the business and strategic perspective is a capability that in the best of cases takes a long time to develop. Some might even suggest that such a perspective is an innate capability that people either have or don't have. Strategic staffing/workforce planning, on the other hand, is a logical process that can be quickly mastered. Thus, it will probably be far easier (and more expedient) for you to select a strategic business leader and teach her workforce planning than to choose an HR professional and develop that person's business understanding and strategic perspective.

Final Thoughts

Here are some final thoughts on this structure and these roles. Note that if they are implemented as described, there may not be large functional units within HR. As is the case with strategic staffing, each HR function may have a small unit that focuses on strategic issues. Figure 16-1 refers to these as "centers of excellence," but they could be just as well be labeled "centers of expertise." These centers are not involved in anything tactical, how-ever. All of the functional support and administration is provided within the structure (and reporting relationships) of the HR service center. Figure 15-2 provides a table that describes how strategic staffing/workforce planning roles and accountabilities might be allocated to various HR positions. It is based on a table that I produced for a client recently. It is fully consis-tent with the ideas in this chapter, but it was developed to meet the partic-ular needs of a specific company. Thus, it may differ slightly in terms of the level of detail it contains. Still, it is a good example of how one organi-zation actually implemented the structure I propose.

Figure 15-2. Sample Workforce Planning Roles for HR Staff.

WFP Process Step	HR Business Partner	Local HR Representative	WFP Lead	Recruiters
1. Identify critical staffing issues	• Review business strategies and plans • Identify staffing implications of facility plans (e.g., replacing and existing facility) • Identify staffing implications of departmental or functional business plans • Identify staffing issues that do not arise directly from business plans (e.g., retirement) • Assess issue criticality and identify those issues that require WFP	• Support the identification of critical staffing issues	• Help to "frame" or define staffing issues appropriately • Support the identification and definition of potential staffing issues that span departments or facilities (e.g., competitive threats)	• Alert HR Business Partners and/or WFP Lead when significant recruiting issues arise (e.g., increased competition for talent, shrinking external talent pools)
2. Define staffing gaps and surpluses	• Provide input regarding staffing requirements	• Support the creation of staffing models • Gather staffing requirements	• Create and "load" staffing models • Provide initial supply information (e.g., current headcount, historic turnover, retirement eligibility)	
3. Develop staffing strategies*	• Provide input regarding staffing strategies • Review proposed staffing strategies to ensure that they are appropriate • Identify possible local implications of staffing strategies (e.g., where one facility may be affected adversely)	• Develop "cross functional" staffing strategies in consultation with managers	• Work directly with HR Consultants to support the development of particular staffing strategies • Work directly with managers, HR Business Partners, and Local HR Reps to develop staffing strategies for issues that span departments or facilities • Identify opportunities to develop staffing strategies that span facilities or departments	• Provide input (e.g., "reality checks") regarding the hiring components of staffing strategies • Suggest recruiting strategies

*Note that staffing strategies incorporate retention strategies

Figure 15-2. (Continued)

WFP Process Step	HR Business Partner	Local HR Representative	WFP Lead	Recruiters
4. Define staffing plans	• Review proposed staffing plans to ensure that they are realistic and cost effective	• Develop staffing plans (in consultation with managers) that allow the most effective implementation of staffing strategies • Document staffing plans • Act as a "broker" to coordinate the work of HR staff (on a cross functional basis) so that staffing plans can be implemented • Define staffing costs • Evaluate the cost implications of staffing plans	• Work directly with Local HR Reps to support the development of particular staffing plans • Work directly with managers, HR Business Partners, and Local HR Reps to develop staffing plans for issues that span departments or facilities • Support the development of staffing cost analyses	• Provide direct input to the development of the hiring components of staffing plans • Provide information regarding recruiting costs • Develop the specific recruiting plans needed to support the implementation of staffing plans
5. Implement staffing plans	• Facilitate staffing moves (of internal candidates) among facilities	• Work with managers to implement the "non-recruiting" components of staffing plans (e.g., identifying individuals to be promoted or redeployed)		• Source candidates needed to implement WFP • Interview and assess these specific candidates • Work with managers to assess and select candidates
Ongoing	• Provide input and feedback to the WFP Lead regarding the WFP process (e.g., opportunities to improve effectiveness) • Keep up to date on changes in business plans (both proposed and actual) in order to identify possible staffing issues • Notify Local HR Reps and/or WFP Lead when new or updated workforce plans may be required • Provide input to selection and retention programs • Educate managers regarding the need for and benefits of WFP	• Monitor/track the implementation of staffing plans to ensure that needs are being met • Educate managers regarding the need for and benefits of WFP • Update workforce plans for the "next cycle"	• Educate managers regarding the need for and benefits of WFP • Maintain the effectiveness of the WFP process (e.g., gathering and incorporating feedback form users) • Maintain tools and supporting resources • Manage the internal WFP "web site" • Modify the structure of existing staffing models when necessary (e.g., adding rows or columns when necessary) • Work with Local HR Reps to update existing workforce plan information • Provide ongoing WFP consulting to managers, HR Business Partners, and Local HR Reps (e.g., helping them apply the process to address complex staffing issues) • Work with HRIS staff to allow the continual flow of required data	• Monitor and evaluate external sources of talent • Coordinate the hiring process with hiring managers

16

Getting Started: Conducting a One-Day "Kickoff" Session

Do you think your organization might be ready to develop and implement an effective strategic workforce planning process, following the system and suggestions included in this book? In my consulting, I often start an organization down the road to effective workforce planning by conducting an intensive, one-day training seminar that allows that company to:

- Create a common, consistent understanding of what an effective workforce planning process includes (e.g., objectives, process steps, implementation context)

- Review and understand the workforce planning process in detail, on a step-by-step basis (including an actual example that demonstrates each step)

- Define how the workforce planning process might be applied within the company for the first time (e.g., identifying actual critical staffing issues, defining staffing model parameters, identifying "next steps" and accountabilities)

This chapter (and the PowerPoint presentations that I have provided at www.amacombooks.org/go/StrategicStaff2E) will allow you to create, tailor, and conduct your own version of this one-day seminar. Every one of the key points that is made in each of the three presentations is already made in detail somewhere in this book. However, to make it a little easier for you to conduct a seminar like the one I suggest, I have provided a description and a bit of a script for each of the three sessions of the seminar.

Each presentation is intended to tell a logical story that has a beginning, a middle, and an end. Needless to say, while the main points should be made in the order in which they are presented, you will probably find it necessary to modify or customize the text of the slides for each presentation so that you can:

- Make the points that *you* want to make, not necessarily those that I think are important.
- "Sell" the concepts and benefits of strategic workforce planning to *your* audience.
- Identify the critical staffing issues that *your* organization is facing.
- Tailor the workforce planning process to meet the objectives and address the critical staffing issues of *your* organization.
- Define the specific next steps that *your* company should take to develop and implement the workforce planning process

If you are attempting to implement strategic workforce planning in more than one organization or unit, you might consider conducting this one-day seminar for each such unit. One word of caution: *You should only conduct this seminar just prior to developing and implementing a workforce planning process*. It is not a good idea to conduct the seminar "in advance of need," so to speak. The concepts of workforce planning are easiest to grasp if they are applied as they are learned. Thus, it is not a good idea to conduct the seminar for a unit and then try to implement the workforce planning process six months or a year later.

For each session, I have also provided a set of objectives and a suggested attendee list. You will see that it is not necessarily a good idea to have the same group attend all three sessions.

Session 1: Developing and Implementing an Effective Process

This session is an overview of what I think effective workforce planning is and what it entails. It is intended to provide a common definition of the workforce planning process and its objectives, a better understanding of the process itself, some ideas for how the process might be applied when business plans are uncertain, and some implementation hints.

Given that this session is an overview, it is usually appropriate to include a broad array of participants, including both senior line managers and HR staff. At a minimum, attendees for this session should include:

- Those HR staff that are responsible for the company's workforce planning efforts
- Senior line managers who are facing critical staffing issues that might be addressed by the initial implementation of workforce planning

- The HR business partners of those line managers
- HR staff from functions that will typically use the results of the workforce plan (e.g., Recruiting, Staffing, Training and Development)

You may also wish to invite representatives of other areas, including:

- Strategic/Business Planning
- Finance (especially when Finance is involved in headcount planning or control)
- HRIS (e.g., to better understand the quality and availability of HR information that might support the staffing models that will be needed)
- HR business partners from units that are not included in the first iteration of workforce planning (e.g., so that they can get an idea of what workforce planning is and how it might apply in their organizations)

Once you have done it a time or two, this section can usually be covered in 90 minutes to two hours.

Here are the key points to make/emphasize in each subsection.

Introduction

- Review what the session will cover.
- Review the simple definitions.
  - —My very broad definition of "staffing" is a critical point. Staffing can have many definitions. To some, it is a process that begins when there is an opening. To others, it is the process that is used to fill jobs internally (as opposed to recruiting, which fills them externally). It is important to use my definition in order to create a common understanding, even if it is only for the duration of the presentation. I sometimes say that my definition of staffing includes any or all managed movement into, around, or out of an organization—including retention. This broad definition of staffing becomes important later, when we define "staffing issues." We want to consider all potential staffing issues, not just those that meet some specific, narrow definition.
  - —When you define "issue," make sure to emphasize that an issue is a specific, measurable difference, not just a "gut feel." To emphasize this point, I sometimes mention that "a lack of bench strength" is not really a staffing issue because at that level it is

neither specific nor measurable. Contrast that with the example of having 10 qualified candidates for an opening but needing 12—that is a specific, measurable difference.

—My definition of strategy is the classic one, with one difference: I always add the tag line that it tells us how objectives will be met. It is impossible for anyone to identify the staffing implications of objectives; we can define the staffing implications only for what is going to be done to meet those objectives. To emphasize the point, get the group to define the staffing implications of being the "low-cost producer" of a good or service. You will probably get a long list. Now ask the group which of the things mentioned will really happen. Needless to say, the group members will be unable to answer that—unless, of course, they define what will be done to become the low-cost producer. Once that is determined, staffing implications can be defined.

—I usually differentiate between data and information by saying that "data are data" (facts, figures, charts, graphs, and so on); data that you use to make a decision are information. The challenge to the group here is that they should eliminate generating, analyzing, or reporting of staffing *data*. There are probably at least some staffing-related reports and analyses—perhaps some that are quite extensive—that don't drive or support decision making (and thus are not *information*). These are not helpful and should be eliminated.

Developing Workforce Plans

• The first slide in this section is intended to generate discussion of what the participants think workforce planning is, what it includes, and why the process is not implemented effectively on a widespread basis (or, for that matter, in your organization in particular).

• The next slide states what I think has to be done differently. I sometimes say, "You have to tweak the process to improve efficiency and drastically change the context within which the process is implemented to improve effectiveness."

• The next few slides address the workforce planning process and its objectives. All of this information is included in the first few chapters of the book.

—When presenting the definition, stress that workforce planning includes both defining and addressing staffing issues—not just defining them.

When discussing the deliverables, present the second one first (short-term staffing plans), since that is what most participants expect to hear. Then present staffing strategies as an important addition to the process.

—The "upside-down T" shows how staffing strategies create the context within which staffing plans should be developed (specifically refer to the space that is at the intersection of the vertical and horizontal bars). In addition, use this slide to introduce the concept of "focus." Remind participants that the objective is not to include all jobs, just those jobs that warrant a strategic perspective (e.g., widening the stem to include half the scope).

—The next slide provides examples of staffing strategies and plans that you can use to cement those concepts—including the difference between them.

• The next group of slides describes the workforce planning process.

—The first slide includes the basic steps.

—The next slide presents a traditional approach—but a wrong one.

—Use the next slide to make the point that this is a bad approach. See if the participants can spot what is wrong with it (i.e., that it is not a good idea to compare current supply to future demand).

...le a "better" approach that includes the ...rement, but state that this process still ...tive approach. If you use this approach, ...wer, but you will need to go through ...e point that this not a very effective ap-

...and make the point that the use of un-...le assumptions can help you get to the ...cribed in the text).

...participants to think about the context ...d improved" process you just described

...detail for this slide is included in Chap-

...the most important slide in the presenta-...this, try this" approach to each bullet point. State why the issue-oriented context works better.

—When you cover the bullet point about staffing issues, skip ahead to the next slide to show what a staffing issue might look like.

—After you show the staffing issues slide, skip ahead to show where these staffing issues might be found. Make sure to mention that these changes could be found in written business plans, but they could also be found in formal planning discussions and "water cooler chats." Return then to the original slide.

—The last slide talks about measurement. Get the group to identify various measures of staffing. Write on a flip chart whatever you hear. When done, point out that the measures that were identified were largely measures of time, speed, cost, or volume—all of which measure efficiency, not effectiveness. None of them take quality into account (e.g., they measure cost per hire, not cost per "good" hire). Make the point that you are doing the "right thing" (e.g., hiring quality people) when the staffing issues you identified are reduced or eliminated. Measuring the effectiveness of the workforce planning process is discussed in Chapter 22.

Dealing with Uncertainty

• The next few slides show how workforce planning can be applied even when business plans are uncertain.

• I usually state that of course the workforce planning process we just described (in the presentation) works well when plans are known, but then ask how it can be applied when plans are uncertain.

• The next slide lists "alternatives to perfect data" (i.e., what we can do when we do not know exactly what will happen), all of which are described in the text.

• The next few slides show the nursing example that is included in the uncertainty chapter of the book. State that while the job category may not fit your organization, the concept itself still applies. Note that these are "build" slides.

—Tell the audience that although the varying curve seems random, there are at least three things that we know: the minimum, the mean, and the maximum.

—The staffing strategy depicted includes three components. The first (up to the minimum) is a known option where staffing requirements are fixed. Thus, staffing plans to meet that fixed need can be certain.

—The second component (minimum to mean) shows a range of staffing needs. Because component 1 always provides 25 FTEs, staffing requirements for component 2 range from 0 FTEs (when only component 1 staff are required) to 15 FTEs (when the patient census hits the mean). The organization was willing to address this level of uncertainty and chose to use its own part-time staff here.

—The third component (mean to maximum) is also a range, from 0 FTEs (whenever the patient census is at or below the mean) to 10 FTEs (when the census is at the maximum). The organization wanted to outsource this level of uncertainty and thus elected to use an external staffing agency to meet this need.

Implementing Strategic Workforce Planning

- I usually begin this section by stating something like, "No matter how well designed a process is, it is only as effective as its implementation."
- On the "hints" slide, there are two key points:
  —I define the roles of the various participants, emphasizing that in the long run, workforce planning is a line management responsibility. Between "now" and "then" (i.e., when managers are actually participating fully), there is a large transition role for HR staff (as described in the bullets).
  —Spreadsheets are absolutely adequate for supporting even some very sophisticated staffing issues and strategies. It is not necessary to buy an expensive package. For most organizations, this will probably be a relief!
- The next slide describes obstacles. Be sure to share the blame! When viewing the HR part of this slide, I sometimes say, "We have met the enemy and it is us."
- Finally, share my implementation bias (approach A vs. B). This concept is described fully in the text. Note that these are "build" slides. I think that these slides (and this concept) are among the most important in the entire presentation.

Staffing Model

If you have an actual example of a staffing model, show it now. If not, delete this slide.

Examples

Leave the participants to review the examples. Do not try to present each one.

Remember to leave time for questions.

Session 2: Tools and Techniques

This session is a detailed description of the workforce planning process. It is intended to be shared with the team(s) that are actually going to develop and implement the process. This is usually a small subset of the individuals who attended the first session. Because of the detailed nature of the presentation, I recommend that senior line managers (and perhaps even senior HR staff) not be included.

The presentation describes each step of the workforce planning process. For each step, I describe what is included and provide a running example of what that step or result might actually look like for a simple case. Normally, all these slides can be covered in 60 to 90 minutes.

If you think that the example will not "speak" to your audience, feel free to change the issues, the row and column headings, the results, and other such elements to something that will. Even if you do make such changes, you will not have to change the numbers or the calculations.

I recently used a variation of this presentation that proved to be an effective learning and credibility-building tool. Prior to the one-day session, I worked with a business unit to create a simple workforce plan that actually addressed a critical issue that the unit was actually facing. I then replaced the simple example in this section with the "real" information from the business unit. This took some effort, but there were two huge benefits:

- Because it used the unit's own information, participants in the one-day session could easily make the leap from concept to reality.
- The process gained credibility among participants because they could see how it was actually applied in a real-world situation in their own company.

There was also an added benefit. The leader of the unit where the process was applied became a real proponent of workforce planning, saying at one point to the group of managers who attended the session, "This is what I need to run my business."

Here are some key points to make during this presentation:

Reminders

The presentation begins with a few reminders of the most critical points that were covered in the first session.

Cover these slides briefly. Use them simply to create a foundation for the presentation that is about to come; don't discuss any of them in detail this time around. If you need some words to use here, refer to the discussion of these concepts in the first presentation.

Detailed Process Discussion

- As with all the presentations, the slides are based on (and sometimes directly extracted from) information that is included somewhere in the book.

- While most of the slides in this section are relatively straightforward (assuming that you have read the book!), several of them require further explanation:

  —The slide labeled "Example: Applying the Matrix" emphasizes that the matrix structure that you just developed (i.e., row and column headings) will be used to structure each and every component of the staffing model (e.g., "supply now," "demand then," staffing gaps and surpluses).

  —Every one of the tools for defining required staffing levels in this presentation is covered in the text. An example of each one is also included in the book; a handout of these examples is included among the computer files you have access to.

  —Use the slide labeled "Example: Gaps and Surpluses Across All Periods" to show how you should review gaps and surpluses across all periods before trying to address them for any one period. Position this as the first step in creating staffing strategies that span planning periods. Choose a box where needs are increasing and show how those needs might best be met through hiring (or some other permanent means). Choose a second box where needs are fluctuating and show how these needs might best be met by using contractors (or some other temporary or contingent source).

  —Walk through the slide labeled "Example: Staffing Plans" to show the participants where the numbers come from. For example, show that promoting 5 Oracle Developers from Lead to Project Manager (in line with the staffing strategy on the previous slide) increases the gap at the Lead level from 7 to 12 (the original gap of 7 plus the additional gap of 5 resulting from promotional losses). Thus, additional promotions from Individual Contributor are needed to fill the increased gap at the Lead level. Note that there are not enough people that can be promoted from the Individual Contributor and entry level positions, and thus some external recruiting is necessary.

Session 3: Applying the Strategic Workforce Planning Process

The objective of this session is to apply the workforce planning process that was described, within the effective context, in your organization. As such, it might be the most critical presentation of the three—although it makes sense only after the previous two presentations have been completed. At the conclusion of this session, you will have:

- Verified that the approach I advocate is applicable to your organization

- Identified the critical staffing issue(s) to be addressed in your initial implementation of the workforce planning process

- Developed a first draft of the staffing model needed to address each critical issue you selected

- Defined the "next steps" and accountabilities for your initial workforce planning implementation

Participants in this session should include the workforce planning team, the line managers that might be your first "clients," and the HR business partners supporting each of those managers. This session should generate a great deal of discussion; don't be surprised if it requires three to four hours. If participants "run out of gas" before that, close the session and add more to the postsession "to do" list.

The slides in this presentation are intended to guide discussion, not to provide detailed answers. Consequently, they are the least detailed of the three sets.

Defining the Context for Strategic Workforce Planning

- This diagnostic is described in detail in the text, including all the arrows and interrelationships.

- This is intended to be a group exercise. Actually ask the participants to answer the questions on the "inventory" slide. Allow them about 10 to 15 minutes; stress that it is better to have a few things in each of the four boxes than to have two boxes full and two boxes empty.

- Ask them to turn to their neighbor (or form a small group) and discuss each of the three questions shown in step 2.

- Share the example with the arrows, starting with the completed matrix.

- Discuss each arrow:

  —Don't spend much time on the first two; I assume that for most organizations, the relationship between long-term business planning and short-term business planning is well developed.

  —Discuss the linkage that each remaining arrow is meant to depict. Note that these are "build" slides.

—Ask the group to summarize its findings (e.g., missing pieces to add, opportunities to better integrate efforts within boxes, ways to add or strengthen arrows).

Developing the Initial Implementation

- Use the outline provided in the slides to facilitate discussion.

- Remember to include not only staffing issues that arise from business plans but also those that don't (e.g., retirements).

- Force the group to narrow its choice to one or two issues initially (if you try to do more than that, you will probably be spreading yourself too thin).

- Sketch out the model as you design it, so that participants can visualize what they are proposing.

- Be specific about the next steps, including "who," "what," and "when."

- Right then and there, gain commitments from participants (i.e., in front of the other participants, for all to hear) that they will complete the steps that they are responsible for.

- Document your next steps and commitments on a high-level project plan (e.g., on a flip chart); distribute a cleaned-up version of that plan as soon as possible (ideally, the next morning).

- Determine when you will meet next.

4

Beyond Staffing Plans: Analyzing and Applying the Results

Using Workforce Planning to Define the Impact of Retirements on Your Workforce

One of the greatest staffing issues currently facing HR and the staffing functions is the large number of potential retirements that could occur in the coming few years. This looming wave of retiring baby boomers threatens to create major shortages in required skills and staffing levels in many organizations, at multiple organization levels. Are you fully aware of the impacts that retirements will have on your organization in the coming years? Have you defined the specific staffing actions you will take to address these needs? Have you begun to actually implement those plans, in advance of those coming needs?

If you are not already doing so, you should act now to identify critical retirement-related shortages, define the impact that those shortages will have on your talent pool, and develop specific staffing and development plans in response. In other words, your company should now be developing and applying the strategic workforce planning process to identify and address these critical retirement issues. In fact, if you are attempting to address these retirement-related issues outside the context of workforce planning (e.g., if you are about to implement generic, across-the-board-type solutions), your effectiveness will be limited indeed.

When it comes to retirement analysis and planning, many companies seem to just spin their wheels, choosing to simply analyze problems at a "high level" (e.g., calculating overall retirement rates for large groups or units of employees) rather than actually solving those problems. High-level solutions are by definition general and generic. As such, these solutions are unrealistic and impossible to implement in any meaningful way. Retirement issues are best addressed through the implementation of specific staffing strategies and plans that are targeted to key issues. HR and staffing departments cannot simply identify and clarify coming retirement issues. They must also create and implement staffing plans that drive the actions that will best address these issues. This chapter describes how workforce planning can be used to identify and actually address the critical staffing issues that retirements may raise in your organization.

Traditional Analyses Will Not Be Sufficient

When it comes to retirement analyses, most organizations operate at a level that is simply too generic to be helpful. Others might use more focused approaches, but their analyses are still not specific enough to drive action. Broad studies (e.g., those that determine that x percent of the overall employee population or y percent of managers above a certain level will be retiring) may seem helpful at first, but it is nearly impossible to do anything constructive based on these overly broad results. They are simply too generic to allow you to create staffing strategies and plans that will drive action. Specifically, what would you actually do differently if you determined that the average age in a particular unit was 58.2 or that 11 percent of your employees in that unit were eligible for retirement in the next five years? Compounding this problem is the very nature of an average, which in some cases might include both IT professionals (where the average age might be less than 30) and production workers (which might include a large number of employees at age 55 or more). An average age across these two groups might be in the forties; if you were to rely on this result, you might not see that a serious retirement issue could be emerging in production.

Here are some examples of mistakes that organizations make when trying to better understand and address the implications of their retirement situations:

- **Overreliance on external data.** Many companies focus their retirement analyses on in-depth reviews of external demographics. These companies often look for overall, industrywide trends that they think may have an impact on their workforce. Others look at statistics for these aging workforces (externally) and try to draw inferences that are relevant to their organizations in particular. While the findings from these external analyses might seem "interesting" at first, they may not even apply to your organization. In any case, recommendations based on external demographics will never be specific enough to help your organization to identify the most critical gaps that you will be facing, nor to define the staffing actions that should be taken to address those particular gaps.
- **An inappropriate focus on large groups of employees.** Some organizations focus their retirement analyses on their own (internal)

workforce, but look at data for large groups of employees (perhaps even the company as a whole). Such broad analyses always yield broad findings that are, at best, difficult to act upon. Studies that identify retirement issues among a company's entire workforce, for example, usually contain data summaries, combinations of jobs, and data compilations that make it virtually impossible to identify any specific, job-related issues or to define effective staffing strategies and plans for addressing those issues. If a study looks at all engineers across a unit, for example, any staffing plans based on these findings are, by definition, for that combined group—engineers as a whole, not by discipline. Thus, specific plans for each discipline (which are needed to guide real action) just cannot be prepared.

- **Looking only at the executive succession and development pools.** A third group of companies includes risk assessments arising from retirements as part of the succession planning processes. While often helpful, this approach is rarely sufficient. What about all the retirements in positions that are not included in the succession planning process? How will they be identified and addressed? In addition, the focus of succession planning is usually on developing candidates. How often do those development plans provide for the transfer of knowledge, experience, and personal relationships from incumbents to candidates?

- **Taking a focus that is too narrow.** Another common mistake that companies make is to attempt to define retirement numbers precisely (trying to forecast who will retire, and when). Often, companies try to predict with certainty what their retirements will be, attempting to improve their accuracy with each iteration. At best, these organizations are simply guessing. An effort like this could be a beneficial part of an overall workforce planning process, but often these analyses are done on a stand-alone basis, where these "accurate" estimates do nothing to address what should be done to mitigate the effects of these predicted retirements. Even where these efforts focus on critical job categories (normally a good thing), they fail to define what needs to be done to address the critical staffing issues.

Integrating Retirement Analyses and Workforce Planning

The big-picture analyses just described are simply not useful—but they are good examples of how HR and the staffing function are missing many opportunities to make a strategic contribution. The following list provides some practical suggestions that your organization can use to move beyond the analysis phase and define the staffing strategies and actions that will address your critical retirement issues most effectively. This approach is fully consistent with the strategic staffing/workforce planning process that is at the core of this book. Here are some steps that you should consider taking:

1. Define appropriate objectives at the start. The overall objective of these retirement analyses is to define the staffing strategies and plans that are required to address critical retirement issues fully. The objective is *not* to just analyze (or better define) retirement issues. To be useful, you must be specific, not generic. Set your sights on developing specific solutions to particular retirement-related staffing issues. You have done the "right" job in your analysis when in the end you have developed specific solutions to your most critical retirement problems, not just better definitions or understandings of what is wrong.

2. Focus your efforts on "at-risk" groups. Instead of one or two broad, overall retirement analyses, conduct a series of analyses, each of which is focused on a specific area or job group where retirements may be a problem (e.g., linemen in an electric utility, senior production workers in a manufacturing company, "hard to find" engineers in aerospace). Here is one method for identifying which job groups warrant this attention:

- Set a guideline percentage threshold above which retirements might become an issue (e.g., 25 percent). This estimate will simply be a number that you will use to screen your data. It should reflect reality, but it does not need to be all that precise. Don't waste time analyzing whether it should be 20 or 25 percent; the results of the screening you are about to do just won't vary enough to warrant such precision.

- Define criteria that you can use to segment your employee population by group and level (e.g., job family and salary grade). Job family works particularly well if the data are available. Function is a perfectly acceptable substitute; organization unit can also be used. Consider segmenting the population by business unit or geography. Retirement rates often differ significantly as a result of company culture, climate, and/or working conditions; For example, those who work outside in harsh conditions are more likely to retire as soon as they are eligible than are others who work inside. Your analyses and plans should take these differences into account.

- Define your retirement criteria. You might use your specific eligibility requirements (e.g., age plus service equals 80 with 10 consecutive years of service) or average retirement age. (A detailed discussion of the pros and cons of these assumptions is included in a previous chapter.)

- Set your planning horizons/time frames. For the purposes of this particular analysis, two planning periods are usually more than sufficient (e.g., now to three years and three to five years).

- Run your data. Create tables that show the percentages of employees eligible to retire (according to whichever assumption you choose to apply) in each category (e.g., Lineman, Salary Grade 30) for each period (e.g., the coming three years). This analysis will show you, for example, that 25 percent of your current population of Linemen in Salary Grade 30 will be eligible for retirement in the coming three years.

- Select your "at-risk" groups. Review the tables you just created. Identify those categories where the percentage of employees who are eligible to retire exceeds the percentage threshold that you set in the first step. Don't try to solve all your problems, especially not all at once. Instead, focus your efforts on those shortages that you think will be most critical and develop staffing plans to address each issue. Identify also any job categories where losses may be few in number, but significant in impact (e.g., losses of key senior managers or experienced technical staff). For these jobs, you will need to create succession/development plans, not staffing models. In addition, you may wish to develop "knowledge transfer plans" to ensure that critical knowledge and experience are transferred from retirees to the employees and staff that remain—before it is too late!

- Identify those job categories where issues are not critical or where your ongoing staffing efforts will probably be sufficient. Prepare no in-depth analyses for these positions.

3. **Create a staffing model.** Create a staffing model that is consistent with the planning parameters and structures defined in the previous step. Focus your analyses solely on your "at-risk" groups. Incorporate your chosen retirement scenario(s) into the model, and calculate the staffing gaps and surpluses that you might expect if these assumptions actually occur. Use the standard workforce planning process that is described so frequently in this book, using the assumptions that you made as your planning parameters. The columns of your model will be job family, function, or organization. Your rows will be salary grade (or whatever data you used to differentiate levels). The process will include defining future staffing requirements for the two periods you chose, identifying current

staffing levels, forecasting future availability (factoring in estimates of voluntary turnover as well as your assumptions regarding retirement), and calculating staffing gaps and surpluses. Review these gaps and surpluses to see where you are most at risk. In some cases, the problem might be related to losing collective experience; in others, it may be the loss of particular individuals.

4. **Build staffing and development strategies and plans.** You may, of course, continue to use the model to help you identify the staffing strategies and staffing plans that will address the retirement issues of each at-risk group most effectively. Review gaps and surpluses across planning periods before deciding what to do in any period. This approach will provide a longitudinal perspective that will allow you to develop the staffing and development strategies that work "best" across the entire planning horizon. For example, you may determine that it would be most effective to replace retiring workers by promoting from within from the next lower level, backfilling the openings that result at each level in a similar way, and replacing at the lowest level through recruiting. If the loss of specific individuals is the problem, incorporate succession and development planning for those positions (even if the positions are not included in your ongoing succession planning efforts). Make sure that you identify the skills and knowledge that must be transferred from one individual to another before retirement occurs. Within the context of your strategy, define detailed staffing plans for each period (e.g., identifying the actual numbers of people to be promoted during that period). Specifically define the development that will be needed to support this movement. Make particular note of instances where accelerated movement will require expedited training and development.

5. **Define all required staffing actions.** Define all required staffing actions, not just recruiting or replacement. Some organizations forecast the number of retirements and think that their job will be done when they recruit that number of people. Usually, the number of staffing actions required far exceeds the number of openings that are expected. Take, as a simple example, an organization that has three management levels. Suppose that 10 managers at the most senior level are expected to retire. It is unlikely that these openings would be filled from the outside. Instead, the jobs will probably be filled through promotion, with the hiring being done at the lowest level. Thus, a minimum of 30 staffing actions would be needed to fill the 10 openings:

- Ten promotions from the second level to fill the ten openings at the highest level.
- Ten promotions from the lowest level to replace those who were promoted from the second level to the highest level.

- Ten new hires to replace the lowest-level staff that were promoted to fill needs at the middle level.

Of course, any retirements at the middle or lower levels (or more than three management levels) would increase the number of required staffing actions even more. In addition to these staffing moves, define the development that will be needed (e.g., to provide some of those that are to be promoted with the skills they will need if they are to be successful in their new roles). Your staffing plans must include all of these actions.

6. Act! Actively implement your plans. Identify the individuals that will be moved. Provide the required development. Implement those moves when the time comes.

In summary, go beyond the traditional retirement analyses that attempt to predict the number of expected retirements with great precision. Instead, address your retirement needs by fully addressing the most critical issues that will arise. Don't try to address all the issues. Identify all the staffing actions that will be required, including but going beyond recruiting. Tailor those plans so that they are appropriate for each issue. I think you will find that the results of your efforts will be much more valuable to your managers and to the organization as a whole.

18

Using Workforce Planning to Support Management Succession and Development Planning

Planning and acting in advance to meet its needs for senior management and key technical talent is clearly one of the most important things that an organization does. Virtually every organization now implements some form of management succession and development planning. Relatively few organizations, however, incorporate into their succession and development processes the specific, quantitative analysis that is typically associated with strategic workforce planning. While shunned by some because it is "too detailed," this more specific, quantitative analysis can actually greatly increase the effectiveness of the succession and development planning process.

A Quick Review of Succession and Development

For most organizations, the succession and development process is implemented to help the organization meet its future needs for executive and management talent. Some of these companies also include key technical or functional positions in the succession and development process. Some implement the process for a small number of key positions; others apply it at virtually every management level.

In nearly every case, the succession and development process includes some version of each of these key steps:

- Identify those critical positions that are to be included in the process. These could be executive-level, management, or key technical/functional jobs.

- Define the capabilities that each of those positions will require in the future. Usually, these required capabilities are selected from some kind of competency model.

- Identify and assess possible candidates for these positions, using the required capabilities as a guide. Usually, each candidate is evaluated to identify development needs (e.g., capabilities not yet mastered) and assessed in terms of readiness for the position (e.g., ready now, ready in one to three years, ready in three to five years).

- Provide these individuals with focused development that will prepare them so that, if desired, they could assume these positions in the future. An action-oriented development plan that describes what will be done to address the most critical development needs is prepared for each candidate.

- Review the results with a group of senior managers. Once candidates have been identified and assessed and development plans have been prepared, a review of the candidate pool(s) is conducted. At this session, executives review and approve (whether formally or tacitly) candidate slates and development plan appropriateness.

Once these steps are taken, the implementation of development plans begins. Needless to say, there is no single "best" way of conducting a succession and development analysis. There are many variations on the succession and development process that organizations have found to be effective. However, one general assumption is true about most of these processes: The succession planning and development process is based largely (if not solely) on contingency planning. That is, the results of the process (at least the part addressing staffing) describe what an organization "could do," "might do," or "should do" if certain circumstances arise. Contrast that to the output of a strategic staffing/workforce planning process, which typically describes what an organization *will do* to address critical staffing needs. Succession and development planning is often primarily subjective in nature (e.g., focusing on skills and capabilities gaps); on the other hand, workforce planning is largely objective in nature (e.g., dealing with quantitative differences in required staffing levels). Is there a way in which the typical succession and development process implemented by most organizations could be strengthened by incorporating some of the objective, action-oriented aspects of strategic workforce planning?

Applying Quantitative Staffing Analysis to Succession Planning

There are several ways in which a quantitative staffing analysis can enhance the effectiveness of an organization's succession and development planning process. To begin with, quantitative analysis can help an organization identify specific areas of vulnerability and determine the "right" size of the candidate pool. Each of these two applications is discussed later in the chapter.

Note that for all of these analyses, your data should be segmented by whatever job categories you are using in your succession analysis. For example, if you are applying succession and development planning at specific job levels (e.g., all vice president– or director-level positions), then the analyses I am about to describe should be segmented by job level. If your succession planning process focuses on specific job titles or positions (e.g., Vice President—finance, General Counsel), then these analyses should be conducted for each job separately.

Here are two examples of how workforce planning methods can be used to strengthen succession and development planning.

Identifying Vulnerabilities and Forecasting Losses

Through quantitative staffing analysis, your organization can analyze management demographics and identify the impact that losses might have on the number of managers and candidates that will be available at various points in the future. Usually, these losses are due to retirements and voluntary turnover. An understanding of what losses might occur when can help you to fine-tune your succession and development plans and ensure that an appropriate number of candidates is being developed (not too many or too few).

Quantitative analyses can strengthen your process in two ways. First, these analyses can help define the number of openings that can be expected in the coming years. This can help you to refine your estimates of the number of candidates that are needed and when candidates with those capabilities should be "ready." Second, they can help to identify those individuals who are most likely to leave (and thus the positions that may require more in-depth analysis).

As you structure this workforce planning–type gap analysis, make sure that you use an appropriate time frame. It is often helpful to consider planning periods that coincide with your estimates of readiness. For example, the first planning period might be from "now" (i.e., the current date) to a point three years in the future (to address "ready in one to three years" candidates); the second planning period might be from three years from the current date to five years out (to capture those candidates that might be ready in three to five years). If you need more details, a more complete description of these retirement analyses is included in an earlier chapter. Here are two areas to focus on.

Forecast Retirements. Retirement analyses often play critical roles in identifying areas of vulnerability. Clearly, very specific succession plans can and should be produced whenever an organization identifies specific individuals who are actually going to retire. What can be equally valuable is a more general analysis that looks at various retirement scenarios on a unit-by-unit or level-by-level basis. Once an organization has gained an overall sense of the retirement losses it can expect, it can make a more realistic determination of the size of the successor pool that it should be developing. This type of analysis is a "tailor-made" application of quantitative workforce planning, using the various tools and techniques described elsewhere in this book.

Some companies base their retirement projections on historical trends. This method is at best unreliable; it applies only when retirements are spread out evenly over a period of several years. In most companies, this even spread just does not occur. Projections should be based on an analysis that considers actual retirement information for the management pool being examined. Here are two methods that can be used to define the expected number of retirees. These methodologies are described in more detail in a previous chapter, but it is appropriate to review them here.

1. Average retirement age. The easiest way to consider retirements is to base your projections on the actual average retirement age. Calculate the average age at which managers in the group you are studying have actually retired. Where possible, consider retirements over the past four to five years when calculating these averages. Remember to exclude from your calculation any individuals who elected to retire early as a result of any "special offers" designed to reduce staffing levels. Try to consider only those individuals who retired "normally." In some cases, average age could be calculated for a large group as a whole (e.g., all managers at or above a given organization level). In other cases, separate averages should be calculated to reflect specific conditions for certain subsets of your population. For example, you may find that managers in difficult overseas assignments or jobs that require extensive travel actually retire sooner than those who work domestically and travel less often do.

Once you have calculated your averages, simply look at your current population and note their ages. For planning purposes, assume that any individual who reaches the appropriate average retirement age will actually leave. Remember to count the number of individuals who will reach the average age during each planning period. Suppose, for example, that your average retirement age for a particular management group is 59 years old. Applying this approach, you would then assume that all managers who are currently 58 or older will retire in year 1 (when they would reach the average age of 59), all who are 57 currently will retire in year 2, all who are now 56 will retire in year 3, and so on.

Needless to say, this assumption may not apply to any specific individual, but it will apply when you look at a group of individuals. After all, that is the basis of an average—some managers may choose to work past the average age, but just as many will choose to leave before they reach that average age.

Also, make sure that you allow for different average retirement ages for different positions. Here are two obvious examples. Linemen who brave winter storms to make needed repairs to downed electric lines will retire at an earlier age than engineers at the same level who work primarily in indoor offices. People in high-stress positions (such as those in law enforcement and air traffic control) will retire at an earlier age than people in less stressful jobs. These differences can prove to be significant.

While simple, the average age method typically yields surprisingly accurate results. For many organizations, this method provides results that are absolutely adequate to support their planning.

2. A retirement "distribution." In some cases, you may need to analyze retirements using a more sophisticated methodology than simply calculating and applying an average retirement age. One really effective way of estimating retirements is to assume that employees will retire over the course of several years, beginning with their initial year of eligibility.

To use this method, you must estimate or assume two things:

- **The number of years over which the retirements are to be spread.** Determine the number of years over which retirements will be spread (e.g., for planning purposes, you will assume that most employees will retire within seven years of their first eligibility date).

- **The percentage of those eligible that will retire in each of those years.** Estimate the number of employees (on a percentage basis) that will retire in each of the years in the distribution as defined in the previous step (e.g., of all the employees who become eligible in any given year, 20 percent will retire in the first year of eligibility, 15 percent in the second year, 10 percent in the third year, and so on). These percentages could be based on actual historical data or on estimated probabilities.

To apply this method to a particular group or job category, first create a list of the managers in the unit(s) that you are analyzing. For each manager, determine their retirement eligibility date by applying the normal criteria (e.g., age plus length of service needs to sum to 80). Print the list, sorting first by job level and then by eligibility date (in ascending order). Now count the number of employees in each category or level that will become eligible to retire in each year. Calculate the expected retirements by multiplying this number of eligible employees by the appropriate percentage for each year and summing across all years. Here is a simple example.

Suppose that we expect most employees to retire within three years of becoming eligible. More specifically, we expect that 50 percent will retire as soon as they are eligible, 20 percent will retire the next year, and 30 percent will retire in the third year. Our sorted list shows that 100 employees will become eligible in year 1, 80 in year 2, and 70 in year 3. How many retirements can we expect in each year?

In year 1, we would forecast that 50 people will retire (i.e., 50 percent of the 100 that became eligible in year 1). In year 2, we expect that 70 employees will retire (i.e., 30 percent of the 100 that became eligible in the previous year plus 50 percent of the 80 that are eligible for the first time in year 2). In year 3, we would expect 79 employees to retire (i.e., 20 percent of the 100 that became eligible in year 1 plus 30 percent of the 80 that became eligible in year 2 plus 50 percent of the 70 that are eligible for the first time in year 3). These calculations are easily handled in a spreadsheet.

Obviously, this is a much more complex algorithm than simply using average age, but it could yield better results. Make sure that the extra precision you obtain justifies the added effort you must expend.

As a final option, you might want to consider talking with the managers of those individuals that you have identified as eligible for retirement. Often, these managers have good insights regarding what these people's actual retirement plans might be (e.g., "John will probably be leaving in the next year or two, but I think that Mary will continue to work long past her retirement eligibility date").

Estimate Voluntary Turnover. In middle-level management positions and below, most openings are created not through retirement, but through voluntary turnover. Consequently, your analysis of vulnerability should include some estimate of the number of managers that will choose to leave your organization (e.g., to take jobs elsewhere).

Unlike a retirement analysis, which tries in some way to identify specific individuals who may leave, an analysis of voluntary turnover should focus on a group or "cohort" of managers, not on any managers in particular. Generally, voluntary turnover is estimated by multiplying an assumed turnover rate by the number of managers in that particular group. For example, if you think that the voluntary turnover rate will be 6 percent per year and there are 50 managers in the group you are looking at, then you might assume that 3 managers will leave during that 12-month period (i.e., 6 percent of the 50). It is important to remember that you are not identifying which 3 managers will leave—just that it is probable that 3 will leave (and may need to be replaced through succession).

When estimating voluntary turnover, try to group managers who have similar characteristics (e.g., look at managers by organization level).

When estimating voluntary turnover, don't just blindly project historical rates. Estimate instead what you think turnover will be for the period in question. It may be helpful to start out by defining a historical rate, but then modify that rate as necessary to reflect the business conditions and economic climate within which you will be operating in the future. Here are two common situations in which historical rates must be adjusted:

- **Changing economic conditions.** If the economy has been strong over the last several years but is now weakening, it is likely that turnover rates will go down. Conversely, when economic conditions are good and opportunities abound, managers are more likely to leave to accept positions elsewhere.

- **Changing competitive conditions.** Needless to say, competition affects turnover. If competition for the talent you need is increasing (e.g., where a competitor is trying to grow significantly and is locating a facility in your area) then turnover will increase. If, however, your industry is retrenching, then turnover is likely to go down.

In either of these cases, it would not make sense to assume that the turnover rates for the future would be the same as those that were seen in the last few years.

Run a Gap Analysis Model. Once you have determined what your assumptions regarding turnover will be, run a modified version of the workforce planning gap analysis to determine the number of possible replacements that might be required and determine the number of candidates that might be needed to provide adequate depth of coverage for the positions you are analyzing. Identify additional candidates where necessary to increase pool size and create development plans for these individuals. Remember that you may want to be developing more than one candidate for each gap that you identify (e.g., your target might be two candidates for each opening). Figure 18-1 diagrams what this process might look like.

Maintaining Candidate Pool Size

Organizations often wrestle with the issue of how large their succession pool should be. For most, this problem is especially difficult because the company really does not know how many management openings it can expect during the planning period.

A quantitative staffing model can be quite helpful in defining the size of the candidate pool that is required in order to support your succession

Figure 18-1. Using a Workforce Planning Approach to Estimate Losses Within a Succession and Development Process.

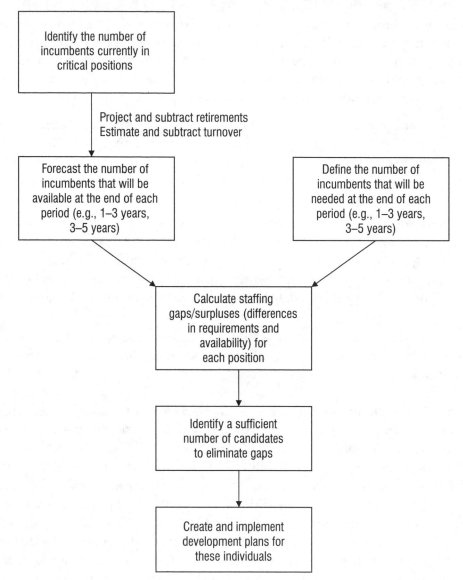

planning objectives. A gap analysis is needed, but it is built in a somewhat different way from the gap analyses that are usually included in a workforce planning process. A well-defined workforce planning–style model can help an organization to better understand the number of positions that are expected to become available at each level at various points in the future. Once these numbers are determined, proper pool size/depth can be defined (e.g., by applying standard ratios such as two candidates per opening).

Most staffing models (including the ones that apply here) include components that allow an organization to define future staffing requirements, identify current staffing levels, forecast future staff availability, and calculate specific differences between requirements and availability. Once these gaps and surpluses are known, the organization can then define the specific staffing plans and actions that are needed to align supply and demand. Usually, however, these processes include all positions and incumbents. Here, the same process is used, but it will be applied only to those individuals who are considered to be candidates.

To create a staffing model that defines candidate pool size and depth, follow these six steps:

1. Define staffing model parameters. First, define the time frame of your model. As stated earlier, this is usually consistent with the estimates of readiness that you use in your succession and development process (e.g., a period of one to three years and a second period of three to five years). Next, identify the population to be analyzed (e.g., the positions to be included in the succession plan and the positions from which candidates for those jobs might come). Finally, create a model structure in terms of columns (e.g., organization units or functions) and rows (e.g., organization or management levels, such as vice president, director, manager, and supervisor).

2. Define actual staffing requirements. In this instance, staffing requirements will reflect the desired size and depth of the candidate pool you have determined that you need. Once the actual number of management positions at each level is defined, you will be able to determine quite easily the size of the candidate pool that is needed at each of those levels (and at each state of readiness, if you take that approach). Create and apply ratios of candidates to positions (e.g., $1^1/_2$ or 2 candidates for each position or 1 candidate at each state of readiness for each position). This analysis will tell you how many candidates will be needed for each time frame (and thus how "deep" your candidate pool needs to be). Simply multiply the appropriate ratio by the number of positions at a given level.

It is the result of this calculation of the number of candidates that defines "demand" (in workforce planning terms, anyway), not the actual number of management positions. Thus, the subsequent gap analysis will define the staffing actions needed to maintain that particular candidate pool size—not simply what needs to be done to fill the openings that are anticipated.

3. Identify current staffing levels. Define the number of candidates (not necessarily incumbents) that are currently in each cell of your model. This will include the number of candidates currently being developed for each position or level, at each state of readiness. This number should reflect "what is," not "what should be."

4. Forecast staff availability. Next, you will need to estimate the number of candidates that you will have at each level in each category of your model at the end of each of your planning periods. Begin with current staffing levels (as defined in the previous step). Next, estimate expected losses in each category as a result of retirement and voluntary turnover (perhaps using one of the algorithms described earlier). You may want to modify overall turnover and retirement rates to reflect what actually happens among candidates (e.g., candidates are more or less likely to leave voluntarily than managers as a whole). For now, do not assume any replacements; let the model tell you how many replacements will be required.

5. Calculate staffing gaps and surpluses. Next, define staffing gaps (where demand exceeds supply) and surpluses (where supply exceeds demand) at each level in your model. Compare estimated requirements (defined by the desired pool size, not the number of management positions) to the forecasted supply of candidates in each category and identify where the pool may be insufficient. Generally, focus on those levels where there are not enough candidates. Don't worry about instances where the pool at a given level may be deeper than is required.

6. Define required staffing actions. Once specific gaps and surpluses are calculated, define the staffing actions that would "best" eliminate these differences and maintain the proper management candidate pool size. Identify what promotions and other job moves will be needed in each year to maintain that pool depth and ensure management continuity. Remember to identify any development that must take place in support of these staffing actions.

Keep your staffing strategies in mind as you define staffing actions (e.g., that to continue to generate a flow of new ideas, you intend to fill 75 percent of the anticipated openings from within and the remaining 25 percent through outside recruiting). This component of the analysis will also allow you to identify and address "cascade effects" (e.g., where promoting a candidate to fill a job at one level creates a new opening that must be filled by promoting a different candidate into the vacancy that was just created).

Figure 18-2 depicts what this version of a gap analysis might look like. Here is a simple example of what this approach might look like for one planning period (e.g., from "now" to the end of the third year). Suppose that your organization has three levels included in your succession plan

Figure 18-2. Using a Workforce Planning Approach to Maintain an Appropriate Candidate Pool Size.

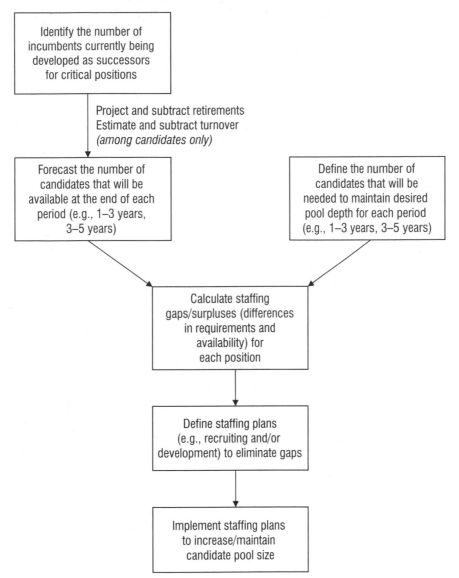

(e.g., executive, director, and manager). Suppose further that your succession planning process incorporates three levels of readiness (e.g., now, one to three years, and three to five years). For the purposes of this example, let's assume that you are evaluating the candidate pool size for all positions in one business unit (you could just as easily do this analysis for all positions across business units). Further, let's say that your company has set the following ratios or targets for the desired number of candidates for each position at each state of readiness:

- One "ready now" candidate for each position
- Two "ready in one to three years" candidates for each position
- One "ready in three to five years" candidate for each position

In an actual case, there might be different ratios for different jobs and/ or levels, but for this example, we will assume that the same set of ratios applies to all levels. Here is a step-by-step example of how this analysis might be structured:

- **Define current headcount.** Identify the current number of candidates that are actually being developed for each position at each state of readiness. These numbers should reflect "what is," not "what should be." Your numbers might look like this:

Current Number of Candidates

	Executive	Director	Manager
Ready now	8	20	60
Ready in 1–3 years	6	34	80
Ready in 3–5 years	5	21	50

- **Estimate voluntary turnover.** Determine the rate of voluntary turnover you expect among the candidates. This will probably be a different rate from that for managers in general. Let's assume that turnover among succession candidates is 5 percent per year. The rate that you would use is then 15 percent (5 percent per year for each of the three years in your planning period). Again, in a real case, rates might vary by level, business unit, or state of readiness. Applying that 15 percent rate to the current number of candidates in the example would yield the following turnover losses:

Voluntary Turnover Among Candidates

	Executive	Director	Manager
Ready now	1	3	9
Ready in 1–3 years	1	5	12
Ready in 3–5 years	1	3	8

- **Forecast retirements.** Next, estimate the total number of retirements you expect to occur from the candidate pool across all three years of your planning period. (Other chapters of this book describe several approaches that you might use.) For this example, let's assume the following retirements:

Retirements from the Current Candidate Pool

	Executive	Director	Manager
Ready now	1		
Ready in 1–3 years		2	1
Ready in 3–5 years			

- **Forecast future candidate pool size.** Next, you will need to forecast what you think the available number of candidates will be at the end of your three-year planning period, given your starting population and the assumptions you made about voluntary turnover and retirements. To get your forecasts, simply subtract voluntary turnover and retirement losses from the starting number of candidates. For the Executive/Ready Now category, six candidates will be available (eight initial candidates, less one voluntary loss and one retirement). For this example, the result would be:

Available Number of Candidates

	Executive	Director	Manager
Ready now	6	17	51
Ready in 1–3 years	5	27	67
Ready in 3–5 years	4	18	42

- **Define required candidate pool size.** Here you apply your chosen ratios. We have assumed that in this example there are 8 executive positions, 22 director positions, and 64 management positions. Now, multiply your chosen ratio (i.e., 1 ready now candidate, 2 ready in one to three years candidates, and 1 ready in three to five years candidate) by the number of positions (not candidates!) to determine how many candidates are needed in each position at each state of readiness. For example, 44 ready in one to three years manager-level candidates will be needed (2 such candidates for each of the 22 management-level positions). When you complete those calculations, you get the following requirements:

Number of Candidates Required

	Executive	Director	Manager
Ready now	8	22	64
Ready in 1–3 years	16	44	128
Ready in 3–5 years	8	22	64

- **Calculate gaps and surpluses.** Finally, compare the number of candidates that will be available to the number that will be required. For example, the model forecasted that 6 executive-level candidates in the ready now category will be available, and 8 will be needed. The gap between these is -2 (always subtract demand from supply to depict a gap as a negative number). Completing this calculation for the rest of the model yields this result:

Candidate Gaps/Surpluses

	Executive	Director	Manager
Ready now	− 2	− 5	− 13
Ready in 1–3 years	− 11	17	− 61
Ready in 3–5 years	− 4	− 4	− 22

- **Define staffing strategies and plans.** Determine what staffing and development actions need to be taken to eliminate the gaps and surpluses that were calculated (thus achieving the desired candidate pool size). This might include identifying and developing additional candidates, recruiting additional talent that has the skills to be successors, identifying individuals working in other companies that could step in, and other such actions. Remember to keep the length of your planning period in mind when creating these plans so that your plans are realistic (e.g., would it really be possible to develop a new candidate in the two years that are available?). Remember too that if part of your solution is to elevate a candidate (e.g., from the three to five years category to the one to three years category), it will be necessary to replace that person with a new candidate in the category she is moving from (i.e., three to five years in this simple example).

Summary

Quantitative analyses can greatly improve the effectiveness of your succession planning process by helping you to move from a "what we should do"/contingency approach to a more deterministic "what we will do" method. These analyses can be used to estimate losses and identify areas of vulnerability (and thus get a better understanding of the number of candidates that will be needed). A more comprehensive staffing model will allow you not only to calculate losses, but also to define the staffing actions needed to create and maintain candidate pools that ensure an orderly succession of talent.

19

"Talent Planning": The Key to Effective Talent Management

For the last several years, it has been difficult to pick up an HR journal without finding an article that addresses some aspect of talent management. Similarly, many conferences and workshops have included the subject; in fact, talent management has been the focal point of many of these events. The high interest in the subject is confirmed when we see the large number of independent consultants and large consulting firms that are offering products and services that support the implementation of talent management programs.

Many organizations have eagerly jumped on the talent management bandwagon. Organizations have tried to fight their "war for talent" by implementing a wide array of talent management "strategies"—innovative approaches for attracting, selecting, developing, and retaining talent. Some organizations have focused these efforts on particular job categories, while others have implemented more generic approaches that are applied on a more widespread basis—perhaps even across the organization as a whole. Figure 19-1 shows a model of a typical talent management process.

But there is a problem with all these good intentions. What is it that separates truly effective talent management strategies and practices from those that are at best only marginally helpful in the long run? By definition, talent management is a collection of innovative actions and solutions that allows an organization to maximize the effectiveness of the talent it employs. However, how can an organization determine which talent management "solutions" will address the most critical staffing issues it is facing? How can it evaluate alternatives and determine which of the array of talent management solutions is best?

In some organizations, HR staff have been quick to adopt innovative talent management practices without first identifying what their most crit-

Figure 19-1. An Example of a Typical Talent Management Process.

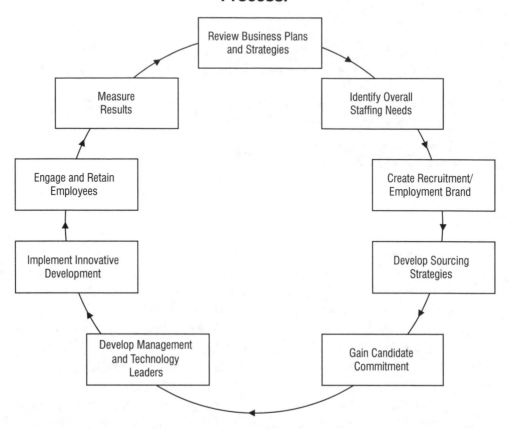

ical issues are or determining which talent management practices (if any) would be the most effective solutions to those most critical issues. Some of these HR staff quickly adopt talent management solutions without first analyzing in depth the staffing and development problems that they are facing. Under these circumstances, talent management truly becomes just another trendy approach that is implemented simply because it is a "best practice"—the very definition of an answer in search of a question.

Just to add an exclamation point, even as I was writing this chapter, I received a flyer in the mail from an HR association that described a perfect example of what *not* to do regarding talent management. It described a classic workshop (always a big seller!) that would allow participants to hear a panel of well-known professors, consultants, and senior HR staff describe how to implement a specific approach to talent management. In this case, the "solution" was a process that included four phases:

- One focused on understanding business strategies and aligning competencies to those strategies

- One addressed the acquisition and "on-boarding" of talent
- One described leadership succession and development
- One addressed employee engagement and retention

In general, the approach that was described in the brochure was not significantly different from the process described in Figure 20-1. Any or all of these phases might be a needed part of an effective solution. What was completely missing from the workshop was any opportunity for participants to learn about workforce planning. Without workforce planning, how could those participants determine what their organization's most critical skills needs would be? What gaps it might be facing regarding required staffing levels? What staffing strategies and plans would be most appropriate? What talent should be acquired, developed, and retained in the first place? Like so many others, this workshop seemed to offer detailed solutions to problems that were never clearly defined in the first place. (All that having been said, I'd bet the session was sold out.)

Talent management strategies are most effective when they are clearly focused on addressing very specific staffing issues—when they are the *best, most effective* solutions to critical staffing problems, not just *good* solutions. They must address specific issues, not simply be generic solutions or "nice to have" programs that address macro-level concerns. To be effective, talent management strategies must consider very particular differences between staffing requirements and staffing availability (both required skills and staffing levels). These strategies must be applied in a discriminating fashion, implementing specific strategies to address particular needs—not generic approaches that try to address "common" needs. They must also take into consideration implementation timing—what needs to be done when. Not every option needs to be (or can be) implemented right away.

To gain the focus needed to implement talent management effectively, your organization should:

- Identify its most critical staffing issues.
- Develop longer-term talent management strategies that address those critical issues most effectively.
- Define specific short-term staffing and development plans within the context of those talent management strategies.
- Implement only those talent management practices that support most effectively the implementation of these staffing strategies and plans.

Do these steps look familiar? They should—they are yet another description of what an effective workforce planning process includes. Put succinctly, talent management is most effective—and in fact may only "work"—when it is implemented within the context of a well-designed workforce planning process. It might be helpful here to envision work-force planning as "talent planning"—a step that must be completed *before any talent management practices are implemented*. Figure 19-2 shows what an effective talent management process should look like—including the workforce planning elements that should precede the process.

Remember that I define workforce planning as the process that organi-zations use to both *define* and *address* the critical staffing implications of their business plans and strategies. This process usually entails defining future staffing requirements, forecasting staff availability, calculating spe-cific staffing gaps and surpluses (both skills and staffing levels), and devel-oping the longer-term staffing strategies (spanning planning periods) and short-term staffing plans (for each planning period) that "best" eliminate those gaps and surpluses.

Figure 19-2. An Example of an Effective Talent Management Process.

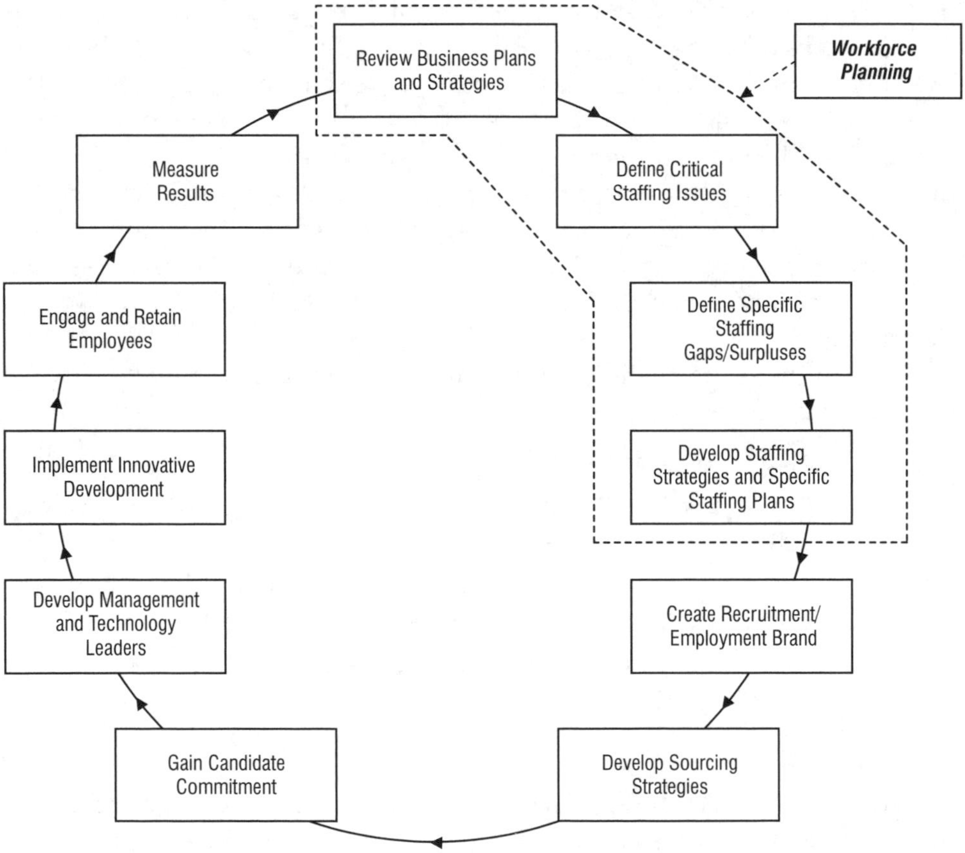

Clearly, effective workforce planning (or "talent planning," just to be consistent with the talent management nomenclature) must precede any talent management efforts. It might even be possible to make the case that unless they are preceded by effective workforce planning, talent management efforts simply will not yield the benefits that are expected. Here are six examples of where talent planning might greatly influence some of the most common talent management practices:

1. **Develop a recruiting/employment brand.** Developing a "brand" or image can greatly facilitate recruiting efforts. This brand is meant to provide potential recruits with an image of what a company is all about (e.g., that the organization values innovation). Most companies tend to cultivate a single recruiting-related brand for the company as a whole. However, can just one brand really be sufficient when the talent to be recruited varies widely? Might it be better to develop different brands that appeal to different target audiences of recruits (e.g., marketing versus engineering)? In an extreme case, is this type of branding even necessary if an organization's future recruiting needs are minimal? Might separate brands, each focused on a particular segment of recruits, be the best answer? However, if separate brands are to be developed to support these varying recruiting plans, then obviously well-defined recruiting needs must be clearly determined before any branding can be done. It is through workforce planning that an organization defines exactly which of its staffing needs are to be met through recruiting—and thus where branding would apply most effectively. Clearly, employment branding without workforce planning just won't be effective.

2. **Develop sourcing strategies.** Once staffing needs have been defined clearly, strategies for sourcing the needed talent can be created. Often, talent management processes assume that most (if not all) of an organization's talent needs will be recruited from the outside. While this can be one valuable source of talent, it is by no means the only source. Critical talent needs can be met by utilizing or redeploying current staff or by using part-time staff, contractors, consultants, and other contingent workers. Staffing needs can also be met through the use of overtime, by outsourcing work (thus eliminating the need for staff in the first place), and through other methods that are not typically thought of as "staffing." All of these possible staffing strategies are included in and flow directly from a well-designed workforce planning process. Once the various staffing strategies are chosen, specific plans for obtaining the needed talent can be created. Note that these sourcing strategies are identified *only* after the staffing strategies have been developed. How many talent management processes consider this wide array of (nonrecruiting) staffing options?

3. Gain candidate commitment. Once sources of qualified external recruits are identified, the specific individuals to be attracted can be identified (assuming, of course, that recruiting is the most effective way to meet staffing needs). The conditions under which these candidates will accept your offer can then be defined. These terms and conditions might touch on such things as salary requirements, flexible work schedules, relocation reimbursement, and commitments to specific development. It is possible that some of these terms need to be very specific; they might even vary from individual to individual. In any case, these commitment terms cannot be set until every staffing source has been identified. Furthermore, some of the sourcing strategies (such as the use of overtime or outsourcing of work) that might emerge from a workforce plan do not even involve individual candidates. Whatever scenario emerges, one thing is clear: None of these options can be defined or agreed to until sourcing strategies are developed and candidates are identified—and both of these steps are part of any effective workforce planning process.

4. Implement innovative learning and development. Learning and development are critical components of any talent management system. Innovative development techniques (some of which are part of talent management) are now available that greatly enhance the effectiveness of the learning process. Yet it makes no sense to apply these innovative techniques across the board or to try to use them to develop everyone in everything. Nor should these techniques be applied (and resources spent) on development solutions that do not address critical needs. Before any innovative learning practices can be initiated appropriately, a company must identify exactly which and how many individuals will require development, and in what. It must also identify when those skills will be needed in the first place. Then, development must be focused so that it addresses individual development needs in the most effective way, with individuals being developed in just those skills that are most critical for the roles they will play. Once these specific skills needs are identified, it is possible to tailor or match innovative development approaches (which are part of talent management) to those particular learning needs. How can an organization best know what specific skills gaps it is facing, and when those gaps are to occur? Once again, this skills gap information flows directly from a well-designed, effective workforce planning process.

5. Engage and retain employees. Often, the best way to fill an opening is to prevent the opening from occurring in the first place. Thus, retention is usually a component of any effective talent management process. However, generic, "corporate" approaches to retention just don't work. Retention efforts that are applied on a widespread basis end up retaining poor performers with obsolete skills who have no realistic career options out-side the organization—exactly the type of employee that should *not* be retained. Retention and "re-recruiting" (whether of specific groups or of individuals) works "best" when it is targeted and is part of an overall staffing strategy (e.g., when retaining those with critical skills is a more effective approach than trying to replace those individuals should they leave). Further, one of the best ways to retain key individuals is to make sure that they are fully engaged in the work they are doing and know that the contributions resulting from that engagement are recognized and appreciated. How does an organization identify those staffing needs that are met most effectively through retention? There is no surprise here. Re-tention strategies—those targeting the specific individuals who should be retained or re-recruited—are a direct output of any well-designed work-force planning process.

6. Measure results. Results measurement is usually a component of a talent management process. After all, it is important to measure the im-pacts of any significant effort, including talent management. Generic mea-sures of results might apply (such as overall impacts on profitability or cost reductions), but it is often difficult to tie these measures directly to the talent management strategies that were implemented. Can an organi-zation really attribute specific cost savings to the implementation of ge-neric talent management practices? On the other hand, organizations whose talent management efforts are linked to workforce planning have two sets of measures that can be used:

- **Efficiency measures**, such as cost per hire, time to fill, and reductions in turnover or vacancy rates

- **Effectiveness measures**, including measuring the extent to which talent management strategies actually addressed the critical staffing issues and reduced the staffing gaps and surpluses that were identi-fied by the workforce planning process

Measures of staffing effectiveness are discussed in more depth in Chapter 22.

One other warning is appropriate. I have never been a big fan of bench-marking your results against the measures of other companies. It is en-tirely possible that your organization might stack up well against another if both are doing the wrong things. At best, benchmarking brings parity; it can never really measure strategic breakthroughs or identify significant competitive advantages. Suppose you are implementing a unique recruit-ing program to attract individuals with skills that are in scarce supply. The program is costly, but it is allowing your organization to attract the talent it needs to support a business strategy that provides a significant strategic advantage. Do you really care at that point what your competitor's cost per hire measures are?

What Should You Do?

So, what is it that you and your organization should do to ensure that all those new talent management initiatives will really pay off?

First and foremost, start by preparing an effective workforce plan that describes the longer-term staffing strategies as well as the short-term staffing actions that *will actually be implemented* to address your most critical talent needs. Now, use those strategies and plans to focus, customize, and adjust your talent management initiatives. Let me summarize my specific recommendations. To implement truly effective talent management practices, you should:

- Develop a series of recruiting and employment brands that directly support the critical recruiting strategies and plans that were the result of your workforce planning process. Avoid generic branding that is not directly aligned with workforce planning results.

- Develop focused talent sourcing strategies and plans that will ensure that you locate a sufficient number of adequately skilled staff (again, as defined by your workforce plans). Remember to include all sources of the required talent (e.g., part-time workers, external contractors, and consultants), not just recruiting.

- Define what you *will* do (not simply what your organization "should" do) on a case-by-case basis to gain individual commitments from the candidates that match your most critical needs, as identified by your workforce plans. Verify that you have the time between "now" and "then" (i.e., when the individuals should be on board) to obtain that commitment.

- Implement innovative learning and development techniques that address important gaps most effectively. Focus on those gaps that are most important—the critical gaps identified in your workforce plans *for which development has been identified as the most effective staffing strategy.*

- Engage and retain needed employees, but not "all" employees. Focus engagement and retention on those whose departure would represent a significant loss to the organization. Such engagement, retention, and re-recruiting opportunities flow directly from the staffing strategies and plans that are the result of your workforce planning process.

- Measure your results, but do not use generic measures or standards or (worse yet) external benchmarking. Instead, measure the extent to which the critical staffing gaps (as identified by your workforce planning process) are being eliminated across planning periods by the staffing strategies and plans that you are implementing. Remember that well-defined issues or gaps are specific, measurable differences between the talent that you will have and the talent that you will need.

Talent management without workforce planning is a bit of a pig in a poke, where success and expected cost savings are by no means guaranteed. In fact, generic talent management solutions that are applied broadly may actually increase costs and leave critical staffing issues unaddressed. Talent management practices that flow from and are consistent with effective workforce planning and "talent planning" processes can allow an organization to focus on just those talent management strategies that will attract, select, develop, and retain exactly the talent needed to achieve business success.

20

C H A P T E R

Structuring Strategic Workforce Planning to Support Common Business Initiatives

Setting Up Relevant Staffing Models for the Changes You Are Facing

There is no limit to the number of business changes and initiatives whose implementation can be greatly facilitated by the application of workforce planning. This chapter describes in detail how workforce planning can be used to help implement three very common business initiatives: a straight-forward growth scenario, a merger/acquisition opportunity, and the opening of a "greenfield" facility (such as a new manufacturing facility). A fourth example is provided that applies when specific skills changes in a particular job family or function are required in order to implement a business strategy effectively. For each of these three examples, I have identified:

- The overall workforce planning approach that should be used
- The most likely staffing issues and implications that will arise from that business strategy or initiative
- What the staffing model itself should look like (e.g., who should be included, what the planning horizon should be, what the rows and columns of the model might denote)
- What longer-term staffing strategies might best address the critical staffing issues that are identified

Specific staffing plans can then be defined within the context of these staffing strategies. Because these plans are so specific to particular change scenarios, I have not suggested any here. Remember that your staffing plans might incorporate internal movement, promotions, recruiting, redeployment, use of part-time staff, use of consultants or contractors, use of overtime, the outsourcing of work, planned reductions in staffing levels, and many other options.

While the approaches described for each of the four initiatives are generic, they will probably apply in large measure (with some customization, of course) to instances in which your organization is trying to implement these business strategies and initiatives. At the very least, they provide a logical train of thought that will give you a real leg up when it comes to developing a workforce planning process that is appropriate for your particular business initiative or strategy.

Business Initiative: A Growth Scenario

Often, organizations anticipate that they will grow significantly over the course of several planning periods. Workforce planning can be instrumental in these cases, identifying the staffing that would be needed to support that growth and ensuring that the needed talent will be available to achieve those growth objectives.

Overall Approach

First, define the type of business growth that is planned. Usually there are two basic types: overall growth (where the organization as a whole is forecast to grow) and targeted growth (where particular segments of the business will grow, but not all segments). Further, growth may come through simply expanding what an organization is currently doing (e.g., selling more of an existing product), through augmenting what the organization does (e.g., selling an existing product in new markets), or through changing what it does (e.g., developing and marketing products that are different from those offered currently).

Once the nature of the growth has been determined, focus your workforce planning process on defining the implications of that growth. You should not attempt to create detailed workforce plans for the entire organization. Instead, concentrate on the parts of the organization that are expected to grow or change (perhaps even only on those that are expected to grow most significantly or most rapidly). In every case, your "now" scenario will reflect your starting point, and your "then" scenario will depict what the organization's staffing needs will be as growth targets of various types are met.

Likely Staffing Issues/Implications

For simple growth scenarios (e.g., expanding existing operations in existing geographies), several staffing issues/implications are most often raised:

- Increases in required staffing levels in growth areas
- Increases in "indirect" staffing (e.g., those supervising and supporting the higher number of staff required)
- Changes in required skills (e.g., a need for first-level supervision skills)
- Changes in organization structure (because of the larger number of employees that are required)

For expansion/growth scenarios (e.g., selling existing products in new geographic areas), these staffing issues/implications might arise:

- Specific increases in the new areas (e.g., new geographies)
- Redeployments from current areas to new areas create staffing gaps in those current areas
- Increases in indirect staffing levels (e.g., additional managers)
- Changes in required skills (e.g., increased need for supervisory skills)
- Changes in organization structure (e.g., staffing of additional business units serving new geographies)

When plans call for growth by augmentation (e.g., new products or services), the following staffing issues are likely:

- Specific increases in the units affected by or supporting the change
- Redeployments from current areas to areas supporting the change create staffing gaps in those current areas
- Increases in indirect staffing levels (e.g., additional managers)
- Changes in required skills (e.g., those needed to develop new products or market new products to different customers)
- Changes in organization structure (e.g., staffing of additional business units developing new products or serving new customers)

Staffing Model Parameters

Create a staffing model that focuses on those job categories, job families, functions, or units that are most affected by the growth or change that is anticipated. Rather than create one big model, create a series of models—one for each major job or organization group that is to be impacted. Create models that include multiple groups (e.g., different job families) only when you truly are going to manage staff across those categories. For each model you build, you will need to define these three planning parameters:

- **Population.** Include in each model the positions that are going to be most affected by the change (e.g., is the finance group really going to grow all that much even if business is expected to grow by 30 percent?). Remember to include possible "sources" of needed talent and potential "uses" for surplus talent.
- **Time frame/planning horizon.** For the "how long" parameter, use the time frame for achieving stated growth targets or implementing required changes. It is sometimes helpful to look one period beyond the stated target date so that you can begin to plan for staffing needs in the more stable period that will follow the growth or change. For the "how often" component, divide the "how long" period into practical milestones (usually quarters or years).
- **Staffing model structure.** Columns should be differentiated to reflect the job groups you decided to focus on. This is usually job family, function, or organization unit. Rows (as usual) should reflect an increasing hierarchy of skill or capability (e.g., Production Worker, Senior Production Worker, Production Supervisor, Manager of Production).

Your ultimate "demand then" matrix (e.g., for planning period 5) should capture the staffing requirements (both skills and staffing levels) that support the final growth objectives. An interim "demand then" matrix will be needed for each milestone that you chose (e.g., the ends of periods 1 through 4).

Staffing Strategies

For any growth scenario, the following staffing strategies might be useful:

- Promotion from within and replacement at the lowest level
- Redeployment of existing staff to newly created positions, developing required skills in advance of need
- Transition plans that manage the movement of staff from "old" to "new" across several planning periods
- Filling newly created positions with a set blend of internal placements and recruiting (e.g., 75 percent internal, 25 percent external)
- Filling openings through internal movement where skills are available and relying on external, experienced talent where internal placement and development would take too long

Business Initiative: Merger or Acquisition

Mergers and acquisitions (M&A) often raise a host of staffing issues. At the very least, there will be two (or more) workforces that need to be as-

similated. Often, this integration creates surplus staff that must be redeployed or reduced. Workforce planning is an ideal tool for managing the
integration of multiple workforces and reducing/redeploying surplus
staff.

Overall Approach

Think of workforce planning as a tool for managing the transition from
two separate workforces to a single integrated workforce. In general, you
will want to create a model in which the "supply now" scenario identifies
the staff that are available in the two organizations separately and the final
"demand then" scenario captures what you think the staffing requirements of the fully combined/integrated organization will be. Use the internal movement component of your model to capture the movement of
employees "from" the two separate organizations "to" the new combined
one. For example, a group of employees might move from Engineer Level
1 in an old organization to Engineer Level 1 in the new organization. Employees that do not move from an old organization to the new organization will be identified as surplus. Staffing strategies to eliminate these
surpluses can then be developed (e.g., movement to other positions, redeployment to some other function with accelerated development, layoffs).

Likely Staffing Issues/Implications

M&A activity typically raises such staffing issues as:

- Workforce integration and assimilation issues (e.g., how best to fill
  opportunities in the new organization using the two pools of employees)
- Identifying surplus staff (especially those that may result from synergy opportunities)
- Potential staffing redundancies
- Capabilities gaps and development issues regarding the product(s)
  being acquired and their markets (e.g., when the company being acquired has expertise or market presence that the acquiring company
  does not have)
- Organization structure changes (resulting from the M&A activity),
  such as new products, new customers, or new geographies

Staffing Model Parameters

At first, given the "macro" nature of a merger or acquisition, it might seem
like a good idea to create an organization-wide model that includes all
positions. In fact, this approach is unwieldy at best and impossible to im-

plement at worst. Avoid this "one giant model" syndrome by adopting one or both of these approaches:

- **Focus your analysis on critical positions.** Not every job in the new organization will be critical; not all will need the strategic perspective (nor merit the work involved) that workforce planning demands. Limit your analysis (at least at first) to those positions that really require the power of workforce planning. If necessary, create new models to address less critical issues once you have completed models for the most critical issues. As examples, your models might include:

  —Positions critical to the success of the combined venture

  —Positions needed to maintain the success or integrity of the acquired products or services

  —Positions for which integration, synergy, or increased efficiency is desired or expected

  —Positions in which redundancies might occur

  —Positions in which surpluses might arise

- **Segment your analyses.** If the number of critical positions is large, don't create one model that includes them all. Instead, create a series of separate models, each of which addresses a "stand-alone" group of critical positions. Include in each group positions among which staff movement is required or desired (e.g., a model for a given function or engineering discipline). Do not include in the same model positions among which movement is not wanted or is unrealistic (e.g., where large capability differences, strong organization boundaries, or great geographic distances really prohibit staff transitions). As an example, engineering and marketing positions might both be critical, but they should be combined in a single model only if significant staff movement (i.e., large numbers of staff, not just one or two isolated instances) between those two functions is expected and desired. Given the great capabilities differences between the two categories, such movement is unrealistic, and thus separate models should be created.

Now, for the models you deem necessary, define the three planning parameters:

- **Population.** Identify those critical jobs that will be included in each model. Remember to include possible "sources" of needed talent and possible "uses" of surplus talent.

- **Time frame/planning horizon.** For the "how long" parameter, use the time frame for completing the M&A. It is sometimes helpful to look one period beyond the stated target date so that you can begin to plan for staffing needs in the more stable period that will follow the completion of the merger or assimilation of the acquisition. For the "how often" component, divide the "how long" period into practical milestones (usually quarters or years).
- **Staffing model structure.** Columns should be differentiated to reflect the job groups you decided to focus on. This is usually job family, function, and/or organization unit. Rows (as usual) should reflect an increasing hierarchy of skill or capability (e.g., Production Worker, Senior Production Worker, Production Supervisor, Manager of Production).

Your "supply now" matrix needs to include available staff from each of the M&A partners. Usually, it is helpful to use separate columns to capture the data for each company and a single set of rows that can be used across companies. Your ultimate "demand then" matrix (e.g., for planning period 5) should capture the staffing requirements (both skills and staffing levels) that support the final growth objectives. An interim "demand then" matrix will be needed for each milestone that you chose (e.g., the ends of periods 1 through 4).

Staffing Strategies

When integrating/assimilating an M&A partner, the following staffing strategies might be considered:

- Staff transition strategies, moving employees from the separate partners to the combined entity
- Capability-based assessments to compare staff from the partner companies in a more objective way and identify development needs
- Internal movement, with recruiting to fill positions where transitions are not possible (or cannot be completed within the required time frame)
- Training and orientation efforts coupled with development to accelerate movement to new positions in the combined organization
- Redeployments (with or without development) to reduce surpluses
- Staffing reductions (especially where attrition is insufficient)

Business Initiative: Opening a Greenfield Site

The opening of a new facility or plant always raises significant staffing issues. Two slightly different examples are described here. In the first example, the new facility is simply replacing an existing facility. In the second, the new facility is augmenting an existing facility. While these examples assume just one existing facility, the same logic would apply in both examples if there is more than one existing facility. In either case, workforce planning is an ideal tool for managing the movement of staff to the new facility.

Overall Approach

As mentioned previously, think of workforce planning as a tool for managing the transition of staff from "old" to "new." If the new facility is replacing an existing one, workforce planning can help you to define all the staffing actions and movement that will be needed to migrate employees from one facility to the other. If the new facility is augmenting the existing one, workforce planning can help you to define the most effective way to staff the new facility while maintaining the talent needed to ensure continuous, efficient operations at the existing facility.

In both examples included here, your "supply now" scenario will include staff currently working at the existing facility. In the case where one facility is replacing another, there will be no "supply now" in the new facility when workforce planning begins (but if there are employees already working at the new facility, be sure to include them).

In the case of a replacement facility, your ultimate "demand then" scenario will probably show no staff at the existing facility and a full complement of staff at the new facility. In the case where a new facility is in addition to an existing facility, your ultimate "demand then" scenario will include all the employees that are required to staff both facilities.

In both examples, your staffing strategies will describe what should be done to move staff effectively while achieving and maintaining adequate staffing at all facilities (e.g., identifying not only the staff that should move to a new facility, but also what—if anything—should be done at the existing facility to replace that talent).

Likely Staffing Issues/Implications

The opening of a Greenfield site will create significant staffing issues at both the new and the existing facilities. These might include:

- Staffing gaps at the new facility
- Staffing surpluses at the existing facility
- The need to fill critical positions at the new facility proactively
- The need for an orderly transition of staff from the old facility to the new one

- The need for accelerated or targeted development to close capabilities gaps created by staff transitions
- The need to fill openings in the new facility when needed talent does not exist in the old facility
- Staffing gaps that are created at the old facility when employees move to the new facility
- Striking the right balance between experienced staff and new hires at the new facility
- Inconsistencies between employee movement policies and practices and staffing objectives (e.g., when more employees want to move to the new facility than is practical or desired)
- Lack of the capabilities needed to implement new technology at the new facility
- Lack of required talent at the new location
- Relocation issues and costs (e.g., where the new facility is located far from the existing one)

Staffing Model Parameters

As always, focus your analysis on critical positions; don't try to include all positions. If the facilities you are analyzing are plants, for example, it is probably not necessary to include maintenance and food service staff in your model. Similarly, if there are two positions of some kind at the new facility and you know that you are going to fill those two positions with two employees that performed that role in the old facility, a detailed workforce plan just is not required. For each staffing model that you build, you will need to define the three planning parameters:

- **Population.** Focus your efforts on critical positions and staffing needs such as these:

  —Jobs that are critical at the new facility

  —Positions (especially at the new facility) that should be filled proactively, in advance of need (e.g., plant manager and plant quality positions)

  —Jobs at the new facility that are probably going to be filled (at least in part) by staff from the old facility

  —Positions where new capabilities will be required (e.g., skills needed to support new technology or operate new, more advanced equipment)

  —Jobs where local recruiting may be required

- **Time frame/planning horizon.** The time frame for your analysis should match the schedule for opening the new facility. For the "how long" parameter, use the projected opening date of the new facility as your target. It is sometimes helpful to look one period beyond the stated target date so that you can begin to plan for staffing needs in the more stable period that will follow the opening. For the "how often" component, divide the "how long" period into practical milestones (usually quarters or years). This will allow you to plan for and monitor the placement of key staff in the new facility in advance of its opening.
- **Staffing model structure.** Columns should be differentiated to reflect the job groups you decided to focus on. This is usually job family, function, or organization unit. Rows (as usual) should reflect an increasing hierarchy of skill or capability (e.g., Production Worker, Senior Production Worker, Production Supervisor, Manager of Production).

Your "supply now" matrix needs to include the staff that are currently working in the existing facility. Your ultimate "demand then" matrix (e.g., for planning period 5) must capture the staffing requirements (both skills and staffing levels) for the new facility. If this is a replacement facility, "demand then" for the old facility should be zero in every category. If the new facility supplements a current facility, future staffing requirements for that original facility must also be determined. An interim "demand then" matrix will be needed for each milestone that you chose (e.g., the ends of periods 1 through 4). These interim milestones will allow you to plan for and monitor the transition of staff from the old facility to the new one.

Staffing Strategies

When staffing a new facility, the following staffing strategies should be considered:

- Transitions from the old facility to the new one
- Redeployments, some with accelerated development to address development needs (e.g., training production staff in new technologies before assigning them to positions in the new facility)
- Internal movement and recruiting to backfill positions in the old facility that become vacant when staff are redeployed to the new facility
- Surpluses that may be created when there are staff with obsolete skills who are unable or unwilling to learn the new required capabilities

- Local recruiting to meet immediate talent needs at either facility
- Changes in job posting or other placement policies/procedures to support the internal movement that is desired/required

Business Initiative: Major Change in Required Capabilities

In some cases, critical staffing issues relate more to skills and capabilities gaps than they do to differences in the number of staff that will be needed. Workforce planning, while usually associated with required staffing levels, can be used to address skills gaps even if staffing levels don't change. Just to be sure, however, your workforce planning process should define both required skills and staffing levels, even if the focus is on capabilities gaps.

Overall Approach

First, identify the job categories, functions, or organization units where critical skills gaps are anticipated. Create and run a staffing model just as you would if you were implementing any workforce planning process. This time, however, pay special attention to the skills that are available and the skills that will be needed in the future. Make sure that whatever tool you use (e.g., a competency model) will allow you to define available and required skills in a way that allows you to compare the two directly to identify critical skills gaps. Remember that even though you are focusing on skills, you will also need to analyze staffing levels. That is the only way in which you will be able to quantify your skills gaps and the plans needed to address those gaps. For example, it is necessary to identify a skills gap relating to the implementation of a new technology, but it is not sufficient. However, to be effective, your analysis must also identify how many employees will need to be developed in that skill, and when (e.g., 15 staff will need to be developed in order to implement the new technology by the end of the year).

Likely Staffing Issues/Implications

Obviously, in this case the major staffing issue will be a capabilities gap. However, several other staffing issues may arise. These staffing issues might include:

- Capabilities differences that cannot be addressed through normal training and development practices
- Capabilities differences that cannot be addressed through development in the time that is available (e.g., to meet immediate or immediately upcoming needs)

- Future capabilities requirements where that talent does not exist at all in the current organization

Staffing Model Parameters

When building a staffing model to address a capabilities gap, the usual three planning parameters must be defined:

- **Population.** Focus on the positions where required skills differences are most critical. Remember that "critical" in this context is not the same as "biggest." There might be positions where a difference of just two or three skills might make or break your ability to implement a business strategy. There might be other positions where a long list of small skills differences exists, but where the differences can be easily addressed through simple training and development interventions (and thus the differences are not critical). Remember to include positions that may be good sources of the new, required capabilities and positions to which surplus employees might potentially be redeployed.

- **Time frame/planning horizon.** The time frame for your analysis should match the need to have fully competent staff in place. Remember that these capable staff often need to be developed and ready even before they will be expected to apply those new skills. For the "how long" parameter, see when business plans will require that those new skills be available. Again, it is sometimes helpful to look one period beyond the stated target date so that you can begin to plan for staffing needs in the more stable period that will follow the need for the new skills (e.g., to begin to create plans for developing those skills on an ongoing basis). For the "how often" component, divide the "how long" period into practical milestones (usually quarters or years). This will allow you to plan for and monitor the development and placement of newly developed staff.

- **Staffing model structure.** Columns should be differentiated to reflect the job groups you decided to focus on. This is usually job family, function, or organization unit. Rows (as usual) should reflect an increasing hierarchy of skill or capability (e.g., Production Worker, Senior Production Worker, Production Supervisor, Manager of Production).

Your "supply now" matrix needs to include the staff that are currently working in the existing facility, documenting the skills that these individuals have. It is usually not necessary to document these skills on an individualized basis. Instead, consider summarizing the skills of the group of incumbents, making simplifying assumptions as necessary (e.g., that any Software Engineer 1 in Unit A that is performing satisfactorily probably has capabilities A, B, and C). Your ultimate "demand then" model (e.g., for planning period 5) must capture the staffing requirements (both skills and staffing levels) that will be required in the future. By definition, required future capabilities will differ from those that are available currently, but required staffing levels might remain unchanged. An interim "demand then" matrix will be needed for each milestone that you chose (e.g., the ends of periods 1 through 4). These interim milestones will allow you to plan for and monitor the staffing and development actions that are intended to eliminate the critical skills gaps you identified.

Summary

These examples are just that—examples. They are meant to give you a leg up when you find it necessary to apply workforce planning to support any of the four common business initiatives that are described. You won't be able to follow these examples blindly (you will need to adapt the ideas presented here), but at least you won't have to start from scratch!

21

Defining Staffing Reductions in a Strategic Context

As business and economic conditions fluctuate, companies sometimes find it necessary to reduce staffing levels. Organizations that are facing major downsizing (e.g., as a result of cost reduction efforts, mergers, or consolidations) are often tempted to look only at the near term when deciding which staff should be kept and which will be asked to leave. Decisions regarding the size (the number of positions to be eliminated), type (the kinds of jobs to be cut), location, and timing of the reduction are often made without regard to the company's longer-term staffing needs. Often, these decisions are based on subjective criteria or somewhat arbitrary financial objectives, not staffing requirements. I have known of companies that have reduced staff to influence short-term profitability—and thus analyst expectations and stock price. While these downsizings meet their near-term targets by definition, they are usually shortsighted. Those seemingly positive short-term reduction decisions and actions can have significant negative longer-term staffing implications. In some cases, these implications are so severe that they negate the effects and intentions of the original reductions.

When consolidation or downsizing is required, it is far more effective to define short-term staffing actions within the context of a longer-term staffing strategy, as produced by the strategic staffing/workforce planning process. Often, implementing a pragmatic approach to strategic staffing can yield the high-quality results that organizations need and expect—and make the results of the downsizing stick.

Using a Staffing Strategy as a Context for Reduction Decisions

As discussed throughout this book, strategic staffing/workforce planning is a process that allows an organization to develop a long-term staffing strategy that is used as a context for defining the most effective short-term staffing actions (see Figure 21-1). Without this long-term context, it is at best difficult to make truly effective short-term staffing decisions—especially those involving staff reductions.

A well-designed staffing strategy can help organizations make reduction decisions that make the most sense in the long run. By defining future requirements (in terms of both capabilities and staffing levels), organizations create a new set of criteria that can be applied when reductions are being considered. As a result, staff reductions can be made in areas that will least affect the organization's ability to implement both its current and its future business plans. For example, individuals with critical skills that will be needed in the future might be retained, even if they are not the most effective performers currently or do not have the longest tenure. The use of strategic staffing/workforce planning also allows the effects of turnover to be factored into each analysis, thus helping the organization to define the actual number of reductions required (i.e., reductions in excess of expected attrition).

Obviously, a staffing strategy can best be developed when there is a realistic, effective long-term business strategy or plan. Consolidations and downsizings should be implemented only after the organization has defined what its future objectives are and how it proposes to accomplish those objectives. Once such a plan has been developed, the staffing needed

Figure 21-1. Defining Staffing Reductions in a Strategic Context.

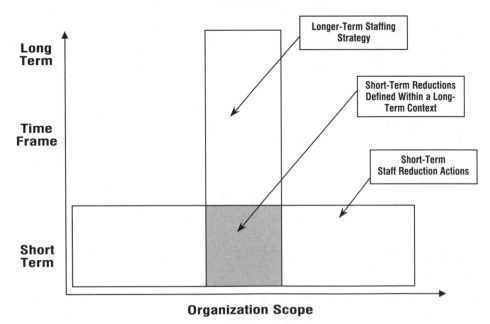

to support that plan can be defined. Staffing reductions that are based on short-term plans (or, worse yet, quarterly objectives) are sure to be detrimental in the long run.

Common Mistakes That Strategic Staffing Can Help You Avoid

Many organizations encounter significant problems when they plan and implement downsizing from a purely short-term (or financial) perspective. Here are some examples of common mistakes that companies often make when staffing reductions are needed.

Reductions Do Not Consider Future Skills Requirements

Organizations often base their staff reduction decisions on performance (e.g., through forced ranking based on current performance), tenure, or analyses of the current skills and capabilities of staff—none of which consider the skills and capabilities that will be needed in the future. Companies that use these criteria often make two separate, but related, mistakes. First, they often end up keeping employees with obsolete skills. Employees who are performing well in their current jobs may no longer perform well if those jobs (and the underlying required skills) change during the planning period. Second, they lay off others who have the capabilities that will be needed in the future. Companies often find later on that the individuals who left actually possessed critical skills that were needed to implement future business plans. Staff with critical skills who are performing only satisfactorily in their current jobs (and who thus are likely to be asked to leave if current performance is a criterion) may actually be needed more than some who are outstanding performers in their current job but whose skills are becoming obsolete. Recently hired staff (i.e., those with the least tenure) may actually have brought desperately needed capabilities to the organization, yet these individuals will be the first to be asked to leave if tenure alone is considered. Older employees (i.e., those who are most likely to accept early retirement when this is offered as a staff reduction tool) sometimes have a depth of experience that will be even more important in a smaller, more focused organization. This needed experience disappears when these people decide (and in some cases are actually encouraged) to leave. A few key individuals with needed skills may even end up working for—and contributing significantly to the success of—a competitor.

An effective staffing strategy defines the skills and capabilities that will be needed to fully implement both current and future business plans.

A company that has developed such a strategy can consider future required skills as criteria when identifying individuals to be let go.

Across-the-Board Headcount Reductions Are Used

Organizations often implement staff reductions (some of them quite large
in magnitude) by reducing staff levels by the same amount in all areas and
locations (e.g., reducing headcount in all units by 15 percent). This approach penalizes effective managers who have worked to keep their staffs
lean. A reduction of this type forces these managers to cut their core of
productive, effective workers. Conversely, managers who have padded
staffing levels or built up surpluses can achieve their reduction targets
simply by eliminating slack and redundancy, keeping most of their staff
(whether productive or not) intact. In either of these cases, the staffing
levels that result often do not match the staffing (i.e., required skills and
staffing levels) that will be needed to implement business plans and strategies.

Companies that have developed staffing strategies have a good understanding of the capabilities and staffing levels that will be needed in the
future. Armed with this information, the organization can achieve its
headcount reduction targets in ways that least affect its future viability.
Instead of across-the-board cuts, the organization can target and focus its
reduction efforts on the areas that are least critical to strategy implementation and minimize reductions in those areas that are most closely aligned
with strategy implementation.

Expected Cost Savings Are Not Realized

The purpose of most staff reductions is reducing operating costs. However, a 20 percent headcount reduction rarely results in a 20 percent savings. Managers tend to achieve the reductions by cutting larger numbers
of lower-level (and lower-paid) staff, resulting in minimal cost savings. A
20 percent reduction in payroll (as opposed to headcount) might actually
require a 40 percent reduction in the number of lower-level staff. On the
other hand, a small reduction in senior management staffing might result
in a reduction in payroll costs that is even greater than 20 percent. In other
cases, managers get "credit" for reducing staff when they cut approved,
but unfilled, positions. Obviously, since these positions are vacant, there
are no actual salaries being paid, and thus no actual cost savings can be
realized.

Some managers get around the system by laying off staff and then
immediately employing "consultants" or contingent workers to do the
needed work. These workers (some of whom may be the company's own
employees who were just asked to leave) are then paid higher rates than

those that were paid to the staff who left. In other cases, some of the individuals that leave actually have skills and experience that are needed in the future. Later on, some of these individuals may be hired back (e.g., attracted away from competitors) at even higher rates of pay. Managers often use external consultants as a "back door" method for working around headcount reductions and freezes, which are usually focused on full-time staff. Reducing 10 positions, then hiring 10 consultants, reduces the full-time staff budget as requested, but actually increases overall staffing costs.

A well-developed staffing strategy identifies the skills and staffing levels that are really needed in order to implement the organization's strategies. Once these are known, the organization can define realistic cost reduction targets that least affect its ability to meet its future, longer-term objectives. In some cases, a staffing strategy may even help an organization identify reductions that actually exceed targets.

Reductions Don't Last

In many cases, staff reductions are made, yet no follow-up changes are made in work practices, volumes, or staffing controls. Thus, a smaller staff is asked to do the same work in the same way as the previous, larger group. People are asked to work harder (and longer), not smarter. Since work practices have not been changed, staffing levels soon creep back up, sometimes to levels that exceeded the original numbers. Managers who lay off individuals to meet short-term reduction targets may shortly begin to work the system to increase staffing levels once again.

Staffing reductions that are made within the context of a longer-term staffing strategy are more realistic and thus are more likely to last. Staffing strategies define the capabilities and staffing levels that are needed to implement strategies effectively. Thus, staffing reductions made within this context are more easily maintained over the long haul.

Summary

A staffing strategy allows an organization to create and implement short-term downsizing plans in the most effective way. The lack of such a staffing strategy (and the long-term context it provides) makes it difficult to define short-term staffing actions/reductions that won't have significant negative impacts on the organization in the future.

22

Measuring Staffing Effectiveness and Efficiency

As you certainly know by now, the strategic staffing/workforce planning process begins when you review your business strategies and plans and identify your most critical staffing issues. Next, you develop a series of staffing strategies that best address your most critical issues. Finally, you define a specific set of staffing plans and actions—those that best support the implementation of your staffing strategies. Figure 22-1 summarizes this process.

As soon as you implement these staffing plans and actions, you will begin to see results. Some people will be hired and others will leave. Some people will be promoted and others will be transferred. But how will you know if these are indeed the right results? How should you measure the results of the staffing strategies and plans that you implement? How will you know that you are better off for having implemented these actions?

Many organizations track staffing performance using such measures as how many jobs are filled, how long it takes to fill each opening, or what it costs to place a new hire. They may also track turnover or retention rates. Such measures can be helpful, but they are by no means sufficient. If you are measuring time, speed, cost, or volume, you are probably measuring efficiency (i.e., doing the job right). Efficiency measures can be helpful, but what tends to be missing from these measures is any indication of quality. The results of your strategic staffing process should also be measured for effectiveness (i.e., doing the right job in the first place). This chapter describes both of these criteria and proposes measures that can be used to evaluate staffing efficiency and effectiveness.

Measuring Staffing Efficiency

It is fairly easy to measure the efficiency of your staffing processes. Any construct that measures time, speed, cost, or volume is a measure of effi-

Figure 22-1. Measuring the Strategic Staffing Process.

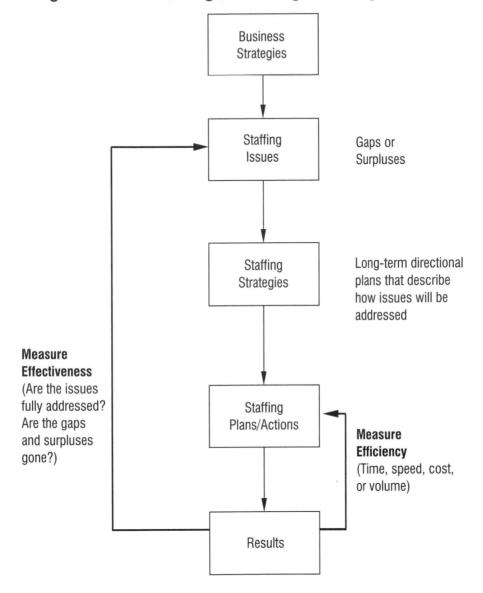

ciency. In staffing terms, the efficiency of your process might be measured in terms of how many openings are filled (a measure of volume), how quickly an opening is filled (a measure of speed), or cost per hire (obviously a measure of cost). Examples of staffing efficiency measures include these:

- Time or speed measures

    Average time to fill an opening (all openings)

    Time to fill (external sources only)

Time to fill (internal sources only)

Number of jobs filled per time period (e.g., month or quarter)

Average time between requisition and acceptance (or start date)

Average time between requisition and interview

- Cost measures (Chapter 23 includes a detailed discussion of how staffing costs can be calculated and analyzed)

  Average cost per hire

  Cost per hire per source (e.g., Internet vs. referral vs. agency)

  Cost per interview

  Cost per acceptance

  Cost per promotion

  Cost per relocation

- Volume measures

  Acceptance rates

  Number of jobs filled (in total)

  Number of candidates per source

  Number of candidates per opening

  Ratio of callbacks to initial interviews

  Job posting response rates

  Turnover rates

  Number of losses

Each of these measures can be tailored to meet your specific needs (e.g., you can define hit rates for specific agencies in order to identify those that are the best sources for a particular type of skill). Also, remember to use measures that focus on the issues you are addressing (e.g., don't use internal measures for jobs that are usually filled through external sources).

Efficiency measures are usually applied in the near term (i.e., within a planning period). To create a more meaningful analysis of efficiency, compare values over time. Calculate values for each planning period for each measure that you use and then compare the measures across planning periods (comparing results from one period to the next).

As you develop and apply efficiency measures, keep in mind these two cautions:

1. Be careful when using overall averages as measures. Averages often mask what is really happening, especially when they include different jobs under different circumstances. In a situation in which one job category is filled quickly and one takes a long time, the average of the two may seem to indicate that the overall time to fill is acceptable when, in fact, the time to fill for that second job category is unacceptably long. The same problem can arise when measuring cost per hire per source. Calculating an average cost across similar sources (e.g., agency hires) might hide the fact that one particular source (in this case, a particular agency) is significantly less expensive than the others. If you do use averages, make sure that you include only equivalent jobs in each group.

   2. **Avoid using absolute measures or standards.** Suppose, for example, that you set a target that all jobs should be filled within 60 days. It is possible that for one type of hard-to-fill job, a time to fill of 90 days or more might be quite acceptable, yet 90 days exceeds the 60-day target. For a different, easier-to-fill job, 30 days may be too long a time, even though that would meet the 60-day standard. Set standards that are appropriate for the jobs being analyzed.

Measuring Staffing Effectiveness

As valuable as they may be, efficiency measures alone tell only part of the story. Most efficiency measures address *quantity* in some way, but none of them address *quality*. What good is it to hire people quickly if those people do not have the skills that are needed to implement your business plans, or if they leave to take another job soon after they come to work for you? What if hiring costs are reduced drastically, but turnover among those who are hired actually increases? Is it really helpful to have a high acceptance rate if the people that are being hired end up being poor performers? What if the least expensive agencies supply individuals with obsolete capabilities? Another set of measures is needed to measure the results of your staffing process fully.

   Clearly, we need to have some way of measuring whether we are hiring, promoting, redeploying, and retaining not just people in general, but the right people in particular. Many organizations try to define the "right people" (or "good hires") in terms of skill, tenure, or performance. A good hire might be one who stays at least three years and achieves higher than average performance ratings. But these proxies are difficult to define and even more difficult to measure on an ongoing basis. Other organizations actually survey managers and ask them to rate the quality of the candidates that they see. These measures of quality are certainly better than none, but do they provide sufficient feedback? Do they adequately measure quality?

   The strategic staffing/workforce planning process described in this book includes a built-in measure of staffing effectiveness (i.e., "doing the right job"). When you implement the process as described, your staffing model will define specific staffing gaps and surpluses. As stated in Chapter 2, in order to define a gap (or surplus), you must define in very particular terms the staff that you will need (in terms of both required skills and staffing levels), forecast the staff that will be available, and compare demand to supply on a category-by-category basis. The differences you identify will be both specific and measurable. Simply stated, your staffing processes are most effective when they eliminate (or substantially reduce) these critical staffing gaps across all planning periods of your planning horizon. You have hired (or promoted or redeployed) the right people (and thus your staffing processes are effective) when the gaps you defined are filled with an adequate number of individuals who have the appropriate skills and experience. Your training programs are effective when they provide employees with the capabilities that close the critical skills gaps that you have identified. All of these are measures that should be included in the staffing models you build.

This approach to measuring effectiveness obviously places a great premium on defining very specific staffing gaps and surpluses. Your staffing models must provide you with an appropriate level of detail. As described earlier in this book, it is not sufficient to simply say that you do not have enough individuals with a particular skill; to use this measure of effectiveness, you must be able to calculate exactly how large that staffing gap or surplus will be. To do this, you will need to specifically define your needs for staff, forecast staff availability at that same level of detail, and compare demand to supply in a very precise way. You will also need to be able to monitor these gaps and surpluses on an ongoing basis to see if your staffing processes are reducing them as you had planned.

Unlike efficiency measures, which can be applied within a planning period, these measures of effectiveness are most valuable when they are applied across planning periods. If a staffing issue that you have identified is truly strategic, you will be unable to address it fully in just one period. It may take three or more planning periods to completely eliminate a critical staffing gap or surplus. Consequently, while you can certainly measure your progress on a period-by-period basis, overall success should be measured across the entire planning horizon.

Measuring Both Effectiveness and Efficiency

When you are measuring the success of your strategic staffing processes, you must analyze both effectiveness and efficiency. Examining either of these alone is insufficient. A process that quickly and cheaply recruits people with the wrong skills may technically be efficient, but it is clearly ineffective. Similarly, a process that places 10 candidates that are perfect fits in a particularly critical job may technically be quite effective, but if you had to interview and consider hundreds of candidates to find that perfect 10, the process is not very efficient.

Tracking Progress

The critical benefit of measurement and metrics comes not at the end of the process, but in tracking progress along the way. Measuring final performance and results can be important, but at that point it is clearly too late to influence what was being done. If you evaluate progress measures at key milestones, you will still have the opportunity to adjust what you are doing—thus increasing the probability that your overall staffing needs will be met efficiently and effectively.

When you are evaluating staffing efficiency and effectiveness, you can measure your progress by tracking the results from period to period or within each period.

Track Results from Period to Period

If the staffing issues that are defined are truly critical, they usually cannot be addressed within a single period. Effort and resources must be expended in every planning period of your planning horizon. The staffing strategies that you develop describe what will be done across planning periods to eliminate key staffing gaps and surpluses. Using these strategies as a long-term context, you then create specific staffing plans that describe what should be done to meet the needs in each planning period. If your plan is well designed and integrated, your final gaps and surpluses will always be addressed if you address the interim staffing needs in each previous period.

Consequently, you should evaluate your progress by measuring the extent to which you have successfully eliminated staffing gaps and surpluses at the end of each planning period. Adjust staffing actions in the subsequent period, if necessary, to ensure that gaps will be addressed. Calculate efficiency measures and compare them to the standards and budgeted levels that you developed initially.

Track Results During Each Period

While measuring results at the end of a planning period is beneficial, such measurement alone is not enough. Progress needs to be measured during each period as well. It is possible to measure the extent to which staffing gaps and surpluses are being eliminated (by implementing staffing plans) as the period progresses. There will be instances, given the short time frame of a single planning period, where it may be better to simply monitor the implementation of your staffing plans rather than the size of your staffing gaps and surpluses. In such cases, ensure that the required staffing actions (as described in your staffing plan for that period) take place as designed and when scheduled. Also, keep track of the resources that are being expended and make sure that these expenditures are in line with budgets and operating plans.

Summary

When you evaluate the success of your staffing processes, it is necessary to measure both efficiency (i.e., anything that measures time, speed, cost, or volume) and effectiveness (the extent to which the staffing gaps and surpluses that you defined were alleviated through the implementation of your staffing plans). As with all plans, it is best to measure and track progress along the way, not just at the end, when the plans are completed. This will allow you to adjust staffing processes throughout the planning period, making it more likely that the plans will have the desired impact.

23

Calculating Staffing Costs and Evaluating Staffing Options

In many cases, it is not enough (or even possible) to simply define one set of staffing plans that should be implemented to support the company's business plan. It is often necessary to develop and evaluate several staffing options that have different cost and timing implications. In other cases, it is necessary to review staffing plans from a big-picture perspective and draw some overall conclusions before the most effective plans and actions can be identified. This chapter defines how staffing costs should be measured and analyzed and describes how various staffing approaches can be evaluated. This analysis and evaluation of options is likely to become a valuable part of your strategic staffing process.

Step 1: Calculate Staffing Costs

Costs must be considered when staffing strategies and plans are being developed. In some cases, it is necessary to calculate the costs of several different staffing scenarios before the selection of the best strategy can be made. In other cases, costs need to be determined so that requested budgets can be prepared and defended. In still other cases, costs must be calculated in order to build coherent business cases for change (as mentioned in Chapter 12).

There are two separate types of staffing costs that should be analyzed: the cost of maintaining your desired workforce configuration, and the cost of making the transition from your current workforce to that desired future state. I sometimes describe these two types as the "cost of being there" and the "cost of getting there." Total staffing costs for any given planning period are the sum of the maintenance and transition costs for that period. Methods for calculating both types of costs are described here.

Workforce Maintenance Costs

Maintenance costs are the costs that an organization incurs when it maintains its workforce in a given configuration. At a minimum, this includes all direct and indirect payroll costs (e.g., salary and benefits). It may also include costs associated with physical space, overhead, and other infrastructure expenses (e.g., personal computers for every employee).

To calculate the cost of a given staffing configuration (e.g., your "supply then" or "demand then" scenario), you will need to estimate the maintenance costs for each job category in your model and then sum these costs across all job categories. Follow these steps:

- Identify all the types of direct and indirect costs that you need to consider for each category (e.g., whether space and overhead will be included).

- Define the appropriate time frame for your calculation (e.g., that you are defining annual or quarterly costs).

- Obtain or project the cost information for every individual in each job category or cell that is included in your staffing model. Make sure that the cost estimates are consistent with the time frame of your analysis (e.g., that if your time frame is one year, you have used annual salary costs). Include in your calculations cost estimates only for positions that will actually be filled. Cost estimates for open positions may need to be included when you are preparing budget estimates, but not when you are calculating actual costs. These open positions will not require actual cash outlays until they are filled.

- Sum these costs across all the individuals in each cell to calculate a total for each job category.

- Sum the costs across all job categories of your model to determine total staffing maintenance costs.

It is always best to base your calculations on real data—that is, the costs that will actually be incurred during the period in question. If you have actual cost information for each employee, use it. If for some reason actual costs cannot be determined, calculate and use weighted averages for each cost (e.g., based on midpoints or "compa-ratios" for that job) for each cell. However, detailed compensation and benefit cost information usually is readily available in your human resource information system.

Finally, remember to consider changes in costs that are to be expected during the planning period in question (e.g., specific merit and overall cost of living increases). Don't base your estimates on current costs (or, worse yet, historical rates), as these are probably much lower than the costs that will actually be incurred. Use whatever costs you think will be appropriate for the period being analyzed.

Figure 23-1 is an illustration that is based on the staffing model example described in Chapter 9. Suppose that we need to calculate the cost of maintaining this "supply then" configuration for a year:

First, determine costs for each job category or cell. Suppose that an analysis of current salary costs shows that the weighted average salary for individuals currently working in the software engineers/project manager job category was $77,295. However, a 3.5 percent average salary increase was also expected for the coming year. That would raise the average salary for this category to $80,000. Estimates for benefits, space, and overhead are also created. Assume that your analysis produces the results shown in Figure 23-2.

We estimate that it will cost the company (on average) $110,000 to employ and support a project manager in software engineering for the planning period in question. To calculate the total cost per job category or cell, multiply the total number of staff that will be in each category (as described in the "supply then" matrix) by the cost per category (as shown in the cost matrix) and sum your results across all job categories (see Figure 23-3).

It will cost this organization $21,055,000 to maintain the workforce configuration described in this particular "supply then" scenario for one year, given the cost assumptions that we made.

One additional adjustment may need to be made in your estimates. It is likely that any new hires that are to be added may be paid at a rate that is higher than that of existing staff. If there are any categories in which you are anticipating significant hiring, you may want to bump up your figures for average salary in order to account for these higher rates of pay (e.g., assuming that base pay for project managers would be $82,000 instead of the $80,000 that we assumed initially).

Figure 23-1. "Supply Then."

	Software Engineers	Object-Oriented Programmers	Total
Project Manager	12	9	21
Lead	25	21	46
Individual Contributor	62	52	114
Entry Level	83	77	160
Total	182	159	341

Figure 23-2. Average Annual Costs for the Coming Planning Period.

	Software Engineers	Object-Oriented Programmers
Project Manager	Salary: $80,000 Benefits: $20,000 Space: $5,000 Overhead: $5,000 **Total: $110,000**	Salary: $75,000 Benefits: $20,000 Space: $5,000 Overhead: $4,000 **Total: $104,000**
Lead	Salary: $60,000 Benefits: $12,000 Space: $4,000 Overhead: $4,000 **Total: $80,000**	Salary: $55,000 Benefits: $12,000 Space: $4,000 Overhead: $3,000 **Total: $74,000**
Individual Contributor	Salary: $50,000 Benefits: $10,000 Space: $3,000 Overhead: $2,000 **Total: $65,000**	Salary: $45,000 Benefits: $10,000 Space: $3,000 Overhead: $2,000 **Total: $60,000**
Entry Level	Salary: $40,000 Benefits: $8,000 Space: $3,000 Overhead: $2,000 **Total: $53,000**	Salary: $35,000 Benefits: $8,000 Space: $3,000 Overhead: $2,000 **Total: $48,000**

Figure 23-3. Total Maintenance Costs.

	Software Engineers	Object-Oriented Programmers	Total
Project Manager	12 × $110,000 = $1,320,000	9 × $104,000 = $936,000	**$2,256,000**
Lead	25 × $80,000 = $2,000,000	21 × $74,000 = $1,554,000	**$3,554,000**
Individual Contributor	62 × $65,000 = $4,030,000	52 × $60,000 = $3,120,000	**$7,150,000**
Entry Level	83 × $53,000 = $4,399,000	77 × $48,000 = $3,696,000	**$8,095,000**
Total	**$11,749,000**	**$9,306,000**	**$21,055,000**

In some cases, such as the one just discussed, it may be appropriate to calculate the costs of your "supply then" configuration. If you use "supply then," your calculations will reflect the costs of the actual staff configuration that will exist if all your assumed staffing actions actually take place. This includes the extra cost of any surplus staff that is being carried; similarly, this approach will not include the cost of any open positions that are not filled by the staffing actions described and included in your plan.

In other cases, you may want to calculate the costs associated with a desired state (i.e., "demand then"), even if that state may not actually be achieved. This situation would arise, for example, when you are comparing the staffing costs of proposed scenarios or solutions before choosing the one to be implemented. If you would like to determine the cost of your required configuration (whether or not all those staffing needs are actually going to be met), the calculation routine just described still applies; however, you will need to base your calculations on "demand then," not "supply then." Calculations based on any "demand then" scenario will not include the cost of surplus staff or the savings associated with open positions.

Transition Costs

Usually, it is insufficient to consider only the costs of maintaining a given workforce configuration. Transition costs and other staffing-related expenses that arise when your organization moves from one workforce configuration to another during a planning period (e.g., the cost of moving from "supply now" to the desired "supply then") must also be calculated.

Your staffing plans (as produced by your strategic staffing/workforce planning process) describe all kinds of staffing actions that are to be implemented to reduce staffing gaps and surpluses (e.g., hiring and redeployment). Each of these actions has a cost associated with it. This typically includes the costs associated with search, recruiting, candidate evaluation, placement, relocation, initial training, outplacement, severance, and early retirement packages.

To calculate these transition costs, first determine the costs associated with each type of staffing action that you plan to implement. Base your estimates on current costs, adjusting those estimates up or down as necessary to reflect what you think those costs will be during the planning period. Wherever feasible, keep the cost estimates for each staffing action separate and distinct. The more specific these estimates are, the more realistic your cost forecasts will be. For example, don't just estimate the average cost of hiring a person into any job; instead, estimate the average cost of hiring a person into a particular job. Better still, estimate what would be the cost to hire a person into a given job from each source (e.g., Internet recruiting vs. external search firms). If this level of specificity is not possible, calculate overall averages. At a minimum, develop estimates for the following:

- The cost of placing an external candidate into each job category or cell of your staffing model. Include costs associated with recruiting, agency fees, relocation, orientation, and initial training. If cost differences between sources are significant, calculate costs for different sources separately (e.g., Internet vs. agency or one agency vs. another). Consider adding in interviewing and candidate processing costs if they can be calculated.

- The cost of placing an internal candidate into each job category. This includes all those who move from one job in your organization to another. Consider relocation, training, and any other related costs. Include estimates of lost productivity if this is significant.

- The cost of having an individual leave a given category. Calculate separate costs for each kind of termination (e.g., voluntary, layoff, and severance). For each type, include costs related to separation packages, severance pay, and outplacement services. There is a section later in this chapter that describes how the true cost of turnover can be calculated.

To calculate total transition costs, simply multiply these estimates by the number of such moves that are expected during the planning period in question (as defined by your staffing plans).

Here is an example of how staffing transition costs might be calculated for the staffing model example described in Chapter 9. Suppose we need to calculate the cost of implementing the staffing plan for software engineers included in that example (see Figure 23-4).

Suppose further that you had developed the cost estimates shown in Figure 23-5 for staffing actions within software engineering.

Figure 23-4. Proposed Staffing Plan.

Type	Staffing Action(s)
Promotions	5 from software engineers/lead to software engineers/project manager
	12 from software engineers/individual contributor to software engineers/lead
	16 from software engineers/entry level to software engineers/individual contributor
New hires	12 into software engineers/individual contributor
	38 into software engineers/entry level

Figure 23-5.

Staffing Action	Cost per Action
Promotion from lead to project manager (including training)	$15,000
Promotion from individual contributor to lead (including training)	$10,000
Promotion from entry level to individual contributor (including training)	$5,000
Hire into individual contributor positions from external sources	$50,000
Hire into entry-level positions from external sources	$30,000

Calculate total transition costs by multiplying the number of actions (as defined by the staffing plan) by the cost per action, as defined in your estimates (see Figure 23-6).

It would cost this organization $2,015,000 to implement all the required staffing actions for the software engineering group. Note that in this example there are no planned losses. If such reductions had been required, the cost of those reductions would have had to be calculated as well (i.e., the cost of each severance times the number of such reductions) and added to the total.

Combine Maintenance and Transition Costs

Usually, an organization needs an estimate of overall staffing costs when making staffing decisions. A complete analysis of staffing costs would include both maintenance costs and transition costs for each planning period. To calculate total staffing costs, it is necessary to add together both types of cost for each planning period. In the previous example, staffing-related costs for the first period in software engineering would equal $13,764,000 (i.e., $11,749,000 in maintenance costs and the additional $2,015,000 in transition costs). Remember that your actual total should in-

Figure 23-6.

Staffing Action	Total Cost per Action
Promotion from lead to project manager	$15,000 × 5 such promotions = $75,000
Promotion from individual contributor to lead	$10,000 × 12 such promotions = $120,000
Promotion from entry level to individual contributor	$5,000 × 16 such promotions = $80,000
Hire into individual contributor positions	$50,000 × 12 such hires = $600,000
Hire into entry level positions	$30,000 × 38 such hires = $1,140,000
Total transition costs	**= $2,015,000**

clude staffing costs for all planning periods, not just for one period (as we just did in the example).

Step 2: Analyze Staffing Costs

Often, there are several staffing plans that might be implemented to address a particular set of staffing issues. Selecting the best approach from among these alternatives usually requires an analysis of total staffing costs. It is not enough to look at just maintenance costs or just transition costs—you must look at the total. One scenario may have lower transition costs than another scenario, but implementing the first solution might result in higher maintenance costs than would implementing the second (i.e., once the staffing moves are made). Since transition costs are usually one-time charges and maintenance costs are ongoing, a scenario that is cheaper in the near term might quickly become more expensive to maintain in the long run. Consequently, you should decide which staffing plan scenario to implement only after you have considered the long-term maintenance costs of each.

Remember that these decisions should not be based on cost considerations alone. Timing is also a key consideration. Suppose, for example, that a given opening can be filled internally at a cost of $10,000 and that filling that same job through an external search might cost $50,000 or more. Based on cost alone, the internal placement might seem more cost-effective. However, an employee who is placed internally might require a year or two to learn what is required and get up to speed in the job, whereas the external placement might hit the ground running and be proficient in six weeks. In such a case, cost considerations alone just don't tell the whole story. If the organization can wait for the employee to produce, then the cheaper alternative is best. On the other hand, if the need must be filled right away, the external placement would be preferred, even though it costs more.

There is one additional benefit of analyzing staffing costs in advance of need: If staffing issues are analyzed in advance of need and staffing plans are developed proactively, it is sometimes possible to reduce overall staffing costs by implementing less expensive staffing solutions. Here are three examples:

- Costing out various staffing solutions can help an organization choose the one that addresses critical staffing issues in the way that is least expensive in the long run.

- Immediate, short-term staffing solutions (such as external searches) are usually more expensive than internal placements, but those internal placements take time. Defining staffing needs in advance allows an organization to develop a pool of qualified talent that can be placed when needed. In almost every case, this kind of placement is less expensive, even when development costs are considered.

- Forecasts of the supply side often identify employees who may be leaving the organization, either through voluntary turnover or through retirement. Proactive staff planning allows an organization to focus its efforts on retaining key individuals, thus avoiding substantial replacement costs later on.

The cost savings that can be realized from proactive staff planning will probably greatly exceed the cost of implementing the strategic staffing process in the first place!

Defining the True Cost of Attrition

Sometimes it is helpful to calculate the cost of attrition (e.g., when justifying a management or staffing process that is aimed at reducing losses). Often, these estimates focus on the costs of replacing individuals who leave and are calculated on a generic basis (e.g., considering average sourcing, recruiting, and/or placement costs, it will cost the organization $20,000 to replace an individual who leaves). These averages, however, provide a distorted view of the real costs. The true cost of attrition should be based on the staffing actions that are actually going to be implemented to fill each opening, not on overall averages.

In some cases, an organization may choose not to fill a particular opening. In these cases, the cost of filling the opening is essentially zero. However, if openings are to be filled, many different solutions are possible (e.g., external recruiting, promotion, or redeployment). The cost of implementing each of these options can be quite different, and thus they should be viewed separately. Furthermore, the cost of filling an opening in one job category may be very different from the cost of implementing that same staffing action in another job category.

Make sure that you consider all the staffing moves that are required to fill each opening. Often, there will be "cascade effects," where several staffing moves will be needed to replace just one individual. Referring to our example, suppose a Project Manager were to leave. It might be that the opening would be filled by promoting a Lead Engineer. That opening at the lead level might be filled by promoting an Individual Contributor; in turn, the opening at the Individual Contributor level could be filled by promoting someone from the entry level. The opening at the entry level would probably be filled through recruiting. Your calculations should reflect that four staffing moves were actually required to "fill" the original opening (three promotions and a hire), and that the recruiting occurred at the entry level (not into the original project manager opening). Of course, your staffing plans would define all these moves.

Complicating things further, required staffing actions (and the costs associated with those actions) may differ from planning period to planning period. For example, it might be necessary to recruit an external candidate to meet a critical need in period 1 (assuming that no internal candidates are available), but if that opening were to be filled in period 2, it would be better to redeploy a qualified internal candidate that would be available at that point. Clearly, the costs associated with these two staffing actions probably vary widely—and thus the actions must be considered separately.

In order to calculate the cost of attrition (or replacement), the organization must first define all the specific staffing actions that will actually be implemented to fill each specific opening. A staffing plan provides exactly this information—it describes these required staffing actions in detail. Use the plan to determine all the actions that will be needed to eliminate a staffing gap in a given job category, calculate the cost of implementing each action, and sum your results across all staffing actions. In this way, you will generate an accurate estimate of what replacement costs for that job category will be.

Finally, this type of analysis can help to define one more attrition-related cost: the cost of making a bad hiring decision. This cost can be calculated by simply considering the cost of filling a position not once, but twice.

Step 3: Evaluate Options and Draw Broad Conclusions

This section describes various kinds of high-level conclusions and probing questions that can be derived from the detailed staffing plans that are typically produced when the strategic staffing process I have described is used. These analyses and questions are meant to provide the user with a better understanding of some of the big-picture issues and implications of the staffing plans that are developed. Two main categories of suggestions have been provided. The first set of suggestions should be applied when a single staffing plan or scenario has been developed. The second set should be applied when one staffing plan or scenario is being compared to another (e.g., to identify major differences between the plans). Often, it is this high-level analysis that determines which scenario or approach should be taken.

A Caution

Most organizations implement the strategic staffing process in order to develop staffing strategies and define staffing plans. The output from the process is usually a list of very specific staffing actions that should be implemented in order to ensure that an adequate number of qualified people will be available to support the implementation of the company's business strategies. Consequently, the primary, most useful output of the process is these detailed staffing plans. While big-picture broad conclusions may help to identify key issues and implications, they should be developed in addition to (and not instead of) detailed staffing plans.

The Overall Approach

Organizations that are relatively certain of their future plans sometimes develop a single staffing scenario and create specific staffing plans that support that scenario. This approach might also be appropriate in situations where companies develop and apply standard staffing ratios or look only at the most likely scenario. When looking for overall conclusions, these companies tend to look for broad staffing implications of that single scenario.

Other organizations define several "what-if" staffing scenarios and develop staffing plans for each. This approach is most appropriate when the future is uncertain. An organization might develop a "best" case, a "worst" case, and a "most likely" case and define a staffing strategy that is the most effective hedge for all three cases. It also might want to define the implications of several possible approaches (e.g., defining the impact on staffing of a move from a 37.5-hour workweek to a 40-hour workweek). Generally speaking, analyses in these cases tend to include comparisons of one scenario with another; broad conclusions usually center on choosing one scenario over another.

Evaluating a Single Scenario

When you are trying to draw broad conclusions from a single strategic staffing plan, I suggest the following approach.

Review Initial Gaps and Surpluses. First, review your initial gaps and surpluses. Identify and focus on those that seem particularly large. At first, don't worry about fixing any of the problems you see. Instead, get a feel for where the problems may be. Focus your efforts on the largest and most significant gaps and surpluses.

Review Assumptions. Review your assumptions to determine the possible causes of the large gaps and surpluses. Where necessary, revise your assumptions and rerun the model.

- **Turnover.** Review the assumptions that you made regarding losses. Are they realistic? Can the losses be reduced for any cell? Might the losses need to be increased in order to reduce surpluses?

- **Planned hiring.** Look at the hiring you have anticipated. Do your plans match your needs? Do your hiring plans reduce critical gaps? Might they be creating unnecessary surpluses?

- **Other staffing moves.** Look at the other staffing moves you have assumed (e.g., promotions or transfers). Are they really needed? Might they be continuing past patterns that are no longer appropriate? Are they addressing gaps and surpluses? Conversely, might they be creating additional gaps or surpluses? Might they be reduced or accelerated?

Compare Supply to Demand. Look at current supply and forecast demand. Identify job categories or cells that show a significant increase or decrease (e.g., 10 to 15 percent).

- **Supply.** Verify that your supply number is correct (e.g., that there is no double-counting and that no people are missed).

- **Demand.** Review your demand assumptions (e.g., the ratios you used). Are they realistic? Are they correct (e.g., have you applied the right assumptions, and are your calculations correct)?

- **Compare supply to demand.** From an overall or total perspective, what is the extent of the change? How large is the change in total population in absolute terms? How large is it in percentage terms? What rows or columns are changing most? Calculate the degree of change. Are these changes warranted? Are they realistic?

Develop Staffing Plans. Once you are sure that your assumptions are realistic and appropriate, rerun the model to update your net needs. Define staffing plans to eliminate gaps and surpluses.

Comparing Multiple Scenarios

When you are drawing broad conclusions across multiple scenarios, I suggest the following approach. First, run a staffing model for each scenario to be considered and define the most effective staffing strategies and plans for each scenario. It is sometimes helpful to establish one scenario as a base case and compare others to it. Review your results, adjust your assumptions, and rerun your models, following the process described for a single scenario. Once you are sure that your initial models are as accurate as possible, begin the comparison of one scenario with another. Here are some comparisons you may wish to consider.

Analyze Demand. Compare the overall total demand for the two (or more) scenarios. Calculate absolute and percent differences. Look for and calculate major differences in row and/or column totals. Look for large differences in individual cells.

Here is an example: Two merging organizations had different workweeks for nonexempt employees. In one, staff worked 40 hours each week; in the other, they worked just 37.5 hours. Clearly, implementing the shorter workweek would have a negative impact on production levels and would thus increase the number of employees that would be required. But by how much? The company's staffing plan that supported the 37.5-hour workweek showed that 2,490 staff would be required to support planned production levels. If the 40-hour workweek was used, only 2,334 staff would be needed. This overall total was valuable in itself, but the company dug deeper. Where did the reductions occur? Were there no reductions at all in some particular job categories and large reductions in others? Or was the difference due primarily to across-the-board reductions?

Compare Net Needs. Compare the total net needs under one scenario to the total net needs under another (calculate absolute and percent differences). Compare row and/or column net needs as well. Look also for large differences in individual cells.

Here is an example: For the merging companies described in the previous example, one scenario (the 37.5-hour week) resulted in an overall gap of 449 staff. In the second scenario (the 40-hour week), the total gap was just 293 staff. Again, this overall difference was important, but detailed analysis was still needed. A review of gaps on a job-by-job basis showed that for some jobs there was no appreciable difference in the size of the gap between the two scenarios. The company concluded that the overall decrease was due primarily to large reductions in a few categories, not to an overall reduction in all categories.

When analyzing gaps, look also at absolute values, not just numeric differences. This approach sometimes provides a more realistic assessment of the amount of change that is actually occurring. Suppose that there was a gap of 10 staff in one job and a surplus of 5 in another. A straight arithmetic sum of the two would show a net gap of 5 staff (and thus 5 staffing problems to be addressed). However, adding the two using their absolute values would result in a sum of 15, not 5. This would show that there are actually 15 staffing problems to address (i.e., reducing the 10 gaps and alleviating the 5 surpluses).

Compare Staffing Plans and Numbers of Actions. Compare the number and type of staffing actions across scenarios. For example, implementation of one scenario might require 210 total hires, whereas implementation of a second scenario might require only 150 hires. Similarly, one scenario might require 122 hires, but another would require only 27 (with the balance being addressed through internal movement).

Summary

When you are developing staffing strategies and plans, the most valuable output is still the detailed staffing plans and actions. However, don't just look at those details. Whether you are analyzing a single scenario or comparing multiple scenarios, step back from the detail and look at the big picture. A broad review of the detailed plans often allows you to reach conclusions and make choices that would not be possible if the detailed plans alone were considered.

Frequently Asked Questions

This section provides some possible answers to questions regarding the development and implementation of staffing strategies.

What makes staffing "strategic" in the first place? Isn't staffing just a process for filling vacancies?

Staffing is much more than a reactive process used to fill existing vacancies or the internal equivalent of external recruiting. Strategic staffing is really a proactive planning discipline, just as strategic planning is. It allows you to anticipate, and thus meet, your staffing needs. First, strategic staffing allows you to define the numbers and types of individuals that will *really* be needed to implement your business strategies and plans. Next, a staffing strategy creates a long-term context that you can use to ensure that your short-term staffing actions are both effective and efficient. Without well-defined needs and that long-term context, you can never be certain that the short-term staffing decisions that you make are those that are most effective for your organization.

I've just been charged with developing a companywide strategic staffing process. Potentially, this seems to be an example of what you say I should not do. How should I proceed?

First and foremost, make sure that what you end up doing will satisfy the managers who gave you this assignment. If they are asking you to create a one-size-fits-all process, try to change their minds. Change the focus of the request from creating a process to providing a solution, addressing an issue, or answering a question. Convince them that it would be more valuable (and more helpful to your clients) to create a flexible process that actually defines specific required staffing actions than it would be to create a standard process that may have little positive impact. If resources are limited, show them that it would be better to solve one problem completely than to provide a process that may (or may not) address multiple issues (use the approach A versus approach B argument that was provided in Chapter 11). Next, try to show them that different staffing issues need different planning parameters (remember the information technology and management depth example described in Chapter 4), and thus that a standardized process would be ineffective. If they are still looking for a common approach, share with them the concept of "workforce planning at 30,000 feet" (Chapter 6) and convince them that this approach provides enough of a uniform approach to meet the corporatewide mandate while still allowing for the focus and flexibility that will permit managers to address the staffing issues that they find to be most critical. Finally, if all else fails, do what they ask, but also do what you think is more effective. Share with your managers the results of both approaches, and describe why your alternative approach is more effective.

My managers don't seem to see the value of strategic staffing. They seem to constantly deal with the urgent, not necessarily the important. They operate with a short-term perspective and don't seem to be interested in avoiding longer-term problems. What should I do?

Most managers are measured and rewarded for achieving relatively short-term goals and objectives, so it is no surprise that they are less interested in longer-term planning. Remember the objective of strategic staffing as defined in Chapter 2 of this book—that it provides a longer-term context within which more effective near-term decisions can be made. Position strategic staffing to your managers as a way of better managing their current situations and helping them avoid problems that may occur on their watch. Do not try to sell the process only as a way of predicting and addressing long-term issues. It's unlikely that managers will care much about that. Chapter 13 includes many suggestions for getting managers to engage in, buy into, and be involved in the strategic staffing process.

I understand the value of the focused approach described in this book, but other human resource staff believe that strategic staffing/workforce planning is something that needs to be applied everywhere. This difference of opinion is preventing any action on the development and implementation of a workforce planning process. What should I do?

Again, start by trying to win them over. Try to get these people to see the benefit of implementing a process that yields real results. Use the arguments raised in Chapters 3 and 4 as a guide.

If that does not work, try to at least get the opportunity to implement the process on a limited basis (e.g., to address one staffing issue that you all agree is critical). Use that example to demonstrate what an effective process looks like and show them the realistic, implementable plans that result.

If this approach is falling on deaf ears, do a bit of an end run. Find a line manager who is facing a critical staffing issue and pitch the process to that person. Get that manager to want to implement workforce planning. That will make it difficult for other HR staff to say no. Make sure that you involve that manager's HR business partner, but do it in a way that allows you the opportunity to discuss the issue and present the process to the manager with the issue—don't try to "dress up" the business partner to meet with the manager in your stead.

One last point on this subject: Not too long ago, I was hired by the head of strategic planning to implement an effective workforce planning process for his organization. The "work team" included that manager, the heads of each of the operating divisions of the company, and the most senior HR person. The businesspeople on the team loved my focused approach. The HR representative was convinced that it would not work and tried to get the team to implement a traditional, one-size-fits-all process. When she was unable to do that, she left the team, sure that the project would fail. It turned out to be one of the most effective projects of my career.

HR staff at my company are convinced that strategic staffing/workforce planning is something that is needed—so much so that they want to implement it everywhere all at once. Is this a good idea?

In a word—no! There may be no worse way to implement workforce planning than on an organization-wide, all at once basis. Remember, the objective here is to identify and address critical staffing issues, not just roll out a capability. While many HR organizations might have the resources to develop and launch a workforce planning process, few of them have the staff that would be needed to work with line managers to implement that process fully (e.g., actually identify staffing issues, develop staffing strategies, and define specific staffing plans). Instead of trying to implement the process everywhere at one time, follow approach B (as described in Chapter 11) and address one issue at a time.

One other caution: While it might be possible, it may not be a good idea to make a big announcement regarding the implementation of a new approach to workforce planning and then roll out that process on an issue-by-issue basis (as I recommend). The announcement will create far more demand for workforce planning (and related HR staff support) than you will be able to handle. You might consider not making a general announcement at all. Instead, build a workforce planning capability and share it with individual line managers who are facing critical staffing issues to which workforce planning applies—on a case-by-case basis. I sometimes tell clients to think about the creation of a workforce planning capability as if it were a "skunk works" during World War II. For example, the best bombsights were invented, designed, and prototyped by small teams working out of individual garages. When the product was perfected, production was transferred to a larger manufacturing facility and the new product was installed on new bombers as they rolled off the line. There was no big announcement—just a new, very effective capability that was developed in secret and rolled out on an as-needed basis. Sound familiar?

My HR peers seem to take a functional perspective—they prefer to operate within the functional "silos" that they are familiar with. How can I get them to work together, in concert with workforce planning, to address complex staffing issues?

Many HR staff "grew up" within a particular function and are indeed more comfortable operating within that single function (e.g., recruiting or development).

Yet the strategic staffing process almost always identifies critical staffing issues that are cross-functional in nature. As a result, implementation of staffing strategies requires that HR staff work together as a cross-functional team to address these cross-functional staffing issues. To make your point with these staff, identify one or two staffing issues that require cross-functional solutions (i.e., those where the solution obviously requires a combination of recruiting, deployment, promotion, and development). Get them to see (and agree) that no one HR function can fully address that issue on its own. Form cross-functional work teams (teams that specifically cross functional, and perhaps organization, lines) and charge those teams with addressing these multifunctional issues. Hold each team accountable for developing and implementing the multifunctional solutions to those critical staffing issues.

My managers are keen on measuring the value and contribution of programs and processes. How can we demonstrate the value of strategic staffing? What measures can we use to document why we are better off using it?

As described in Chapter 22, it is important to address both *efficiency* (i.e., "doing the job right," as Peter Drucker would say) and *effectiveness* (what Drucker defines as "doing the right job"). Simply stated, anything that measures time, speed, cost, or volume measures efficiency. Thus, most typical measures of staffing are efficiency measures (e.g., time to fill, cost per hire, and number of openings filled). On the development side, typical efficiency measures include number of training hours per employee, number of employees trained, and cost per training day. However, none of these are measures of effectiveness. All of these efficiency measures ignore quality. It does you no good to hire someone who is not qualified or who leaves soon after joining the organization. Similarly, it does not matter how quickly or cheaply you are training people if you are providing them with the wrong skills. One of the real benefits of identifying staffing issues is that you have a built-in measure of effectiveness. Simply stated, your staffing practices are effective to the extent that they eliminate the staffing gaps and surpluses that you identified. Remember that it is important to measure both effectiveness and efficiency.

My management team thinks that because of its importance, strategic staffing should be done for all units of my company, using the same format. How can I get management to consider the more targeted approach you suggest?

This question is similar to the previous one-size-fits-all question. Don't fall into this trap. First, make sure that your managers know that it will take a fair amount of work to create effective staffing strategies, especially if you work at the level of detail needed to prepare action-oriented staffing plans. Next, convince your managers that it's not really necessary (or feasible) to develop staffing strategies for all jobs. Position strategic staffing as a powerful tool that needs to be applied selectively, where it will have the most value. Remember to focus on only those jobs where the company needs time to react or where it needs to be proactive. If this argument doesn't work, look at your available resources. You probably don't have the time and horsepower you would need if you were to implement a complete strategic staffing process everywhere. Since you don't, get management to prioritize and identify those job categories that should be addressed first.

As for the one-size-fits-all approach, convince the management team that various job categories require different planning parameters and thus different models. Again, use the IT versus management depth example in Chapter 4. That example demonstrates that at least the planning horizon (if not other planning parameters) for those two staffing issues needs to be different. Also, consider implementing a version of "workforce planning at 30,000 feet" (see Chapter 6) on an organization-wide basis, thus giving managers the flexibility they need to identify critical staffing issues and develop staffing strategies and plans at a level of detail that makes sense to them.

My business plans already have a staffing component, including headcount projections. Why can't I just use those?

You can, and perhaps you should—but only if that information is reasoned and insightful. Often, those numbers are based on the headcounts that the finance function will allow (as opposed to the staffing levels that are really needed). In other cases, staffing projections are based on unrealistic management guesses or assumptions that are probably not very useful. In almost no case does the staffing information included in a business plan say anything about the skills and capabilities that will be needed. Use the concepts discussed in Chapter 7 to develop your own projections of staffing requirements. Review the section of Chapter 12 that describes the two-way arrows that connect business planning and staffing planning (in both the long and the short term). That section provides some ideas on how to position what you think is required (the right-to-left arrows) with the headcounts that finance thinks should be provided (the left-to-right arrows). Compare and contrast your staffing projections with these numbers. Present a logical argument that your projections are better or more realistic, not just that the numbers in the plan are "wrong." Don't forget to add in the information on required skills and capabilities. Changing skills requirements are critical issues in their own right. They often affect required staffing levels and are never even identified in most headcount planning or headcount allocation processes.

I understand that strategic staffing is important, but right now I'm too busy addressing short-term needs like recruiting to fill immediate openings. What should I do?

It might just be that the reason you are in such a predicament is that you did not create staffing strategies in the past! The lack of that long-term context will make it difficult (if not impossible) for you to make effective staffing decisions in the near term. It's easy for me to say (and hard for you to do), but you really should take the time to create staffing strategies, even if only for your most critical positions. Not only will that ensure that the short-term staffing actions you create are most effective, but it will probably also reduce the time and effort that creating those plans requires.

How can the strategic staffing process support the development and implementation of diversity initiatives?

Not only can strategic staffing support diversity planning, but it may be a mandatory component of diversity planning. Many organizations set somewhat arbitrary goals for diversity and create a separate set of staffing and development plans aimed at achieving those goals. Diversity planning works most effectively when it is an integral part of the strategic staffing process, not when it is simply an add-on. Use the process to define the number of staffing gaps ("opportunities") that will occur, then use these opportunities to increase diversity. As part of your ongoing strategic staffing efforts, specifically define the number of openings that you expect will occur in each category in which you are trying to increase diversity. Then determine how best to allocate these opportunities to various types of employees to achieve your diversity objectives (e.g., reserving 50 percent of the opportunities in a particular category for diversity candidates). Remember to look at diversity across all your planning periods, not simply the current one. It is quite likely that diversity goals can be met only in the long term.

You can also use strategic staffing to define your diversity goals initially or to ensure that any goals that you have already set are realistic (i.e., that they can actually be attained within the time horizons that were set). Again, use your staffing model to determine the number of openings (opportunities) that are expected in each planning period. When you are setting goals for the first time, determine how many of those opportunities can realistically be allocated to diversity candidates and then calculate a target that reflects this number (e.g., the new ratio of diversity candidates to total incumbents). Calculate the representation that would result if you were to allocate the maximum number of anticipated opportunities to diversity candidates. Compare this number to the goal that exists. In many cases, diversity goals that have been set outside the staffing process cannot be met—even if every anticipated opportunity is allocated to a diversity candidate. If your stated goals exceed the number you just calculated, you will need to either define a more aggressive approach (e.g., adding positions for diversity purposes) or reduce your diversity objectives to levels that are realistically attainable.

I work for a small organization (or I am considering developing staffing strategies for a smaller unit of a large organization). Can I still use the type of staffing strategies and plans that you describe? Wouldn't I need a large number of employees in the models to make them work properly?

Actually, staffing models can be built for and applied to all populations, including smaller ones. The law of large numbers applies when you want to draw conclusions about a population as a whole even though you have looked at only a small sample. That is not what you are doing when you implement strategic staffing.

You are not trying to infer anything. You are not looking at some subset of staffing actions and trying to draw conclusions about all staffing actions. Instead, you are trying to describe what the results will be if your planning assumptions occur. When implementing workforce planning, you are actually accounting for each and every kind of staffing action that you think will occur—you are not trying to infer anything. Instead, you are using the process to describe individual required staffing actions. The reliance on being descriptive—and the complete lack of any inferences—means that the law of large numbers just does not apply. The number of staff included in the model in no way affects the usefulness of your results. Consequently, the strategic staffing process described in this book applies equally well whether the number of positions and staff is large or small.

There is one component of the process in which the law of large numbers may apply, however. When you estimate voluntary turnover, you typically forecast a rate and apply that rate to the population in question. For example, if a job category includes 40 staff and the turnover rate is 5 percent, you would probably estimate that 2 staff would leave voluntarily during the period (i.e., 0.05 times 40 equals 2). But what if there were only 4 staff in that category? How would you account for a loss of just two-tenths of a person (i.e., 0.05 times 4 equals 0.2)? In cases like these, where the population in any cell of your model is small, voluntary turnover rates won't apply and different assumptions regarding turnover must be made.

My managers embrace the qualitative staffing analysis that you suggest, but they are resisting the implementation of the quantitative part (e.g., the detailed staffing models). What should I do?

First of all, make sure that you at least continue to do just what you are doing. Having managers analyze and address staffing needs from a qualitative perspective (e.g., defining and addressing capabilities gaps) is better than doing no strategic staffing at all. Try building on that foundation.

First, try to identify the root cause of their resistance. Some managers feel that quantitative models are solely tactical and should not be part of a strategic approach. Others may resist implementing the quantitative component of the planning process just so that they cannot be held accountable for meeting or not meeting their staffing goals. This is a difficult issue to address. It is unlikely that you will be successful if you confront the managers who feel this way; instead, emphasize all the positive reasons why strategic staffing must be both qualitative and quantitative in nature.

Show these managers that it is extremely difficult to implement plans that are solely qualitative in nature. Qualitative plans lack scope, and without some measure of scope, the best solution cannot be defined. If there is a skills gap, for example, the best solution if there were 5 anticipated openings would clearly be different from the best solution if there were 500 such openings. Chapter 18 expands on this thought.

Another reason to include a quantitative component is so that progress can be measured. Suppose that your organization needs more people (with qualitative plans, we can be no more specific than that) in quality engineering, and we hire five such people. How well are we doing in meeting our need? Clearly, it is impossible to tell. Defining staffing needs in quantitative terms allows you to determine just how much progress you are actually making. Hiring five when you need six in total tells one story; hiring five when you need a hundred tells an entirely different story.

There is one last reason for including quantitative analysis in your strategic staffing process. Ironically, this reason tends to be one of the major impediments to implementing a quantitative approach. Defining needs in quantitative terms and evaluating progress against those goals allows you to hold managers specifically accountable for meeting staffing needs and implementing staffing plans. Without quantitative measures, it will be impossible to do this. In some (hopefully rare) cases, managers will realize this.

Using the Strategic Staffing Templates from the Web Site

By now it is clear that a spreadsheet-based staffing model is a tool that can be very useful. Included among the files on the book's web site are two strategic staffing templates that you can use for this exact purpose. They are generic models that can be tailored to address a host of staffing issues. The templates are real models that you can actually use—they are not just examples.

Your first impression may be that a more complex model or algorithm is required, but these spreadsheets are sufficiently flexible and powerful to support most strategic staffing applications (especially of the type described in this book). The generic Excel™ spreadsheets that are included have been specifically formatted and developed to support strategic staffing. Each spreadsheet consists of a series of matrices into which relevant calculations and links have already been built (e.g., calculating "supply then" as well as staffing gaps and surpluses). Figures B-1 and B-2 describe the process that is embedded in each of the spreadsheet templates.

There are two separate versions of the staffing model templates. The methodology for calculating gaps and surpluses is basically the same for each version. What varies are the options that can be used to eliminate gaps and surpluses:

- **Staffing Model Template 1 (Without Contractors).xls** is the simpler version. It allows you to eliminate staffing gaps and surpluses by manipulating internal movement into and out of jobs, external transfers into and out of other jobs in the company, new hires, overtime, part-time staff, consultants, outsourcing work, involuntary terminations, and other planned losses. This version does not include regularly scheduled contractors (although you may choose to use the "consultants" category to capture contractors that are used occasionally). It can be used when analyzing either "whole people" or full-time equivalents (FTEs).
- **Staffing Model Template 2 (with Contractors).xls** is similar to Template 1, but it allows you to consider the use of regularly scheduled contractors, temporaries, and other contingent staff in addition to regular, full-time em-

Figure B-1. The Strategic Staffing Process Embedded in the Spreadsheet.

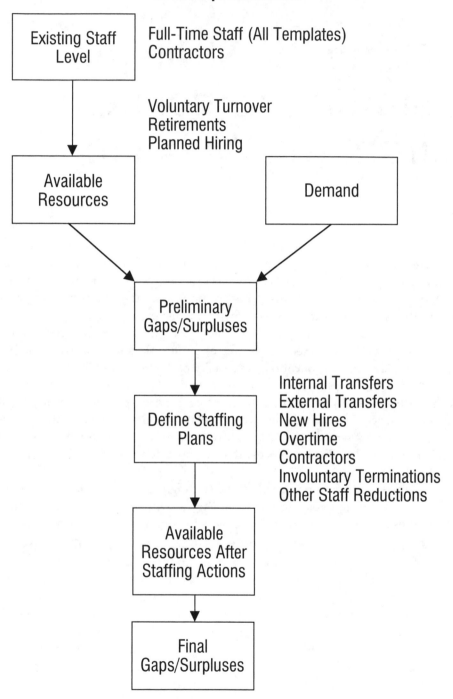

Figure B-2. The Strategic Staffing Process Embedded in Template 2.

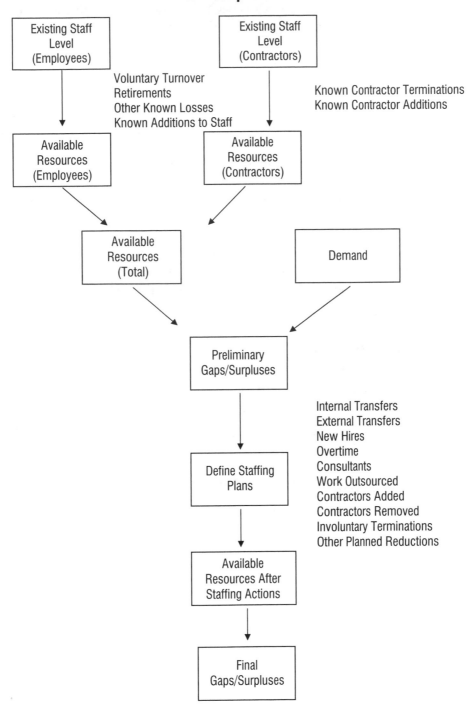

ployees. This version does indeed differentiate between permanent employees and contractors. It allows you to eliminate staffing gaps and surpluses by manipulating either employees (e.g., internal movement into and out of jobs, external transfers in and out, new hires, involuntary terminations, and other planned losses), contractors (e.g., adding and removing contractors as required), or both. It can be used when analyzing either "whole people" or FTEs.

Both of the templates include only those components that are needed to support that particular version of the analysis. Each template is a series of linked matrices that are designed to contain information on staffing requirements, availability, gaps and surpluses, and staffing actions. The templates can accommodate models whose basic matrix structure includes up to 25 columns and 70 rows. Each template is actually a workbook that includes five separate spreadsheets, allowing you to develop staffing plans for up to five separate planning periods. In each case, the five periods are linked appropriately (e.g., the employee supply at the end of one period automatically becomes the employee supply at the beginning of the next period). The templates must be used in conjunction with Microsoft Excel (or another package that recognizes Excel spreadsheets); they cannot be used on a stand-alone basis.

Terms and Conditions

The templates included in the computer files that accompany this book (and the models that you derive from the templates) may be installed on only one computer, either a stand-alone PC or a single server. If multiple copies of the templates are needed (e.g., for additional users or other business units), simply purchase additional copies of this book.

Initial Model Setup (Both Template Versions)

The overall modeling approach is the same for both templates. In general, every time you need a model, you should make a copy of the appropriate template and then customize that copy so that it reflects your particular needs. This will ensure that your basic template will remain "clean," allowing you to use it over and over again. There is no limit on the number of staffing model templates or copies that you can make.

The following eight steps should be taken to customize a template for a particular organization or issue *no matter which template is used*. Specific instructions for using the different capabilities of the two versions follow. All the customizing described uses only standard Excel functions and operations. Refer to the program's documentation if you need assistance with those functions.

1. **Select and copy the appropriate template.** Select the template that includes the staffing options that are most appropriate for your staffing practices (e.g., select the one that includes contractors if that is a valid staffing

alternative). Create a new version of the template for each new model that you need to develop. Open the template (e.g., Staffing Model Template 1 (Without Contractors).xls) in Excel. Using the Save As command (found on the File menu), save the template, using a new name. Usually, the name should describe the model or scenario that you are addressing (e.g., "Manufacturing Staffing.xls"). Close the original template so that only your new copy is active.

Note that you should never edit the original template itself (i.e., Staffing Model Template 1 (Without Contractors).xls). This way, you will always have clean, uncorrupted templates on which you can base future models. You may, of course, fully edit the copy that you create.

2. **Determine the number of planning periods.** Determine the number of separate planning periods for your model (e.g., four quarters or three years). Remove from your model any unneeded planning periods, deleting worksheets where appropriate (e.g., deleting period 5 if your model has only four quarters). To do this:

   - Click on the tab at the bottom of your model that describes the period you wish to delete.

   - Click on the Edit option on the task bar.

   - Click on the Delete Sheet option on the pull-down menu that appears.

Repeat this for each unneeded sheet/period.

3. **Edit the column headings.** Once you have determined the column headings for the model you wish to create, edit the columns of the template you have created (i.e., the copy) to reflect those headings. Initially, the columns of the template are labeled "Col 1" through "Col 25". Use the Replace command (found under the Edit option on the tool bar). First, "find" Col 1 and "replace" that text with the first column heading you wish to use. Be sure to choose the "Match Entire Cell Contents" option that appears when you click the "Options" button in the Find/Replace window (e.g., so that you will not find Col 11 when you are searching for Col 1). You may wish to choose the Replace All option. Also, be careful to avoid typos (e.g., the command won't find "Col25" when you are really looking for "Col 25"). Be careful not to edit the "total" column.

Once the heading changes are complete, delete all unneeded columns. Select the column(s) to be deleted and select Delete from the Edit option on the toolbar. This one change will remove unnecessary columns from all matrices in the model. For example, highlight columns Q through Z if you wish to delete 10 columns. Be sure that you have included all necessary columns before deleting any—it will be time-consuming to add columns back in later on.

Remember to change the column headings and delete unneeded columns from the matrices included in each period in your model, editing each worksheet as described here. You will need to change each period individually.

4. **Edit the row headings.** Once you have determined the row headings for the model you wish to create, edit the rows of the template to reflect those headings. The rows of the template are initially labeled "Row 1" through "Row 70." Again, use the Replace command (found under the Edit option). First, "find" Row 1 and "replace" that text with the first row heading you wish to use. Be sure to choose the Match Entire Cell Contents option that appears when you click the "Options" button in the Find/Replace window (e.g., so that you will not find "Row 11" when you are searching for "Row 1"). You may also wish to choose the Replace All option. Again, be careful to avoid typos.

Once you have made all changes to your row headings, delete unnecessary rows *from each matrix* in the model (e.g., the Existing Staff Levels and Demand matrices) by selecting the rows to be removed and choosing Delete from the Edit option on the toolbar. Make sure that you delete entire rows, not just some cells. It will be necessary to remove rows from each matrix separately (e.g., Starting Staff Level and Voluntary Turnover Rate). Be sure that you have included all the rows you will need before deleting any—it will be time-consuming to add rows back in later on. Make sure that you do not delete any of the "total" rows that appear at the bottom of some matrices.

Don't be alarmed when error messages appear in some calculated fields of your model while you are in the process of deleting rows. The model is simply indicating that (temporarily) it can no longer perform a given calculation. Just keep on deleting. All the error messages should disappear once you have deleted the appropriate rows from all of the matrices in your model.

5. **Scan the model to verify that the headings are correct.** Scan through the model (simply by pressing Page Down) to ensure that all the headings (for both rows and columns) now reflect the ones that you want to use. Verify that there are no error messages. Make sure that you look at the model for each planning period.

6. **Edit the model components.** In some cases, you may wish to delete from the model specific components that you do not need (e.g., deleting the overtime matrix if overtime is a staffing option that you will not use). First, review the various matrices that are included in the template. Determine which ones are needed for your model (e.g., if you employ part-time staff, you'll want to include the part-time matrices) and which ones are not needed (e.g., if you do not wish to include involuntary terminations). Select the rows that include the components to be deleted (remember to include the row heading and the blank row between matrices). Next, select the Edit option from the toolbar and click on the Delete command from the menu that appears.

If you delete matrices, there will be an impact on calculated fields in

subsequent matrices. For example, if you delete the Involuntary Terminations matrix, you will get an error message on the available resources matrix. This is because the calculation built into the available resources matrix
includes a reference to the Involuntary Terminations matrix that you deleted. To correct this error, place the cursor in the first cell of the matrix
that includes the error (usually Row 1/Column 1). The equation used to
calculate the value for this cell appears in the window at the top of the
sheet. Place the cursor on the term of the equation that includes the
"error!" message and delete only that term. This will take out of the equation the reference to the matrix you deleted. If you have deleted more than
one matrix, you will need to remove all the other "error!" terms in a similar
fashion. Press Enter to record the changes. Now copy the cell with the
revised equation to every other cell of that particular matrix of your model.
Judicious use of the Copy command will make this apparently daunting
task much easier. Make sure that you eliminate any and all such errors in
the calculated fields. Remember also to make these changes to all periods
of your model.

Sometimes deleting components from the template models is difficult
and time-consuming. While these changes improve the efficiency and ap-
pearance of the model, they need not be made. Rather than deleting unnecessary components, you may choose to retain the unneeded matrices in the
model and simply keep them blank. Doing this will eliminate the need for
editing equations and will not affect the calculations in any way.

7. **Copy the format to subsequent periods.** Once you have made all the necessary changes to period 1 of your model, you will need to copy that format into each subsequent period. Follow these step by step instructions
exactly. The process may seem a bit unwieldy at first but you will get the
hang of it quickly.

To begin, click on the Period 2 tab at the bottom of the model. Next,
edit the row and column headings of the Starting Staff Level matrix so that
they match the format you used in period 1. Be sure to remove unneeded
rows and columns. Make the same changes to the Starting Staff Level matrices in all remaining periods.

Now you will need to edit the formulas included in the Starting Staff
Level matrix for period 2. Click on the Period 2 tab at the bottom of the
model. Place the cursor in cell B7 (make sure that you are looking at the
model for period 2). Look at the formula that appears at the top of the
spreadsheet. At first, this formula will include all the temporary staffing
actions (described later in this appendix) that were listed initially for period 1. If you deleted any of the temporary staffing alternatives for period
1, the formula will include one or more "Error!" terms. Place the cursor in
the formula line and simply delete each "Error!" term and the minus sign
that precedes it. Now, copy this revised formula from cell B7 and paste it
into all the remaining cells of your Starting Staff Level matrix. Once you
have completed this step for period 2, repeat the step for all other periods
included in your model.

Finally, click on the Period 1 tab at the bottom of the model. Highlight/ select all of the matrices included in period 1 except Existing Staff Level. Click on Edit, then Copy. Next click the Period 2 tab at the bottom of the model. Place the cursor in the cell in column A that is two rows under the last row of your revised Starting Staff Level matrix. Click on Edit, then Paste. The remaining matrices for period 2 will appear. Repeat this Paste step for all remaining periods of your model so that each period includes the same matrices.

8. **Save the edited template.** Once you are sure that the template has been formatted correctly, save it. In some cases, it may be helpful to create several different models with the same format (e.g., when you are defining staffing plans for more than one scenario). If this is the case, make a template of your template; that is, keep the customized version of the model that you just created as another template (e.g., Manufacturing Staffing Template.xls). You can create additional versions of this new template by saving it under different, more descriptive names (e.g., creating Manufacturing Staffing Version 1.xls and Manufacturing Staffing Version 2.xls). By saving the new template this way, you will create a foundation on which you can build other scenarios. For example, if, later on, you wish to create a Manufacturing Staffing Version 3.xls, you need only open Manufacturing Staffing Template.xls and resave it under the new name. The new model will already be formatted correctly.

Note: If your various scenarios use common data (e.g., if they all have the same starting headcount), you may find it more convenient to load those data into the template (see the following steps) before you create new models. If you do this, each subsequent model that is created from the template will include the common data.

Finally, you need to transfer the staffing model format you have created to subsequent periods. Copy all the matrices of your customized model (beginning with Voluntary Turnover Rate) and paste them to the model for each additional period. Note that the template already includes the matrices for starting headcount, including certain linkages (described below).

Defining Staffing Plans

Once the appropriate model format has been created, the work of defining staffing plans can begin. While the basic approach for doing this is the same for both templates, there are some differences. Therefore, separate instructions for using each version are provided for each. On the one hand, this may seem to create unnecessary redundancy; on the other hand, separate instructions allow you to review just those steps that are needed for the approach you select. Comment fields have been added to each matrix that describe the data to be entered or the calculations that are being made. These comments are brief and are intended to guide you along the way; they are not intended to replace these detailed instructions.

Note that the mechanics of the process are described here, not the underlying reasoning. For example, this section describes how voluntary turnover information should be entered into the model, but it does not discuss how assumptions regarding voluntary turnover should be developed in the first place. That kind of information is provided in earlier chapters of this book.

Using Template 1

Staffing Model Template 1 (Without Contractors).xls should be used when regularly scheduled contractors should not be considered as staffing resources. When using this version, the following steps should be taken.

Step 1: Load Initial Data and Run the Model. The following data should be loaded into the appropriate matrix as a first step. You must enter data for existing staff levels, but all other data are optional.

- **Existing Staff Level.** Click on the Period 1 tab at the bottom of the worksheet. Enter into each cell of this matrix the number of staff actually in each category at the beginning of the planning period ("supply now"). The model can contain either "whole people" or FTEs. Make sure that the choice you make is consistent throughout all the matrices in the model (i.e., all are FTEs or all are "whole people").
- **Voluntary Turnover Rate.** Enter the voluntary turnover rate to be used for each category in each cell. A rate should be entered for each cell for which there is information in the existing staff level matrix. Rates can vary for each cell. A 10 percent rate should be entered as .10. Remember to adjust rates so that they are consistent with the length of your planning period (e.g., use .05 if the annual rate is 10 percent and your planning period is six months or .01 if your annual rate is expected to be 12 percent and the planning period is one month). The model will calculate voluntary turnover and place the results of the calculations in the subsequent voluntary turnover matrix.
- **Retirements.** Enter the number of individuals from each cell that you expect to retire during the planning period. Use whatever retirement assumptions you think are appropriate (e.g., average retirement age or actual eligibility). Include only "normal" retirements, not any early retirements you anticipate. Since early retirements are "controllable" staffing actions, they should be captured in one of the other losses matrices near the end of the model.
- **Other Known Losses.** Enter the number of losses that you know will occur for reasons other than voluntary turnover or normal retirements. Remember that you are capturing only "uncontrollable losses." This might include transfers that have been finalized but that have not yet occurred or employees taking approved leaves of absence.
- **Known Additions to Staff.** Enter the number of additions to staff that you know will occur during the planning period. These should be "uncontrollable actions," not those that you plan to make. This category would include

individuals to whom offers have already been extended and who are committed to joining the company during this planning period, but who are not on board yet. It would also include any employee transfers that have been agreed to but not finalized and any employees known to be returning from leaves of absence. It should *not* include "controllable" staffing options, openings that are authorized but that won't be filled during the period, or any additional hires that may be needed to address various staffing gaps that the model may identify later on. Once the data are entered, the model will calculate "supply then" for each cell and place the results of that calculation in the subsequent available resources before staffing actions matrix.

- **Staffing Requirements.** Enter the total number of staff (individuals or FTEs) that will be required in each category in order to implement your business plans/strategies. This number can be entered directly or called from another spreadsheet that you may have created to calculate demand based on various assumptions that you have made (e.g., calculations based on staffing ratios). Once these data have been entered, the model will automatically calculate staffing gaps and surpluses for each category. This is displayed in the Preliminary Gaps and Surpluses (Before Staffing Actions) matrix that appears next.

Step 2: Review Preliminary Results for the First Period. Once all preliminary data have been entered, the model will first calculate the available resources (before staffing actions) matrix by subtracting voluntary turnover, retirements, and other known losses from existing staff levels and adding in any known additions to staff that you have included. The model also calculates preliminary gaps/surpluses for each job category by comparing available resources (before staffing actions) to staffing requirements. Review these preliminary results, but do not try to fix any of the gaps or surpluses at this time.

Step 3: Run the Model for Subsequent Periods. The various planning periods included in your model are already linked appropriately (e.g., the Starting Staff Level for period 2 is related to the available resources (after staffing actions) for period 1).

Note that the available resources are not simply carried forward "as is." The model takes into account "permanent" staffing actions, but subtracts out any staffing resources that were provided from or by temporary sources (including overtime, part-time staff, consultants, and outsourced work). This is done so that these temporary solutions are not "institutionalized." For example, it might be that in the previous period, a need of 0.5 FTE was met by using part-time staff. Suppose that in the next period, demand for staff in that category increases by an additional 0.5 FTE. In reality, the need in that subsequent period is a full FTE—a need that might best be met through hiring. If the original 0.5 FTE part-timer was "built in," then the need in the subsequent period would seem to be another 0.5 FTE—a need that would also be likely to be met through the use of part-time staff. However, this would mean that two 0.5 FTE staff would be on board, and it is likely that one hire would be a better (cheaper) option than two part-timers.

You may, of course, use any solution you wish during the subsequent period, but the model's methodology forces you to make a conscious decision to do that.

For each subsequent period (e.g., periods 2 through 5), you will need to enter all information other than the starting staff level (e.g., voluntary turnover rates and retirement projections for each period). First, click on the Period 2 tab at the bottom of the worksheet. Next, enter the information that corresponds to the uncontrollable staffing assumptions that you are using, including:

- Voluntary turnover rates
- Retirements
- Other known losses
- Known additions to staff

Once these data are entered, preliminary staffing gaps and surpluses will be calculated for that period. Next, enter these data for all remaining periods, one period at a time. If this is the first time that you are going through this process, do not include information for any controllable staffing actions (e.g., internal transfers, external transfers, or recruiting). That information will be added later on.

Step 4: Enter Staffing Plan Data for Period 1. As described in this book, the next step in the process is to review staffing gaps and surpluses across all planning periods and develop staffing strategies that best address these needs across periods. Once this has been done, you can define the specific staffing actions (within the context of your staffing strategies, of course) that should be taken in each planning period. Enter the staffing plan information that reflects the staffing that you think needs to take place during period 1 to eliminate the staffing gaps and surpluses shown in the Preliminary Gaps/Surpluses matrix. The following options are open to you:

• **Internal Transfers Out and Internal Transfers In.** These two matrices capture movement from one cell of your model to another cell of your model (e.g., promotions or lateral moves). They should not be used to capture people that are moving onto or off of the model (that comes in the next step).

Determine the number of such moves that are required to address staffing needs. If, for example, two people are being promoted from supervisor to manager, enter a ''2'' in the supervisor category (you will also need to enter a ''2'' in the manager category on the internal transfers in matrix described next). You will need to enter the total number of people leaving each cell for all other cells in the Internal Transfers Out matrix. If, for example, you are expecting that two people *from* a given cell will be promoted and three other people *from* that same cell will make lateral moves, enter 5 in that cell (2 + 3).

Enter the total number of people entering a cell from all other cells in the Internal Transfers In matrix. This is where you would enter the ''2'' in the manager cell to complete the promotions in the simple example just described above. Again, enter the total. If, for example, you are expecting that three people will be promoted *into* that cell and one person from another cell will make a lateral move *into* that cell, enter 4 in that cell (3 + 1).

Every individual that moves from one cell in the model to another cell in the model must be deducted from the first cell and added to the second (almost like double-entry bookkeeping). When you have finished defining all internal transfers, verify that the total number of people leaving all cells equals the total number of people entering all cells.

• **External Transfers Out.** Enter the total number of people leaving each cell to take jobs in the organization that are not included on the model you are now working with.

• **External Transfers In.** Enter the total number of people joining each cell of the model you are working with from other jobs in the organization that are not included on your model.

• **New Hires.** Enter the number of new hires that will be needed in each cell to meet staffing needs *over and above* those already included in the known additions to staff matrix (described earlier).

• **Overtime.** Enter the number of overtime FTEs that will be used to eliminate staffing gaps in each job category.

• **Part-Time Staff.** Enter the number of part-time FTEs that will be used to eliminate staffing gaps in each job category.

• **Consultants.** Enter the number of consultant FTEs that will be used to eliminate staffing gaps in each job category. You may also capture contractors here, provided they are scheduled only on occasion. If you utilize contractors on a regular, scheduled basis, you should consider using the Template 2 version of the model (described next in this appendix).

• **Staff Equivalent of Work Outsourced.** If you plan to reduce the demand for staff by outsourcing work, use this matrix. Enter in each category the number of FTEs that would be needed to support the amount of work that is being outsourced.

• **Involuntary Terminations.** Enter the number of involuntary terminations that are expected for each cell (if any).

• **Other Planned Staff Reductions.** Enter the number of other reductions (i.e., reductions that are not the result of voluntary turnover, retirements, or involuntary terminations) for each cell.

Step 5: Review Results. Once all these data have been entered, the model will first calculate available resources (after staffing actions) for each cell of your model. This calculation starts with available resources (before staffing actions) and:

• Adjusts cells up or down to account for internal transfers.
• Subtracts out external transfers out, involuntary terminations, and other staff reductions.
• Adds in external transfers in, new hires (recruiting), overtime, part-time staff, consultants, and outsourcing.

Next, the model compares the available resources (after staffing actions) matrix to the staffing requirements matrix and calculates final gaps/surpluses (after staffing actions). Ideally, if the staffing actions you entered are correct, every cell of the final gaps/surpluses matrix should be zero (or a gap or surplus that you find acceptable). If this is not the case, it is likely that you will need to modify your staffing plans. Determine what staffing actions need to be added, deleted, or changed. Edit the matrices in step 4 to reflect these changes and again review the final gaps/surpluses matrix.

Step 6: Enter Staffing Data for Subsequent Periods. Once period 1 is final, look at the preliminary gaps and surpluses that have now been created in period 2. These gaps and surpluses will reflect all the staffing actions you entered for period 1. Define the staffing plans that you think best meet these needs in period 2 (consistent with your staffing strategies, of course) and enter that information in the appropriate matrices in period 2. When period 2 is "done" (e.g., when final gaps and surpluses are all zero or some other acceptable number), repeat the process for period 3. Repeat for all subsequent periods.

Using Template 2

Staffing Model Template 2 (with Contractors).xls should be used whenever regularly scheduled contractors are used to meet staffing needs. In these cases, at least some staffing gaps can be eliminated by employing contractors on an ongoing basis, not simply once in a while, "as needed." When using this version of the template, the following steps should be taken.

Step 1: Load Initial Data and Run the Model. The following data should be loaded into the appropriate matrix as a first step. You must enter data for existing staff levels for both employees and contractors, but all other data are optional.

- **Existing Staff Levels/Employees.** Click on the Period 1 tab at the bottom of the worksheet. Enter into each cell of this matrix the number of employees that are actually in each category at the beginning of the planning period ("supply now"). The model can contain either "whole people" or FTEs. Make sure that the choice you make is consistent throughout all the matrices in the model (i.e., all are FTEs or all are "whole people").
- **Existing Staff Levels/Contractors.** Enter into each cell of this matrix the number of contractors currently working in each category at the beginning of the planning period ("supply now"). Use FTEs if part-time contractors are used.
- **Voluntary Turnover Rate/Employees.** Enter the voluntary turnover rate to be used for each category in each cell. These rates will apply only to employees (contractors that leave are handled in a separate matrix), so a rate should be entered for each cell for which there is information in the existing staff levels/employees matrix. Rates can vary for each cell. A 10 percent rate should be entered as .10. Remember to adjust rates so that they are consistent with the length of your planning period (e.g., use .05 if the annual rate

is 10 percent and your planning period is six months or .01 if your annual rate is expected to be 12 percent and the planning period is one month). The model will calculate voluntary turnover and place the results of the calculation in the subsequent voluntary turnover/employees matrix.

- **Retirements/Employees.** Enter the number of employees from each cell that you expect to retire during the planning period. There are no retirements allowed for contractors. Use whatever retirement assumptions you think are appropriate (e.g., average retirement age or actual eligibility). Include only "normal" retirements, not any early retirements you anticipate. Since early retirements are "controllable" staffing actions, they should be captured in one of the other losses matrices near the end of the model.

- **Other Known Losses/Employees.** Enter the number of losses among employees that you know will occur for reasons other than voluntary turnover or normal retirements. Remember that you are capturing uncontrollable losses. This might include transfers that have been finalized but that have not yet occurred or employees taking known leaves of absence.

- **Known Additions to Staff/Employees.** Enter the number of additions to staff that you know will occur during the planning period. These should be "uncontrollable" actions, not those that you plan to make. This category would include individuals to whom offers have already been extended and who are committed to joining the company during this planning period, but who are not on board yet. It would also include any employee transfers that have been agreed to but not finalized and any employees known to be returning from leaves of absence. It should *not* include "controllable" staffing options, openings that are authorized but that won't be filled during the period, or any additional hires that may be needed to address various staffing gaps that the model may identify later on. Once the data are entered, the model will calculate "supply then" for each cell and place the results in the subsequent available resources before staffing actions/employees matrix.

- **Available Resources Before Staffing Actions/Employees.** The number of employees that will be available in each job category will be calculated and displayed in the matrix that follows. These numbers will equal existing headcount minus losses (voluntary turnover, retirement, and other known losses) plus known additions to staff.

- **Voluntary Turnover Rate/Contractors.** Enter the rate at which you think contractors will choose to leave your organization. This should reflect unanticipated losses, not the losses associated with the completion of a contract. Use the same data entry procedure described for the voluntary turnover/ employees matrix (above). The resulting turnover will be displayed in the Voluntary Turnover/Contractors matrix that follows.

- **Known Contractor Terminations.** Enter the number of contractors in each job category whose contracts will expire during the period (and not be renewed).

- **Known Contractor Additions.** Enter the number of contractors that will be added to each job category during the planning period. These numbers should reflect actual, known commitments (and thus are "uncontrollable"), not additions that are planned (and thus are "controllable"). Planned additions can be entered later in the model.

- **Available Resources Before Staffing Actions/Contractors.** The number of contractors that will be available in each job category will be calculated and displayed in this matrix. These numbers will equal existing contractor headcount minus known contractor terminations plus known contractor additions.

- **Available Resources Before Staffing Actions/Employees + Contractors.** The total number of staff available in each job category is displayed in this matrix. It is equal to the sum of available employees plus available contractors in each job.

- **Staffing requirements.** Enter the total number of staff that will be required in each category in order to implement your business plans/strategies. This number should include the total of all positions, whether held by employees or contractors. There should *not* be separate demand numbers for employees and contractors. This number can be entered directly or called from another spreadsheet that you may have created to calculate demand based on various assumptions you have made (e.g., calculations based on staffing ratios). Once these data have been entered, the model will automatically calculate staffing gaps and surpluses for each category. This is displayed in the Preliminary Gaps and Surpluses (Before Staffing Actions) matrix that appears next.

Step 2: Review Preliminary Results for the First Period. Once all preliminary data have been entered, the model will first calculate available resources before staffing actions/employees + contractors, summing the result across both categories of workers. The model also calculates preliminary gaps/surpluses for each job category by comparing available resources before staffing actions/employees + contractors to staffing requirements. Review these preliminary results, but do not try to fix any of the gaps or surpluses at this time.

Step 3: Run the Model for Subsequent Periods. The various planning periods included in your model are already linked appropriately. The existing staff level/employees matrix for period 2 is linked to numerous matrices for period 1. It shows the number of employees in each category at the beginning of period 2 (assuming that all the staffing actions planned for period 1 actually take place). The Starting Staff Level/Contractors matrix for period 2 is also linked to matrices for period 1. It shows the number of temporary staff in each category at the beginning of period 2 (again assuming that all the staffing actions planned for contractors for period 1 actually take place).

Note that the available resources for employees are not simply carried forward "as is." The model takes into account "permanent" staffing actions, but disregards any staffing resources that were met using temporary sources (including overtime, part-time staff, consultants, and outsourced work). This is done so that these temporary solutions are not "institutionalized." For example, it might be that in the previous period, a need of 0.5 FTE was met by using part-time staff. Suppose that in the next period, demand for staff in that category increases by an additional 0.5 FTE. In reality, the need in that subsequent period is a full FTE—a need that might best be met through hiring. If the original 0.5 FTE part-timer was "built in," then the need in the subsequent period would be shown as another 0.5 FTE—a need that would be likely to be met through the use of part-time staff. However, this would mean that two 0.5 FTE staff would be on board, and it is likely that one hire would be a better (cheaper) option than two part-timers. You may, of course, use any solution you wish during the subsequent period, but the model's methodology forces you to make a conscious decision to do that. The model also adjusts the starting number of contractors, incorporating all contractor additions and terminations that occurred during the previous period.

For each subsequent period (e.g., periods 2 through 5), you will need to enter all information other than the existing staff levels for both employees and contractors (e.g., voluntary turnover rates, retirements, and known losses and additions). First, click on the Period 2 tab at the bottom of the worksheet. Next, enter the information that corresponds to the uncontrollable staffing assumptions that you are using, including:

- Voluntary Turnover Rates
- Retirements
- Other Known Losses/Employees
- Known Additions/Employees
- Known Contractor Terminations
- Known Contractor Additions

Once these data are entered, preliminary staffing gaps and surpluses will be calculated for that period. Enter these data for all remaining periods, one period at a time. If this is the first time that you are going through this process, do not include information for any controllable staffing actions (e.g., internal transfers, external transfers, recruiting, or contractors added or removed). That information will be added later on.

Step 4: Enter Staffing Data for Period 1. As described in this book, the next step of the process is to review staffing gaps and surpluses across all planning periods and develop the staffing strategies that eliminate these gaps and surpluses most effectively. Next, define the specific staffing actions (within the context of your staffing strategies, of course) that should be taken during period 1 to eliminate the staffing gaps and surpluses shown in the preliminary gaps/surpluses matrix. With this version, the following options are open to you:

- **Internal Transfers Out and Internal Transfers In/Employees.** These two matrices capture movement of employees from one cell of your model to another cell of your model (e.g., promotions or lateral moves). They should not be used to capture people that are moving into or out of the model (that comes in the next step).

Determine the number of such moves that are required to address staffing needs. If, for example, two people are being promoted from supervisor to manager, enter a 2 in the supervisor category (you will also need to enter a 2 in the manager category on the Internal Transfers In matrix described next). You will need to enter the total number of people leaving each cell for all other cells in the Internal Transfers Out matrix. If, for example, you are expecting that two people *from* a given cell will be promoted and three other people *from* that same cell will make lateral moves, enter 5 in that cell (2 + 3).

Enter the total number of people entering a cell from all other cells in the Internal Transfers In matrix. This is where you would enter the 2 in the manager cell to complete the promotion in the simple example just described. Again, enter the total. If, for example, you are expecting that three people will be promoted *into* that cell and one person from another cell will make a lateral move *into* that cell, enter 4 in that cell (3 + 1).

Every individual that moves from one cell in the model to another cell in the model must be deducted from the first cell and added to the second (almost like double-entry bookkeeping). When you have finished defining all internal transfers, verify that the total number of people leaving all cells equals the total number of people entering all cells.

• **External Transfers Out/Employees.** Enter the total number of employees leaving each cell to take jobs in the organization that are not included in the model you are now working with.

• **External Transfers In/Employees.** Enter the total number of employees joining each cell of the model you are working with from other jobs in the organization that are not included in your model.

• **New Hires/Employees.** Enter the number of new hires (employees) that will be needed in each cell to meet staffing needs *over and above* those already included in the known additions to staff matrix (described earlier).

• **Overtime/Employees.** Enter the number of overtime FTEs that will be used (among employees) to eliminate staffing gaps in each job category.

• **Part-Time Staff (noncontractor).** Enter the number of part-time FTEs (excluding regularly scheduled contractors) that will be used to eliminate staffing gaps in each job category.

• **Consultants (noncontractor).** Enter the number of consultant FTEs (excluding regularly scheduled contractors) that will be used to eliminate staffing gaps in each job category.

• **Staff Equivalent of Work Outsourced/Employees.** If you plan to reduce the demand for staff by outsourcing work, use this matrix. Enter in each category the number of employee FTEs that would be needed to support the amount of work that is being outsourced.

• **Contractors Added.** Enter the number of regularly scheduled contractors that will be added to each job category during the period to eliminate staffing gaps.

- **Contractors Removed.** Enter the number of regularly scheduled contractors in each job category whose contracts will expire or be canceled during the planning period (e.g., to reduce staffing surpluses).

- **Involuntary Terminations/Employees.** Enter the number of involuntary terminations (among employees) that are expected for each cell (if any).

- **Other Planned Staff Reductions/Employees.** Enter the number of other employee reductions (i.e., reductions that are not the result of voluntary turnover, retirements, or involuntary terminations) for each cell.

Step 5: Review Results. Once all these data have been entered, the model will first calculate available resources (after staffing actions) for each cell of your model. This includes both employees and contractors. This calculation starts with available resources (before staffing actions)/employees + contractors and:

- Adjusts cells up or down to account for internal transfers.
- Subtracts out external transfers out, contractors removed, involuntary terminations, and other staff reductions.
- Adds in external transfers in, new hires (recruiting), overtime, part-time staff, consultants, outsourcing, and contractors added.

Next, the model compares available resources (after staffing actions)/employees + contractors to staffing requirements and calculates final gaps/surpluses (after staffing actions). Ideally, if the staffing actions you entered are correct, every cell of the final gaps/surpluses matrix should be zero (or a gap or surplus that you find acceptable). If this is not the case, it is likely that you will need to modify your staffing plans. Determine what staffing actions need to be added, deleted, or changed. Edit the matrices in step 4 to reflect these changes and again review the final gaps/surpluses matrix.

Step 6: Enter Staffing Data for Subsequent Periods. Once period 1 is final, look at the preliminary gaps and surpluses that have now been created in period 2. These gaps and surpluses will reflect all the staffing actions you entered for period 1. Define the staffing plans that you think best meet these needs in period 2 (consistent with your staffing strategies, of course) and enter that information in the appropriate matrices in period 2. When period 2 is "done" (e.g., when final gaps and surpluses are all zero or some other acceptable number), repeat the process for period 3. Repeat for all subsequent periods.

Retrieving the Book's Computer Files

By purchasing this book, you are granted access to several computer files that may help you to design, develop, and implement your strategic staffing/workforce planning process. These files include:

- A simple (yet complete) example of a staffing model
- Two different staffing model spreadsheet templates
- Three presentations to help you to educate managers, train your team, and apply the strategic staffing/workforce planning process within your organization
- Examples of various methods for defining required staffing levels (which you may choose to use as handouts during the presentations)
- Several tools that you can use to evaluate the effectiveness of your strategic staffing/workforce planning process
- An example of the type of detailed staffing plan that might be created by the strategic staffing/workforce planning process

To retrieve these files:

- Go to the web site www.amacombooks.org/go/StrategicStaff2. You will see a list of the files that are available.
- Right click on the file that you would like to download. Select the Save Target As . . . option in the window that opens.
- Select the folder on your computer that you would like to download the file to and click on Save.

If you have any questions or problems, contact AMACOM customer service using the link that is provided.

Index

absolute measures, 291
accountability, 75, 154, 175, 194
aerospace (example), 163
assessments
    sharing via web site, 210
    strategic staffing/workforce planning
        process, 293–294
attrition costs, 286–287, 303–304
averages, as measures, 290–291

banking (examples), 103–105, 147–156
branding, in talent planning, 265, 268
budget cycle
    budget process and, 174–175
    staff planning in, 37–38, 154
business context, 177–190
    diagnostic framework for, 178–189
    downsizing and, 283–287
    growth scenario, 271–273
    integration with strategic staffing/
        workforce planning, 177–178,
        184–186
    major change in required capabilities,
        280–282
    merger or acquisition, 115, 273–276
    opening greenfield site, 276–280
    of reduction decisions, 283–285
    of strategic staffing/workforce plan-
        ning, 22–40, 178–179, 236–237
business plans
    discussing with managers, 202–203
    integration with staffing plans, 76,
        177–189
    staffing issues and, 44–47

call centers (example), 96–97
capabilities analysis, 48, 61–62, 129
cascade effects, 256, 303–304
case studies and examples, 28–31, 81–84,
    125–140, 141–164
    aerospace, 163
    banking, 103–105, 147–156
    call centers, 96–97
    computer hardware, 30–31
    consulting, 123–124
    engineering/construction (examples),
        26, 31, 37–38, 104
    of gap analysis, 125–134, 143–144, 145
    health care, 25–26, 81–84, 117–120,
        163–164

high-technology, 125–140
information technology (IT) operations,
    28, 31–32, 81–84, 141–147
insurance industry, 29, 34, 81–84, 96,
    115, 162–163
mergers and acquisitions, 115
oil industry, 33–34, 122–123, 190
pharmaceuticals, 29–30, 141–147
restaurants, 109–110
retailing, 104
of staffing model, 125–140, 141–164
of staffing profiles, 103–110
of staffing ratios, 94–97, 109–110,
    117–120
of staffing requirements, 108–110,
    117–121
state government, 27–28, 120–121
of surplus analysis, 125–134, 143–144,
    145
telecommunications, 161–162
utility, 156–161
centers of excellence, 152
change
    in context, 20
    critical staffing issues and, 46–47
    cross-period, 70–71
    discussing with managers, 202–203
    focus on, 201
    headcount, 83–84, 286
    pace of, 19
    in required capabilities, 280–282
    in roles and positions, 88
    staffing implications of, 6, 36–38
collaboration, web site in building, 207
communication
    interviewing managers, 199–204
    of strategic staffing/workforce plan-
        ning, 78, 199
    traditional approaches to, 205
    web site in, 205–213
competency models, 62
computer hardware (example), 30–31
consistency, balance between flexibility
    and, 77–84, 193–197
consolidated staffing plans, avoiding,
    35–36
consulting
    example, 123–124
    role of short-term consultants, 151, 153,
        286–287

context of strategic staffing/workforce
planning, *see* business context
contingency plans, 115–117
contractors, 11, 70–71, 144, 146
controllable staffing, 53–54, 55, 63–64,
286–287, 303–304
cost measures, 290, 295–308
analyzing staffing costs, 302–304
calculating staffing costs, 295–302
in downsizing, 286–287
evaluating options and drawing conclusions, 304–308
staff cost ratios, 154
staff planning in budget cycle, 37–38,
154
workforce maintenance costs, 296–299,
301–302
credibility argument, for implementation
approach, 171
critical issues, *see* issues
cross-functional plans, 185–186
cross-unit staffing strategies, 28
curvilinear regression analysis, 90

data
alternatives to perfect, 112–121
external, overreliance on, 241, 267–268
information versus, 10, 24–25, 230
lack of adequate, 19
web site and, 205, 210
see also cost measures
deliverables, in strategic staffing/work-
force planning, 78
demand for staff, 8–9, 60–62, 129, 134, 139,
153–156, 277, 279, 282, 299–302, 306,
307
development
review of, 247–248
in staffing model, 57–58
in talent planning, 266, 268
training plans in, 146
diagnostics
for analyzing business context, 178–189
sharing via web site, 210
direct staffing ratios, 92–94
downsizing, 283–287
mistakes to avoid in, 285–287
staffing strategy as context for, 283–285
downtime, adjusting for, 159–160

e-coach, on web site, 211
education argument, for implementation
approach, 171–172
effectiveness
efficiency and, 292–293
measuring, 267, 269, 291–293
of talent planning, 267, 269
tracking progress of, 293–294

efficiency
cost measures, 290, 295–308
effectiveness and, 292–293
measuring, 267, 269, 288–291, 292–293
of talent planning, 267, 269
time or speed measures, 289–291
tracking progress of, 293–294
of traditional workforce planning, 20
volume measures, 158–159, 290
elapsed time argument, for implementation approach, 171
engineering/construction (examples), 26,
31, 37–38, 104
examples, *see* case studies and examples
expertise, sharing via web site, 205–206,
210–211
external transfers, 138, 140

feedback, from managers, 204
flexibility, balance between consistency
and, 77–84, 193–197
forecasting
available resources, 62–66, 133
retirements, 64–65, 66, 132–133, 140,
240–246, 286–287, 303–304
of staffing availability, 62–66
traditional approach to, 23, 24, 192
forms, on web site, 210
frequently asked questions (FAQs), 82,
211, 309–316
full-time equivalents (FTEs), 11, 119–120,
157, 160
future
discussing with managers, 203
skills requirements in, 285–286
see also forecasting

gap analysis, 42, 48–68
for all remaining periods, 67–68
case studies and examples of, 125–134,
143–144, 145
for first period, 67
in measuring staffing effectiveness, 292
reviewing across multiple periods,
69–71
in scenario analysis, 305, 307
in succession planning, 253, 256, 260
government (example), 27–28, 120–121
greenfield site, staffing model for opening,
276–280
growth scenario, staffing model for,
271–273
guidelines for strategic staffing/work-
force planning
define issues on ongoing basis, 36–38
feed other HR functions, 38–39
focus on issues, 26–31
focus on particular positions, 33–35
keep plans separate, 35–36

"kickoff" session, 227–237
proactive, planning perspective, 25–26, 33–34
solve problems, 38, 113–114, 210–211
tailor process to issues, 31–32, 79–81, 196
at 30,000 feet, 77–84, 193–197

headcounts, 83–84, 286
health care (examples), 25–26, 81–84, 117–120, 163–164
high-technology (examples), 125–140
horizontal approach, to implementation, 167–168
HR staff, 214–225
    engaging line managers in strategic staffing/workforce planning, 191–197
    HR business partner, 218–221, 225–226
    HR service center, 216–218, 225–226
    human resource information system (HRIS) and, 62–63, 65–66, 223
    in implementation of strategic staffing/ workforce planning process, 176
    overall structure of HR, 215–224
    roles and responsibilities of, 173–175
    skills needed by, 218, 219, 222–223
    strategic staffing/workforce planning "center of excellence," 221–224, 225–226
    strategic staffing/workforce planning role in feeding, 38–39
    talent planning and, 261–269

impact argument, for implementation approach, 166–167, 170–171
implementation, 166–237
    effective framework for, 166–173, 233
    horizontal approach to, 167–168
    obstacles to effective, 175–176
    in one-day "kickoff" session, 237
    roles and responsibilities in, 173–175, 191–199
    of talent planning, 263–264, 268–269
    vertical approach to, 169–170
    web site and, 207, 211
incremental approach, to staffing, 99–101
indirect staffing ratios, 94
information
    data versus, 10, 24–25, 230
    sharing via web site, 209, 212–213
information technology (IT) operations (examples), 28, 31–32, 81–84, 141–147
insurance industry (examples), 29, 34, 81–84, 96, 115, 162–163
internal movement, in staffing model, 57, 135–138, 140
interviewing managers, 199–204
    conducting the session, 201–202

interview guide for, 202–204
    preparation for, 200–201
intranets, 207
involuntary terminations, 139, 140, 286–287, 303–304
issues
    defined, 8–9, 229–230
    defining on ongoing basis, 36–38
    discussing with managers, 203
    examples of, 27–28
    focus on, 26–31
    in staffing process, 8–9, 42, 43–48, 78, 195
    tailoring process for, 31–32, 79–81, 196
    types of, 27

kickoff session, 227–237

learning and development, see development
leverage argument, for implementation approach, 172
longer-term perspective, 10–12, 13–15, 27, 43–44, 180, 181–182, 183, 184–185, 186–187, 189

maintenance costs, 296–299, 301–302
management depth, 151–152, 153
managers, 191–204
    accountability of, 75, 154, 175, 194
    engaging in strategic staffing/workforce planning, 191–197
    interviewing, 199–204
    penalizing effective, 286
    role in strategic staffing/workforce planning process, 175–176, 191–199
    talent planning and, 261–269
    see also succession planning process
measurement
    of staffing effectiveness, 267, 269, 291–293
    of staffing efficiency, 267, 269, 288–291, 292–293
    of staffing efficiency and effectiveness, 292–293
medical care (examples), 25–26, 81–84, 117–120, 163–164
mergers and acquisitions
    example, 115
    staffing model for, 273–276
message boards, 211
Monte Carlo approach, 121–124
multiple regression analysis, 89–90, 91

net needs, 307
new hires, 138–139, 140

oil industry (examples), 33–34, 122–123, 190
outsourcing, 11, 70–71

pharmaceuticals (examples), 29–30,
    141–147
planning horizon, 31–32
    for business plans, 178–189
    longer-term, 10–12, 13–15, 27, 43–44,
        180, 181–182, 183, 184–185, 186–187,
        189
    short-term, 10–12, 14–15, 180, 181, 182,
        185–186, 187, 188, 189
    for staffing model, 55–56, 127–128,
        178–189
policy development, 152, 154–155
population, for staffing model, 56–58, 127,
    275, 278, 281
PowerPoint, in conducting "kickoff" ses-
    sion, 227–237
proactive approach, 25–26, 33–34
problem-solving approach, 38, 113–114,
    210–211
productivity, 116–117
proficiency, 116–117
progress measures, 155, 293–294
project-based staffing, 99–101
    examples of, 26, 31–32
    incremental approach to, 99–101
    zero-based approach to, 99
project probabilities, 121–124
promotions, 52, 63–64, 140

recruiting
    in staffing model, 57
    in talent planning, 266–267
redeployment, in staffing model, 57
reduction in staff, see downsizing
redundancy, 183–184
regression analysis, 89–92
    curvilinear, 90
    limitations of, 92
    multiple, 89–90, 91
    simple, 89, 90–91
reports
    documenting staffing plans, 74–75, 82
    of staffing transactions, 24–25
resources
    forecasting available, 62–66, 133
    sharing via web site, 212–213
    see also supply of staff
restaurants (example), 109–110
retailing (example), 104
retention, in talent planning, 266–267
retirement analysis, 64–65, 66, 132–133,
    140, 240–246, 286–287, 303–304
    integrating into strategic staffing/work-
        force planning, 242–246
    retirement age in, 250–251
    retirement "distribution" in, 251–252
    in succession planning process, 242,
        245, 249–252, 258–259

traditional approach to, 241–242
    see also succession planning process

scenario planning, 114–115, 305–308
    multiple scenarios in, 306–308
    single scenarios in, 305–306
scope, of implementation, 166
sensitivity analysis, 117
short-term perspective, 10–12, 14–15, 180,
    181, 182, 185–186, 187, 188, 189
simple regression analysis, 89, 90–91
skills
    development of, 57–58, 146
    future requirements, 285–286
    of HR staff, 218, 219, 222–223
    web site in building, 206–207
sourcing strategies, in talent planning,
    265, 268
span of control, 94
specialization, 152
speed measures, 289–290
spreadsheets, 90, 91
    knowledge of, 223
    templates for, 82, 210, 211
    on web site, 210, 211
staffing, defined, 7–8, 229
staffing drivers, 45–47, 87–89, 94–97
staffing levels, 48, 62
staffing mix, 8, 48
staffing model, 14, 49–54
    "best" approach to, 52–54
    "better" approach to, 50–54
    defining gaps and surpluses in, 67–68,
        125–134
    defining parameters for, 54–60, 127–128
    defining staffing requirements for, 60–
        62, 94–124
    examples of, 125–140, 141–164
    forecasting staffing availability in, 62–66
    for growth scenario, 271–273
    for merger or acquisition, 273–276
    for opening a greenfield site, 276–280
    for retirement analysis, 244–245
    simple approach to, 49–50
    structure of, 58–60, 128, 142–143
    traditional approach to, 31, 78–79
staffing plans
    accountabilities in, 75, 154, 175, 194
    contents of, 73
    cost measures in developing, 290,
        295–308
    creating, 140
    defined, 7, 15
    defining, process of, 42, 72–76
    developing, 306
    documenting, 74–75, 82
    guidelines for effective, 23–40

integration with business plans, 76, 177–189
  repeating process in, 76
  reviewing, 76, 182–186
  sample, 75
  scenario analysis and, 114–115, 305–308
  support activities and infrastructure in, 75–76
  time frames in, 75
  traditional approach to, 22–23
staffing profiles, 103–105
  examples of, 103–110
  nature of, 103
staffing ratios, 92–97
  developing, 94–97
  direct, 92–94
  examples of, 95–97, 109–110, 117–120
  indirect, 94
  nature of, 94–95
staffing requirements, 60–62, 94–124
  alternatives to perfect data, 112–121
  case studies and examples of, 108–110, 117–121
  foundation for, 86–87
  interviewing managers to determine, 199–204
  overview of, 87–89
  project-based staffing and, 99–101
  regression analysis and, 89–92
  staffing profiles and, 103–110
  staffing ratios and, 92–97
  in uncertain environment, 112–124, 232–233
staffing strategy
  business strategy versus, 9–10
  as context for reduction decisions, 283–285
  defined, 7, 230
  defining staffing needs, 68–72
  developing, 10–13, 42, 68–72
  guidelines for effective, 23–40
  longer-term, 10–12, 13–15, 27, 43–44, 180, 181–182, 183, 184–185, 186–187, 189
  nature of, 17–18
  organizational level in, 181
  short-term, 10–12, 14–15, 180, 181, 182, 185–186, 187, 188, 189
  staffing, defined, 7–8, 229
  strategy, defined, 9–10
  traditional approaches to, 19–20, 22–23, 31, 40, 78–79
standards, 291
state government (example), 27–28, 120–121
strategic staffing/workforce planning
  balance between consistency and flexibility in, 77–84, 195–196

business context, 22–40, 178–189, 236–237
for common business initiatives, 270–282
common impediments to, 18–19
defined, 6
engaging managers in, 191–197
guidelines for effective, 23–40, 228–233
integrating retirement analysis into, 242–246
integration with business context, 177–178, 184–186
"kickoff" session, 227–237
objectives of, 7, 10–13, 178, 197–198
overview of process, 13–14
process of, *see* strategic staffing/workforce planning process
as rare, 17–18
selective application of, 12, 13
staffing, defined, 7–8, 229
strategy, defined, 9–10
at 30,000 feet, 77–84, 193–197
traditional approaches to, 19–20, 22–23, 31, 40, 78–79
web site for, 205–213
see also staffing plans; staffing strategy
strategic staffing/workforce planning process, 41–76
  assessing, 293–294
  balance between consistency and flexibility in, 77–84, 193–197
  case studies and examples, 28–31, 81–84, 108–110, 125–140, 141–164
  communicating, 78, 199
  critical staffing issues in, 28–31, 42, 43–48, 78, 148–152, 195, 280–281
  identifying other staffing issues, 47–48
  interviewing managers in, 199–204
  "kickoff" session, 227–237
  manager involvement in, 175–176, 191–199
  measuring both effectiveness and efficiency, 292–293
  measuring staffing effectiveness, 267, 269, 291–293
  measuring staffing efficiency, 267, 269, 288–291, 292–293
  overview of, 41–42
  staffing gaps and surpluses in, 6, 11, 14, 42, 48–68, 69, 125–134, 139, 153–156
  staffing plans in, 15, 72–76
  staffing strategies in, 14–15, 68–72
  tracking progress of, 293–294
  upside-down T in, 11–12, 42, 209, 231
strategic workforce planning, *see* strategic staffing/workforce planning
succession planning process, 247–260
  maintaining candidate pool size, 253–260

succession planning process (*continued*)
   quantitative analysis in, 248–260
   retirement analysis and, 242, 245, 249–252, 258–259
   review of development and, 247–248
   voluntary turnover in, 252–253
supply of staff, 8–9, 59–60, 62–66, 129–130, 133–134, 139, 153–156, 277, 279, 281–282, 297–302, 306
surplus analysis, 42, 48–68
   for all remaining periods, 67–68
   case studies and examples of, 125–134, 143–144, 145
   for first period, 67
   in measuring staffing effectiveness, 292
   reviewing across multiple periods, 69–71
   in scenario analysis, 305
   in succession planning, 256, 260

talent planning, 261–269
   implementing, 263–264, 268–269
   importance of, 261
   process overview, 262–268
technology firms (examples), 125–140
telecommunications (example), 161–162
temporary staffing options, 11
terminations
   involuntary, 139, 140, 286–287, 303–304
   see also downsizing; turnover
time frame
   for business plans, 178–189
   defining, 75
   for determining workforce maintenance costs, 297–299
   to respond to staffing needs, 34
   for staffing model, 55–56, 143
   for staffing plans, 55–56, 127–128, 178–189, 276, 279, 281
   for tracking progress, 293–294
   see also longer-term perspective; short-term perspective
time measures, 158, 159, 289–290
tools
   sharing via kickoff session, 233–235
   sharing via web site, 206, 209–210
   for strategic staffing/workforce planning, 79, 82, 196

training, *see* development
transfers
   external, 138, 140
   internal, 57, 135–138, 140
transition costs, 299–302
turnover
   controllable, 53–54, 55, 63–64, 286–287, 303–304
   patterns of, 24
   rates of, 130–132
   traditional approach to, 23, 24
   uncontrollable, 52, 55, 63, 65, 130–132, 140, 258, 286–287, 303–304

uncertain environment, staffing requirements in, 112–124, 232–233
uncontrollable turnover, 52, 55, 63, 65, 130–132, 140, 258, 286–287, 303–304
upside-down T, 11–12, 42, 209, 231
utility (example), 156–161

values, 184
vertical approach, to implementation, 169–170
volume measures, 158–159, 290
voluntary turnover, 63, 130–132, 140, 252–253, 258, 286–287, 303–304

walk-throughs, 210–211
web site, 205–213
   designing, 207–209
   frequently asked questions (FAQs), 82, 211, 309–316
   need for, 205–207
   sharing information via, 209, 212–213
   strategic staffing templates from, 317–334
   in strategic staffing/workforce planning, 83
"what if" plans, 115–117, 305
workforce maintenance costs, 296–299, 301–302
workforce planning, *see* strategic staffing/workforce planning

zero-based approach, to staffing, 99

Recommended SHRM Resources

Staffing Management magazine

For the latest techniques and trends in recruiting and retaining employees, HR experts turn to *Staffing Management*—the essential resource on recruiting and staffing. Subscriptions are $35 per year United States and its territories; $55 per year Canada; $85 per year international (via airmail). Visit www.shrm.org/staffingmanagement/magazine/ to order.

The Practical HR Kit

Solving the Compensation Puzzle: Putting Together a Complete Pay and Performance System
> By Sharon K. Koss, SPHR, CCP

Proving the Value of HR: How and Why to Measure ROI
> By Jack J. Phillips, Ph.D., and Patricia Pulliam Phillips, Ph.D.

Legal, Effective References: How to Give and Get Them
> By Wendy Bliss, J.D., SPHR

Investigating Workplace Harassment: How to Be Fair, Thorough, and Legal
> By Amy Oppenheimer, J.D., and Craig Pratt, MWS, SPHR

The Source Book Kit

Employment Termination Source Book
> By Wendy Bliss, J.D., SPHR, and Gene Thornton, Esq., PHR

Performance Appraisal Source Book
> By Mike Deblieux

Hiring Source Book
> By Cathy Fyock, CAP, SPHR

Trainer's Diversity Source Book
> By Jonamay Lambert, M.A., and Selma Myers, M.A.

HIPAA Privacy Source Book
> By William S. Hubbartt, SPHR, CCP

TO ORDER SHRM BOOKS

SHRM offers a member discount on all books that it publishes or sells. Bulk purchase discounts are also available for SHRM-published books. To order these or any other book published by SHRM through the SHRMStore:

ONLINE: www.shrm.org/shrmstore

BY PHONE: 800-444-5006 (option #1); or
770-42-8633 (ext. 362); or
TDD: 703-548-6999

Recommended SHRM Resources

Staffing Management magazine

For the latest techniques and trends in recruiting and retaining employees, HR experts turn to *Staffing Management*—the essential resource on recruiting and staffing. Subscriptions are $35 per year United States and its territories; $55 per year Canada; $85 per year international (via airmail). Visit www.shrm.org/ staffingmanagement/magazine/ to order.

The Practical HR Kit

Solving the Compensation Puzzle: Putting Together a Complete Pay and Performance System
   By Sharon K. Koss, SPHR, CCP

Proving the Value of HR: How and Why to Measure ROI
   By Jack J. Phillips, Ph.D., and Patricia Pulliam Phillips, Ph.D.

Legal, Effective References: How to Give and Get Them
   By Wendy Bliss, J.D., SPHR

Investigating Workplace Harassment: How to Be Fair, Thorough, and Legal
   By Amy Oppenheimer, J.D., and Craig Pratt, MWS, SPHR

The Source Book Kit

Employment Termination Source Book
   By Wendy Bliss, J.D., SPHR, and Gene Thornton, Esq., PHR

Performance Appraisal Source Book
   By Mike Deblieux

Hiring Source Book
   By Cathy Fyock, CAP, SPHR

Trainer's Diversity Source Book
   By Jonamay Lambert, M.A., and Selma Myers, M.A.

HIPAA Privacy Source Book
   By William S. Hubbartt, SPHR, CCP

TO ORDER SHRM BOOKS

SHRM offers a member discount on all books that it publishes or sells. Bulk purchase discounts are also available for SHRM-published books. To order these or any other book published by SHRM through the SHRMStore:

ONLINE: www.shrm.org/shrmstore

BY PHONE: 800-444-5006 (option #1); or
                      770-42-8633 (ext. 362); or
                      TDD: 703-548-6999